A SECURITY ADVISOR IN IRAQ

John Heron

authorHOUSE®

AuthorHouse™ UK Ltd.
500 Avebury Boulevard
Central Milton Keynes, MK9 2BE
www.authorhouse.co.uk
Phone: 08001974150

First published by AuthorHouse   10/20/2010

ISBN: 978-1-4520-8254-7 (sc)

This book is printed on acid-free paper.

'Baghdad – Given by God' (Iraq)

Located on the river Tigris, the city dates back to the 8th century and was once the centre of the Muslim world.

On 30 July 762 the caliph Al Mansur founded the city. Mansur believed that Baghdad was the perfect city to be the capital of thee Islamic empire under the Abbasids. Mansur loved the site so much he is quoted saying, 'This is indeed the city that I am to found, where I am to live, and where my descendants will reign afterward.

The city's growth was helped by its location, which gave it control over strategic and trading routes (along the Tigris to the sea and east-west from the Middle East to the rest of Asia). Another reason why Baghdad provided an excellent location was due to the abundance of water and its dry climate. Water exists on both north and south ends of the city gates, allowing all households to have plentiful supply, which was very uncommon during this time.

Baghdad reached its greatest prosperity during the reign of the caliph Harun al-Rashid in the early 9th century. Baghdad eclipsed Ctesiphon, the capital of the Persian Empire, which was located some 30 km to the southeast, which had been under Muslim control since 637, and which became quickly deserted after the foundation of Baghdad. The site Babylon, which had been deserted since the 2nd century BC, lies some 90 km to the south. Once one of the greatest centres of learning and culture in the Islamic world, Baghdad has a long and illustrious history. Once a favoured destination on the 'hippie trail' and packed full of sights; since the 'war on terrorism' of 2003, Baghdad has since become one of the most dangerous cities on earth.

IRAQ

Courtesy of the University of Texas Libraries,
the University of Texas at Austin

GLOSSARY

AK47	7.62mm short, Soviet designed assault rifle
COMMS	Communications
CONTACT	Situation in which an enemy attacks your position
COT	American fold up bed
CP	Close protection
ERV	Emergency rendezvous
FOB	Forward operating base
FIRE FIGHT	Gun battle
GPS	Global positioning system
IED	Improvised explosive device
MSR	Main supply route
OP	Observation post
RECCE	Reconnaissance
RPG	Rocket propelled grenade
RV	Rendezvous
SOP	Standard operating procedure
VBIED	Vehicle borne improvised explosive device

PREFACE

I think this would be a good time to give a very short explanation of why I have chosen the title and omitted a certain term from this book, starting with the title. Security men out here are called 'contractors' or 'advisors' purely because they advise clients on security related problems. The war which everyone thought was over is still being fought out here in Iraq and a large part of it has involved the security contractor. Put Iraq and security advisor together and that is where the title comes from, very simple. Security advisors work within 'The Circuit' wherever they are in the world. The Circuit in recent years was quite secretive in its activities and unless you were part of it you wouldn't really know it existed. The activities include a vast array of services to many clients, these include Kidnap and Ransom response, anti surveillance and counter surveillance, risk analysis and close protection (body guard in layman's terms) in hostile environments to name but a few. Contracts are outsourced from both commercial clients and also governments. Since 9/11 many commercial companies realized that they required close protection for their workers in foreign lands, governments also realized that they required the services in many hostile countries. This gave rise to the PSCs (Private Security Companies).

Secondly in the early days in Iraq I often heard the word 'mercenary' used by the media, a term as offensive as it is untrue. Mercenaries are hired guns and sell their services to the highest bidder. They have no loyalty, moral foundation or sense of duty to their own country, never mind other countries who hire them. If the price was right a mercenary would take up arms against his own government.

I have been on the circuit for ten years and completed many assignments before the Iraq conflict. I have never accepted any contract that would bring me up against the police or government of any country I have worked in.

All images and forms are the property of the author and for security reasons faces and names/dates/phone numbers/signatures have been blacked out.

Authority has been obtained from P.G, M.C, M.A and J.S to show their images with eyes blacked out.

All images showing Saddam on his capture were taken by an unknown American soldier.

Introduction

This book is in memory of all the guys with whom I served, men who died while trying to make this world a safer place for our children and our people. To the many hundreds of guys who I met on the "surveillance circuit" and "the circuit," to the many guys who lost their lives in Iraq in terrible conditions. I have had the pleasure of meeting some extraordinary guys over the years, brave guys who have lived and died in some of the worst conditions imaginable. To the guys who are still working in Iraq or elsewhere in the world, I will always be your friend; to the guys who have died, I will always remember you.

Here is a little of my background so that people who read this book don't think we advisors are a bunch of misfits just looking for a fight. People in my profession need to have military experience, technical and mechanical skills, the ability to improvise, physical toughness, great grit and courage, and a higher tolerance for risk than the great majority.

I was born in November 1958 in Gateshead, Tyne and Wear in the Northeast of England. I was one of a large family of nine children. My father was a military man all his working life, and my mum was a housewife who also worked at various factories. My childhood was fantastic because I had five brothers. With my dad in the Army, we followed him all over the world. We six lads would play war games while our sisters, three of them, would play girlie games. I was trouble from the outset and caused my parents much worry and heartache throughout my childhood. All I wanted was to be outside exploring; I hated being inside the house. I needed the excitement of being in the open so much that I began running away from home at the age of eight. How my dad kept his hands off me when I eventually got caught each time amazes me to this day. My mum would become upset to the point of a nervous breakdown; however, Dad never once hit me. Instead he used his voice. Getting a bollocking from him was very scary, to say the least; it was terrifying. However bad I was, he never struck me once.

At the age of eight, I really didn't know what sort of worry and heartache I brought my parents because I wanted only to be outside, whether in sun, rain, or snow. I loved the outside. We lived in Shrewsbury, a beautiful county in the Midlands, at the time of my escapades. At times I even convinced a couple of my brothers to go with me and live rough; nevertheless, the police always caught us after a few days. We would sleep rough and steal food and milk off doorsteps, for in those days people were trusting and left the milk money under the empty milk bottles on the doorstep. I knew this, and early in the morning, I would steal the cash to buy food and sweets.

Eventually my parents couldn't take it anymore, and my dad urged the courts to have me sent away to a children's home. I was ten at the time and can still remember going to court in Shrewsbury. My parents escorted me to the solicitor's office, then into court; I really didn't know what was going on at that age and couldn't see that I was causing any problems at all. To me it was just an adventure. In court, the judge and my parents met in private while I remained just outside the courtroom with the usher or a guy with a black cape on over his suit. Eventually I was asked to enter, and the caped guy took my arm and led me in. I cannot remember what the judge said, but immediately after he said it, my mum burst into tears while my dad looked out the window and down at the street. My mum grabbed me and hugged me so hard it nearly knocked the wind out of me; she was crying and kissing me, and it felt like she didn't want to let me go. In the end, a woman came in and managed to get me out of my mum's arms and lead me out of the courtroom. Still the penny didn't drop, and I didn't have a clue what was happening. We got into this woman's car, and she drove off out of Shrewsbury.

Eventually we ended up at this huge mansion-type building in a town called Wellington. I was introduced to the man who ran this place, and whilst the woman was still there, he gave me the ground rules that I was expected to abide by. Later on that day, I met up with all the other children, who had just finished school. This was a children's home right in the middle of a town, and the kids went to school on their own and came back on their own. The first night there, the penny dropped, and I cried my eyes out; I sobbed in bed that

2

night and thought I would never see my parents or family again. I just couldn't understand what I had done wrong and why that judge had sent me away from my family.

As time went by, I began to get used to being there and started mucking in with what the other kids did. I even went to school and found I quite enjoyed it. However, the open fields that we passed on our way to school were calling. In school one day, I got hold of a map and realized that Wellington was not all that far from Shrewsbury and my family, so that night after school; I decided to try and get there. I remember my dad giving me map-reading lessons when I was young, and I thought that if I followed the main road, I would hit Shrewsbury.

It was drizzling rain when I set off on my own in my school uniform. I decided not to stick to the main road because I knew the police would be looking for me. I made my way across the country. I walked through fields, along tracks, and over any obstacle between myself and Shrewsbury. After walking all night, I hit the outskirts of Shrewsbury, and I knew exactly where I was. It was early morning when I arrived at my family's house, so I decided to stay away until everyone was up. I remember when I knocked at the door and my mum answered; she threw herself on me and kissed and cuddled me on the doorstep. Then she got me inside the house, and after a while she asked me what I was doing there. I gave some cock-and-bull story about the authorities at the home letting me out for the day. That story obviously didn't work, for the police came about an hour later and took me away. Captured again, I decided that next time I wouldn't make my capture so easy for them.

Over the years, I accepted what I had done to my parents and settled into life at the children's home. My parents and family moved back up to the Northeast and settled there; my dad left the Army and got a job, but I was still down in Wellington. One Christmas I heard that I was going to leave the home and live with my grandmother. She was lovely, and I always liked visiting her when I was a toddler. I was sent by train from Wellington to the Newcastle station. There my dad picked me up and took me home to my grandmother's house, where I would live from then on. I did not need to worry about my mum because she lived just down the street. These were happy days, but I still needed something to do, something exciting. One day a friend and I decided to build a raft and row from the Gateshead side of the River Tyne to the Newcastle side, and halfway across, the bloody raft fell apart and drifted downstream. We had to swim to the Newcastle side and then walk back over the Tyne Bridge, soaking wet. Great days!

In 1975, at seventeen, I decided to join the Army; I passed the test at Gunner House, Newcastle, and within three months I was heading by train to Winchester to join the Royal Green Jackets. The training was eighteen weeks long and hard, but I loved it sometimes. Sometimes I hated it, especially when we had to do classroom work; I hated classroom work. I was happier when we were in the hills, learning how to survive and attack enemy positions in any condition the weather could throw at us. I got married to a lovely woman called Joanne when we were both eighteen. We lived together in Army married quarters throughout my career. We had two boys, John and Andrew, at an early age. Both our sons are now doing well and serving their queen and country.

Looking back on my Military career I realise how lucky I was to have joined the Green Jackets, they were very family orientated and the Senior NCO's and officers spoke to you like any other person would speak to you. Officers or Senior NCO's never spoke down to you unlike other Regiments. I started my Military career in 'C' Company and served in Gibraltar. After two years in Gibraltar we were posted to Tidworth in Hampshire where we got back to proper infantry training. The Battalion had orders for a four month tour of South Armagh, Northern Ireland. Training began immediately. I was now in the Close Observation Platoon. The role of the C.O.P was to watch suspected terrorists from hidden observation points or follow them in unmarked civilian vehicles, very risky to say the least as we only worked in four man teams with no back up whatsoever. All our tasks were secret to the members of your team. A term we used to use was "opsec" which meant operational secrecy. Christmas 1977 we arrived at Belfast docks on a troop carrier, we unloaded all our specialist equipment from the ship, loaded it into landrovers and headed off south to a village called Bessbrook. Bessbrook was where the HQ of the Battalion would be stationed for the duration of the tour with the other rifle companies based in Forkhill, Crossmaglen, Newton Hamilton and Newry. We, as the C.O.P, would find ourselves working in all these locations. A few "jobs" we carried out spring immediately to mind. One job we carried out was in Newry. We had to place an "op" in such a position so we could watch a supermarket which was going to be robbed by the IRA. The only place we could watch the supermarket safely was from the top floor of a disused bank. My boss, a Captain, and me drew short straws with the rest of the team and found ourselves in the bank where we would have to stay day and night for the duration of the operation. The bank was very secure with bars on all the ground floor windows, a huge thick oak front door and a reinforced steel rear door; well that's what we thought. Night two the boss and I changed over watch and I was just settling down on the floor in the corner of the room in my sleeping bag when we were both startled by a bang of some sort down stairs. The boss immediately told me to go down and investigate the bang to which I replied that he was on duty so he should go. A few minutes of arguing I found myself inching down the stairs with two pistols. As I reached the bottom I heard rustling in a room to the right of the stairs. What I really wanted to do was to go back upstairs and come back down as a pair but decided to take the bull by the horns and get this sorted by myself. The door to the room was open and I was right next to it with my back to the wall, I was shaking and cold with fear because I didn't know what I was going to be confronted by. I counted to three then quickly moved into the doorway only to be met by a little fat man with white hair and a white beard. We just stared at each other for a few seconds, eyes wide open, when all of a sudden the little man shrieked loudly nearly at the same time as me. Just before I turned to run back up the stairs the little man dropped to the floor but I took no notice and ran as if my life depended on it back to the top floor. The boss was waiting at the door to the room we were using and asked what the fuck was going on. I told him as best I could what I had seen and what had happened. The boss then told me to get myself together and to follow him back downstairs. Arriving at the bottom floor the little man was still lying on the floor where I left him. The boss immediately went over to him and after a quick check told me he was dead. I went over and checked his pulse only to find he did not have one. I certainly didn't shoot him. In the end we had to call the Military, Police and Ambulance. When they arrived we managed to get the front door open to let them all in, the operation was obviously called off at this stage. One of the paramedics told me it looked like the man had died of a heart attack. When I think back over the events of that night I come to realise that anyone seeing me with long hair and a face full of camouflage cream in a building which should have been empty may well have died of a heart attack. The poor bloke was a tramp and had somehow gained entry into the building where he was hoping to get somewhere dry and out of the rain and snow. It's a wonder that both of us didn't have a heart attack because it certainly put the shits up me. Another job we were tasked with was to watch an unmanned border crossing between Southern Ireland and Northern Ireland. The intelligence we had was that the IRA where bringing weapons over from the south and they would be crossing at the border crossing point. Having carried out day time and night time reconnaissance we found the only place we could set up an "op" was in a disused pig pen in the corner of a field. A track led from the pig pen down to a fast flowing river, along the length of the track was a very thick hedge. We set off from Forkhill base with heavy bergans very early one morning and crossed grassed fields and ploughed fields before reaching the river. We looked up and down the river for a safe crossing point before I finally found a point where we could cross. The crossing was boulders which were up above the top of the water. I volunteered to go first and stepped out onto the first boulder which wobbled slightly. I then gingerly put my other foot onto the second boulder and promptly went straight into the icy water right up to my chest. The water was absolutely freezing due to the wintery conditions and I was quite rapidly going downhill with the cold, the guys on the river bank saw the funny side of this and laughed their heads off. Eventually they dragged me out, got me out of my wet clothing and into dry clothing before setting off towards the pig pen. We settled down into "op" routine and monitored the crossing point. The third night we opened fire on IRA terrorists bringing weapons from the south. Two terrorists made a run for the river and seemed to cross it without any problem. I called my boss on the radio and told him that I was going to have a go at those two guys and ran down the track heading towards the river. As I was running I could hear the shooting and realised I was the target because I saw sparks on the track pebbles, with that I jumped head first to my right which should have taken me through the hedge, unfortunately inside the hedge was a dry stone wall which my head made contact with. I found myself on my arse on the ground and quickly got back to my feet and headed off again to the river, more determined to get these bastards. I crossed the river with difficulty and set off over a ploughed field in the direction of the two terrorists. A quarter of the way across the field I gave up, not because I was on my own or anything like that but purely because I couldn't move due to the amount of mud that was on my boots. When I think back to those days I laugh quietly to myself at the fun we used to have. I served in Northern Ireland for a total of six years during my career and I don't care what anyone says about the Irish because I found them very friendly people, even the Catholics although some of them needed to be locked up for ever. We knew who was IRA and who wasn't and if we saw an IRA man on the street we would make conversation with him even though he wouldn't talk to us because we knew fine well that each one of them were being watched by the IRA Security Cell, so talking to them put them under suspicion straight away. In all it was just one big game, a very dangerous game but nevertheless a game of cat and mouse. Every tour I did in Ulster I gained experience and enjoyed every moment. I carried out quite a number of exciting jobs in the Army including a six month attachment with "spooks" based in Olympia Stadium, West Berlin, from here we used to go over into East Berlin and take pictures of East German and Russian tanks, armoured personnel carriers and anything else they brought in from Russia. We would go over to East Berlin via the notorious Checkpoint Charlie. Once across into the east we would head to, supposedly, secret railway lines and wait in cover for trains to come to drop off its cargo, here is where we took most of our pictures. Other places would be the actual military camps. Our vehicles were black Mercedes "G" wagons with a cupola in the roof. We would drive right up to the camp wall which was out of view of the guardroom, jump up onto the roof through the cupola (hatch) and take pictures of everything we could in the camp. One day it was my turn but unbeknown to us we had a shock in store. I got up onto the roof and started to take my pictures when one of the guys inside the vehicle shouted *drive, drive, guard at the rear.* The driver immediately put his foot down and the vehicle lurched forward throwing me off the top and onto the street. Luckily for me the camera that I was holding fell into the vehicle. Although I was dressed in military clothing I knew if I was caught it would end up as an international incident and possibly a long stretch in jail for me. I ran as fast as I could up a street and away from the camp. At the top of the street I saw four blocks of high rise flats and ran towards them. I reached the flats and ran right to the top of one of them. Even though we wore military clothing we had civilian clothing underneath and also a lost procedure plan. The lost procedure plan was quite simple, once I had my bearings and knew my exact position I had to make it to a pre arranged landmark, known as an emergency rendezvous point or ERV, by a certain time, if I missed that time then I would have to go to the next ERV position and so on until I was picked up. If I missed the last cut off time I would have to stay overnight and hide out until the following morning when a vehicle would be at a ERV at eight o'clock, the vehicle would only wait two minutes before it moved to the second ERV and so on and would carry on all day until it either picked me up or meant I had to stay another night hiding. Up in the flats I quickly discarded my uniform and walked to the far end and went down the stairs as far as the first floor. I looked over the balcony and saw soldiers searching the first block so I ran down to the ground floor and disappeared towards Berlin city centre. I got to the first ERV but realised I was late and so immediately moved to the second ERV hoping to get picked up there, unfortunately I was late again so had to move again to the third ERV. At this point I knew I was not going to be picked up because time was against me so I decided to stay out overnight and hide away. Here I was in a country that was unfriendly with the rest of the world and scared out of my wits, I had to get as close as I could to the morning pick up and wait. I managed to find an open back door at the rear of some derelict buildings. It was getting late by this time so I went inside, found a room and made myself as comfortable as possible. I stayed awake all night because I was cold, hungry and scared of being caught so I spent the night listening to the sirens of Police or Military vehicles passing up and down the road outside the buildings. At seven thirty in the morning I moved out of my hiding place and made for the ERV where I would hopefully be picked up, in my haste to get there I arrived too early and even though it was rush hour I had the feeling everyone was looking at me. I had to move away from the pick up point area so as not to compromise it because there were still Police cars moving around the area, some slow and some fast. At eight I saw the "G" wagon approach the pick up point so I moved towards it at a quick pace, a pace that would not get me noticed but get me into a safe place quicker. The door swung open and in I jumped inside getting right down on the floor while the driver drove off. The passenger was a good friend of mine and laughed when he saw me because I must have looked a right state, he handed me a uniform which I put on straight away, he then handed me a razor and while the vehicle was on the move I tried as best as I could to have a quick shave. Once all done I was given a flask full of hot tea. Nearing Checkpoint Charlie all the doors were checked to see if they were all locked and everyone settled down and tried to relax because any hint of looking nervous would alert the guards and we would be stopped in the checkpoint. We drove through the first barrier and had to halt in front of another barrier while the guard gave a visual check inside and a thorough check under the vehicle which was the normal procedure. Once cleared the guard motioned for us to proceed, the driver was just moving off when another guard stopped us and walked right down to my window and looked inside, he knew something was wrong but couldn't put his finger on it but it didn't take him long to realise that whatever time this vehicle went through from West to East earlier this morning it only had three people inside, now it had four. We had to stay inside the vehicle for three hours waiting for a British Army Liaison officer to arrive and talk the East Germans into releasing us and all the time the guard tried their hardest to get us to open the door for a chat, smoke, tea or even a look at some sexy magazines. We all knew that if the doors ever did get open we would all be arrested. Eventually the Liaison Officer arrived and within half an hour we drove over into the west. Fucking awesome I thought, we had beaten them even though they knew one of us had stayed in their part of Berlin overnight and they had missed their chance of an arrest. I remained in West Berlin for another four months and carried on my work over in the East of the city, great times, absolutely great.

In 1992 the government made a big mistake by downsizing the forces, and phase 1 and phase 2 voluntary redundancies were introduced, a huge mistake. If you look back in history, you find that

Great Britain has been caught with its trousers down on a number of occasions. After WW I, the government downsized, only to be caught out by the onset of WW II. Korea was next. Then again the country got caught short, and with these cuts in the forces, I dare say we will get caught short again with Iraq and Afghanistan. Another Islamic country, such as Iran, may also be on the cards.

I decided to leave the Army and settle into civilian life purely because my regiment was being transformed and cut. I had joined the 2nd Battalion, the Royal Green Jackets, and that is how I wanted to go out.

I had always loved camping. I started to look around the country for a cheap site to buy and develop. I found an ideal caravan and camping site in Ayr, Scotland, which was being sold for a song and dance at £60k. I decided that this was what I wanted to do and immediately signed off from the Army.

I had about nine months to serve and threw myself into finding out more of this site. I visited the site, spoke to the old couple who were selling, and told them I would like to buy it. It was an absolute gold mine, right on the tourist trail. As the weeks turned into months, I found everything was going well with my future purchase and really looked forward to getting my teeth into the business. If it fell through, I could always take my signing-off papers out and remain in the Army, although this was not what I wanted. In the past I had heard horror stories about guys leaving the Army after completing their twenty-two years and not finding a suitable job or ending up on the dole, a situation that was not for me. A month before I was due to leave, I got a letter from the couple's solicitor; they had decided to raise the price from £60k to £190k.

Not knowing anything about the housing/business market in Scotland, I pulled out. In hindsight, I should have gotten my solicitor to sue them under Scottish law. However, I didn't know about that possibility, so I didn't sue them.

I packed up my married quarters and left the Army the following month. My wife, my sons, and I headed out into the unknown, Civvy Street, not knowing what lay ahead. I found it hard to settle into civilian life and went from job to job, trying to find my feet. Leaving the Army was going to be far worse than I feared, at least there I knew what I was doing but civvy street was a different matter altogether because I wasn't qualified in anything. Just to get on the work ladder I took a job as a security guard but when I saw how lax the other guards were I left. I had various jobs from Insurance salesman, which I soon realised was a con on the public, right up to a labourer on a building site, here was a great job, demolition and refurbishment of older buildings. The guys were great and the banter was very similar to that In the Army. I remained as a labourer moving from site to site for a few years before moving into the surveillance circuit.

I always instilled into my two lads the need to tell the truth and never get involved with gangs of any sort. One night my eldest lad came home late and said he had been riding a motorbike around some waste ground. I remembered how my dad would handle this sort of problem and told my son to get into my car and wait for me. Then I drove to the local police station, where I told the duty sergeant what had gone on and asked if she could help me. She agreed to speak to my son about his ways. She took him and me into a room and proceeded to give him the biggest bollocking of his life! Needless to say, he never did anything like that again. As I got older, I found out that my dad decided to have me put away to save me from myself. I don't hold what he did against him. I fully support him; if he had not done what he did, I would certainly have ended up either dead or in jail. It couldn't have been an easy decision for him to make, and I know I couldn't make that sort of decision. Sadly, both of my parents are dead, but not a day goes by that I don't think of them, my memories of growing up, the hardships our family went through, and the anguish my parents went through because of me. I hope that when I meet up with them again, I will have done enough to earn their respect and their forgiveness.

The surveillance circuit turned out to be a job right up my street and somewhere where I could put some of my Military training into practice. This job involved monitoring people who filed false insurance claims for feigned injuries. After a couple of years at this job, I decided to start my own business up and got my first break doing a drugs job for the Hastings Police. My partner was an ex-Royal

Marine called Rob, a good steady lad who was also from the Northeast. The job was a success; the Police arrested a female on a tip off from us who was in possession of drugs she intended to sell. This female was a true professional who obviously made her living from the sale of drugs. When we started the job we carried out the normal background checks and confirmed she lived at the address given. There are so many different ways of finding out who lives in a property and confirming the target was inside the property. If the target was at work I could also find out where he or she worked by just talking to neighbours of their partner, very simple. The best way to carry out a surveillance job on some unsuspecting person was a car and a small van, a good combination of vehicles. The OP was from a van which was parked up the street from her house with a car as back up. The car had a duel role in that it watched the van and if and when the target left the house she would be followed either on foot or by vehicle. We saw the target early on in the morning and she had black hair, when she came out later on in the morning she had dyed her hair red. She drove from Hastings to London, carried out the deal and drove back at speed to Hastings. What she didn't know was that she was being followed and filmed throughout. A trap was set up about ten miles outside of Hastings in the form of a VCP where she was arrested. As she drove around a bend she was confronted by a large VCP of about four Police cars and a dog unit. The car was stopped and searched and initially nothing was found, however when the dog unit began their search the drugs were found. The Hastings Police were overjoyed with the result. About two months after that job, we carried out a job for the Glasgow police department in the area of the Goebbels Estate, a really rough area. Again the target was a young 21 year old female. After speaking to her at her front door we confirmed she lived at the property with her mother and also she did not have any form of emplyment, the main thing though was we knew what she looked like. The first couple of days was just followed her round the estate on foot and recorded who she visited and at what time, we also found that she sold the drugs behind a Police station next to some derelict shops, here she had all round vision and was safe from being mugged by just running straight into the station. The observation point would be in building rubble directly across the road from the derelict shops and outside in all elements. The Police initially wanted me to take an officer into the OP but after a heated discussion the request was dropped. A successful OP is small and compact, if we had of had an officer in the OP with us the it would have doubled in size and therefore far easier to be compromised. Rob and me would have a hard time in the OP because of no fires or hot food, exercise would be down to a minimum with the only movement being in the dark hours. All film and reports would be put into what is commonly known as a dead letter box. This includes everything that needs to be taken out and includes all ablutions. A large plastic container for urine and small sealable bags for the number two's. the dead letter box was to be about six hundred metres away from the OP, this gives the operative some exercise and keeps the OP safe from prying eyes. Getting fresh kit into the OP comes in the form of a live letter box. This is where we collect cold food and a flask of tea or coffee, new film and observation logs which had to be filled out on a daily basis. Other items would be plastic bags and a clean plastic container. We moved into the OP at three in the morning after being dropped off by an unmarked Police car. After setting the OP up with cover from view and also cover from rain we settled down and waited to see what sort of activities she carried out. During the daytime we never saw the target but at about four each afternoon she appeared by the derelict shops with her friends and a handful of small plastic bags containing her deal where she sold to many customers. As the days went on we both realised how big of an operation she had because the amount of youngsters she had keeping a look out was doubling in size each day. I realised that we would need quite a few box's of film and loads of observation logs. All our dead and live letter box's were carried out between two and three each morning and at a different location. The main worry for us was animals in the form of dogs, we only had a couple of problems with them when they were with their owners, luckily when their owner called them the dogs left us and went back to them. One dog got more excited and wouldn't listen to what his owner was saying, in the end the man came over to see what the dog was getting all worked up about and stood right next to us without seeing anything of our OP, after cursing the dog he headed back onto the pathway and out of sight. After two weeks of surveillance, we managed not only to get the female drug dealer in the bag, but also all her dickers – what a result. The dickers were youngsters and all they had to do was keep an eye out for any Police activity, if they saw any they would alert the dealer. It turned out that the police didn't even know most of these people were involved with drugs, though they knew all of them by name for other crimes. We completed hundreds of other jobs, but none as exciting as those two. One job we did down south in Portsmouth we followed a Police Officer who was shirking work. He walked about two miles from home into Portsmouth city centre and went into a large furniture store. Rob and me set up a position across the road in an alleyway and watched for further movement. About half an hour later I heard the unmistakable sound of sirens coming down the road and said to Rob that it looked like someone was going to be in the shit because there were quite a few Police cars involved in whatever was happening. To our utter shock the Police cars stopped on the road right in front of us and within seconds Police had us both up against the wall and the area sealed off. We were searched and then questioned on the spot. I told them exactly what we were doing but omitted to tell them our target was a serving Police Officer and then gave them a phone number to call with a reference number. One of the Police Officers walked away from us and made a call, two minutes later he came back and said we could go as our story checked out and he was happy. Curiosity got the better of me and I asked how this all came about, he pointed to the buildings left and right or us and told me they were banks and that a shop keeper thought we were casing the joint with a view to robbing it. Well I had to laugh at that as I walked out onto the front street and sure enough, there was Barclays Bank on the left and the National Westminster Bank on the right. The Police left the location and Rob and I moved position further down the road. An hour later our target emerged from the furniture store and none the wiser at what just happened. We followed him back to his house and watched the front door for any further movement until it began to get dark when we called it a day and left the area.

I got hired by a well known brewery and was informed that stock to the value of thousands of pounds was going missing from one of their warehouses and could I help. What a challenge, of course I could help. We rented an apartment about twenty miles away from the target area for four months and set up all our kit. A fee was agreed and we set about preparing the job which turned out to be very difficult because we could not access the site and therefore could not get into the warehouse. As much as we tried it always ended up the same way so I called the brewery and arranged a meeting. At the meeting I told them of the problems we were experiencing and told them of a plan that would enable both me and Rob to gain access and find out what was going on, it meant the brewery had to employ us both with one of us doing the day shift and the other doing the night shift. After a long discussion it was agreed and so the very next day Rob and I turned up at an office where we filled in forms and both given an identity card. Unfortunately I got the night shift after drawing straws with Rob. It didn't really bother me about doing night shift because I knew that as the weeks went on we would change shifts. The job was now on and after a couple of weeks neither of us could identify anyone who might be involved. We now had to change plans and get right into the ribs of potential targets and try to get out for a beer with them. This worked a treat because one guy I went out for a beer with showed he was not all he was cracked up to be and came across as a bit of a rogue. I followed his lead and told him I had been arrested a couple of times for 'possession of stolen goods' which just ended up with me paying a hefty fine. I noticed the guy was very interested in what I was telling him, even though I have never been arrested in my life for a crime like that. Over the next few days I got closer and closer to this guy, to the extent of being invited to his house for an evening meal, and meeting his wife and kids. After meeting his family I was hoping this guy had nothing to do with anything illegal at the warehouse but it was not to be, he was the ring leader. Because he was the floor manger and also the man who reported the stores going missing he managed to take the spot light off him and therefore found it far easier to steal the stores that were going missing.

Out for a pint one night the man asked me if I was interested in a little job he had going as a sideline to which I replied 'yes I was'. He told me he had a certain thing going at the warehouse and that it was fool proof and that I would make a load of money from it and if I wanted in on it he would introduce me to the others. I told him I would think about it and made the excuses that I didn't want to be involved with the Police anymore to which he assured me we would not get caught. I told him I would think about it and give him a definite answer the following day. Returning to the apartment I told Rob of what had been said and worked out a plan to get everything on record, both film and speech.

The following day I met up with the floor manager and said we should meet after work to discuss how I would be involved and what was in it for me. That night I prepared myself with a covert microphone and got Rob to stay off sick so he could film us in the bar. All was set and the meeting began. I asked the floor manager loads of questions about what stores he managed to get out of thee warehouse, how he got it out, who he delivered it to and what sort of price he managed to get, I even went as far as asking him who else was involved making the excuse that too many people could cause problems and did he trust everyone. The entire conversation was being taped and the poor bloke told me everything. I really felt gutted that this guy was the head of the operation because he had such a good future with his company but greed obviously outweighed the risk. I informed my contact from the company that we needed to meet up and discuss what we had so far. At the meeting I replayed the tape of our conversation and watched for some reaction. The guy didn't know who the voice belonged to and when I said the name of the person he nearly fell off his chair. I then asked him how far he wanted us to go with this because the evidence we had so far would not stand up in court and was nothing compared to what we could get. He made a phone call in private then returned to us stating 'take it as far as we could'.

Rob resigned from his position but I remained in mine, this was purely so Rob could get everything on video tape when he followed us around the area dropping off the stores.

The first part of the job was to receive the stores into the warehouse by a delivery truck, the second part was to check and sign the forms which the truck driver supplied, part three was to get rid of the truck driver and then bring in a white van in for loading with cigarettes, of all types spirits, beer and the usual crisps and nuts. How he made all that disappear from the shelves in the store I will never know but I suspect it was hidden in a mass of paperwork somewhere.

Once the van was fully loaded it was driven out of the site and parked up on a side street. The next morning we clocked off and left the site, the floor manager told me to meet him at one in the afternoon next to the van. At the apartment Rob and I worked out a plan and from then on the game was on. Arriving at the van I saw another two small white vans waiting. The floor manager told me what to put in each van while he took the driver to one side for payment. Once finished the drivers got into their vans and drove away. All I was hoping while all this was going on was that Rob got everything on tape because I only wanted to do this once and then hand over what we had and get the fuck away. The floor manager and I got into our van and drove out of the area. I asked him who those two guys were and couldn't believe it when he told me their names and what pubs they managed, what a result. He then told me all the pubs we were going to visit that day and asked me to get into the back and separate the stores into piles on the floor which would mean we could just arrive at a pub, drop off the goods and then get going to the next pub. While I was in the back I managed to text all the pubs to Rob so at least he was in the picture of where we were going, nothing worse than being blind on a surveillance job. We drove around the area and dropped all the stuff off at various pubs, collected thee money and then when it was completed I got dropped off at my car. From there I drove out of the area and headed for the apartment. By this time I was quite tired and just wanted a bath and get some sleep but I knew that was out of the question because we had to type up everything from the Dictaphone and also edit the video tapes. This part of the job is very boring and time consuming and took us about eight hours to complete. Once we had everything sorted I made a call to my company contact and arranged to meet the following morning, I was not going into work that night and called in telling them I had pulled a muscle in my back and needed to get to the doctors first thing in the morning. The floor manager called me and asked if everything was alright to which I replied 'everything was fine other than my back', I told him I just needed a couple of days and rest and was not used to humping heavy boxes from one shelf to another. He told me that the next drop offs would be the following week and was I up for it, 'yes of course I was'. The conversation ended and Rob and I went out for a Chinese meal and a couple of beers. Early the following morning Rob and I met up with our contact in a hotel. The contact was accompanied by two other men also dressed in suits and where introduced as management from a higher level. We showed exactly what we had, which as far as I was concerned was fantastic, even though Rob was on his own he managed to get some very incriminating evidence and also managed to get all number plates and full facial shots of everyone involved in the drop offs. He even managed to get in such a position that he got the handover of money on film. The three suits watched and read everything we had but never changed the looks on their faces. A couple of hours later and with everything read and watched one of them said that what we had would be handed over to the police for further investigation and that the job we had done was far more than they expected. I was informed that we were not needed any longer and thanked by all three, I enquired about my invoice and if they could tell me if I had to deduct our weekly wages which we had earned while working for them, one of the men started to laugh and said we should invoice the full amount and to accept the wages as a bonus. With that we parted our ways, the three suits went back to their offices, I and Rob headed north and home.

A Policewoman was off work due to a back injury. She lived in East Kilbride just south of Glasgow. We both turned up at the job and Rob decided to knock the front door to confirm she lived there and more importantly that she was in the property, nothing worse than sitting watching an empty house. Confirmation that she was inside the property and that she was going out at ten o'clock was good enough for me and we set up just off the estate where she lived and waited. Just before ten we saw her drive her car out of the estate and heading in the direction of Glasgow. At a large roundabout she turned up a dusty track and out of sight. We gave her a couple of minutes and before I drove up the track to see where she was and what she was doing. To my utter joy I saw that she was at a golf club and getting ready for a game of golf. Golf courses are normally quite easy to be able to watch the target playing but this one was surrounded by a duel carriageway and was becoming quite a nightmare to watch. In the end I decided to take the bull by the horns and give a last attempt at getting film which I badly needed. I grabbed my camera and bag and walked to the reception desk where I spoke to a very nice woman. I told her that I was doing a sports degree and that my subject was golf of which I knew nothing about would it be ok if I filmed some golfers and asked them some questions on the game. At first the woman was not comfortable with my request and I thought she was going to ask me to leave but just when I was going to plead with her my target and two other females came out of a changing room. I decided to ask them if they would mind and explained everything to them, after a little chat they all agreed to help me and agreed for me to follow them and film what I wanted but that I shouldn't interrupt their game with too many questions. Wow, I just could not believe my luck, an invitation to film my target. I followed the three women round the course but only filmed my target when she took a shot. After they finished they went straight into the restaurant for something to eat and drink. I followed them in and began asking golf questions before asking names which I said I needed to complete the task, all names were given to me and I departed. That was one of the easiest jobs we did.

It never suprises me of how trusting some people are. We had a job to watch this guy who was supposed to be bedridden. Rob knocked the front door a couple of days before we went on the job to see what, if anything, the guy was up to. It turned out the guy wasn't bedridden at all and was quite active, he even had a job and left his house at 7.30 in the morning to catch his bus. A couple of days later we set up and watched the house, Rob in the car and mme stood further down the street outside some shops. We watched the target leave his house and stand at the bus stop but something just did not look right because he was looking all over the place, up and down the road and at everyone that walked passed him which only said one thing to me, something had spooked him. I called Rob and he said much the same and that we should be very careful with this guy. As we were talking a bus turned up and the target joined the queue. I made my way to the bus stop and stood behind the target, I didn't have a clue where he was going and tried to listen to what he said but heard nothing, once he had paid his fair and went to sit down I looked at the driver and said, same again please. He gave me a ticket and I went to sit down. In my hand I had a bag with a covert camera hidden inside and was lucky enough to get a seat directly opposite the target. Placing my bag on my lap I filmed the target. Watching him out of the corner of my eye I noticed he was very alert and kept looking out of the back window, obviously concerned about the car following behind. I text Rob to drop back away from the bus so the target would settle down. No sooner had I said that when the target got on his phone and called the Police stating that he was being followed and even giving the registration of the car to them, we had already booked in with the Police earlier that morning and just hoped they didn't say anything to the target. I looked at the target and asked him if everything was alright as he looked quite worried, he told me that he was being followed by a surveillance team because he had a large insurance claim in, he also told me how he was conning the insurance company and that he had been working since day one of the claim, he told me where he worked what he did in his past time and basically everything about him and his family. What this guy did not realise was I was the other half of the surveillance team and was filming him, with sound. After getting off the bus we both walked to his place of work where he showed me round inside the factory. He even made me a cup of tea. What a bloke, so trusting.

Another job that ended up with Rob running down the road with a mad Jock chasing him and me laughing my head off. We went on a job in Inverness and had to watch the activity of a male who lived with his partner and had connections in the drug trade. We followed this guy to a shopping mall in separate cars and when he parked up he seemed to be looking around the car park for someone or something. I parked my car a few rows behind the target while Rob went further down the car park to park. As soon a Rob emerged from his vehicle this guy ran for him and for some unknown reason instead of him getting back into his car he started running away from this guy. Rob is a fit bloke and had no problem running and keeping ahead of this guy and basically ran him round the car park while I filmed everything and chuckling to myself because it looked so funny.

I was still working on the surveillance circuit in 2003 when I got a phone call from a friend inviting me to a meeting in London regarding work in the Middle East, I was given no further details save for an address and date to turn up at and what forms to bring with me. I arrived at the meeting at the date and time I was told and then ushered into a small conference room where I saw about another thirty or so other guys. We were all told to sit down and listen to what was going to be said and that if anyone had any problems and wanted to leave they could. We were told what was happening and that the country in question was Iraq. We were informed as to what our job would entail, what the daily rate would be and also what the dangers were, we were then given a full hour long intelligence brief and the stopped for a tea and coffee break. The break was purely put in so anyone who wanted to leave could do so without any embarrassment, this worked quite well because when we went back into the room I noticed quite a few empty seats. From here we were to be called into a room individually and go through a sort of mini interview, nobody would be told that day whether they had the job or not, this would be by phone call over the next few days. Two days later I received my call and offered a job, well, what could I do but accept? I packed in my job the day after and got ready to deploy to Iraq. My days working on the surveillance circuit I enjoyed very much but as they say - all good things come to an end.

Chapter 1 (2003)

Basra Oilfields burning

Thursday, 27 September 2008, I left home at 1500 hours to get the train from home, to Manchester Airport. My wife drove me to the station; she parked the car in the car park and helped me out with my bag. She asked me if I wanted her to stay with me until the train came, and I said no. I knew, even after all these years that she would cry, and I hated seeing her upset. We had a kiss in the car park, and I picked up my bag and walked away. I looked back once and saw her crying in the car. I continued to the station, found my platform, sat down on the bench, and waited. It was a cold day, and I huddled up in my fleece and started to recall Iraq again.

I had been in Iraq since August 2003 and had carried out many different jobs. I started doing PSD, or private security detail. A PSD is comprised of four armed men who look after VIP clients in hostile countries, much like four bodyguards. Four is the minimum number; it could be quite a lot more, but that depends on which country you are operating in and what the threat there is. I then took over the QM job for Control Risk Group. I was a private security consultant, one of a thousand ex-Army men who could not find their way in civilian life and took the call from private security firms to assist in the rebuilding of Iraq. I took off from RAF Brize Norton and landed at Basra Airport along with six other men.

After two nights sleeping on the tiled floor at Basra, we jumped on a flight to Baghdad. I wasn't sorry to see the back of Basra Airport. Basra had taken a fierce beating at the hands of the British in the war, and they controlled everything. The airport was controlled by the British Royal Military Police, and the C130 Hercules aircraft were controlled by the movement's cells, who were British soldiers. Landing at Basra, we were told to make our way inside the building and book in with movements, these people arrange all flights, trains and vehicle movements for the British Army. Once booked in, we were given a flight to Baghdad. However, our flight would not leave until two days hence, and because we couldn't move outside the airport building, we had two rough nights on a tiled floor in the main terminal. The lighting was supplied by a generator. Tea and coffee were plentiful, but the food was for British soldiers only, not for security contractors. The military cookhouse was on the first floor, and one had to get past an armed guard at the bottom of a flight of stairs to gain access to it. The first night, we six were pretty hungry and started talking of ways to get past the guard. We were all ex-British military men, and we were not short of ideas. In the end we decided to just 'blag' it with a story of us being military; we wouldn't tell the guard which unit we came from. We would let him make his own mind up.

We approached the guard and gave him some hard-luck story of being stranded in Basra for two nights; he asked what unit we came from, but we said we couldn't say because we were heading to Baghdad, and our location had to be kept quiet. He asked if we came from

Hereford, home of the S.A.S, and again we just kept quiet. He gave us a good looking over, and what he saw was a bunch of unshaved, scruffy men. He then said we could go; before we went past him, I told him to keep very quiet about us and gave him a wink, and he said we shouldn't worry about that. He wouldn't say anything to anyone other than the guard who took over from him, so we wouldn't have any trouble. I thanked him, and we set off upstairs to the dining area. Once at the hotplate, we had to sign in on a sheet of paper. Each one of us wrote down our name and *M.O.D London*. The chef was happy with that and asked us if we were MI5 or MI6, and again we said we couldn't say and that he shouldn't broadcast our presence. He assured us he wouldn't. We served ourselves and sat down to a hearty meal, the first we had for nearly twenty-four hours. After the meal we sat in some easy chairs and watched a bit of sky television before leaving and heading downstairs to our accommodation, the tiled floor.

Most of us had sleeping bags, so we stripped off and got our heads down. It was quite hard to get a full night's sleep because the airport was in constant use by the military with troop movements, troops coming into the country, troops leaving the country, and troops being moved around Iraq itself, so every couple of hours or so, we would be wakened by the noise of these lads. Through the daylight hours, we had to stay inside the terminal building. It was far too dangerous to move outside, especially as we were not armed. We got some cards out and played various games for a few hours, then lay down to read and nearly always dropped off to sleep.

Evening came again, and we headed up to the cookhouse area for our evening meal; again we talked our way past the guard and again ate a hearty meal before watching some television and returning to our sleeping area. I am not saying the lads on guard were slack or unprofessional by any means. The story we gave, our accents, and the fact that we were British didn't help him one bit. If he had had any doubt at all, he could have stopped us. The fact that he really did not know what unit we came from and that he had never encountered a security guy before, made it very easy for us to get past him. I honestly hope the lad had a safe tour and got back home to his family safely, and I wish him well. I don't think for one moment he was really taken in by our story, but I thank him for using his common sense and letting us eat. I also know that we should have seen the unit RQMS or QM and gained permission to eat. However, having served in the British military, we all knew the system, and we knew the unit RQMS and QM would have told us in no uncertain terms what we could do. At the end of the day we were all ex servicemen who had been trained and had served our country, all we were doing here was putting that training into practice. We were called forward by the movement's guys and given a boarding card for the flight to Baghdad; the flight was leaving around midnight and would take an hour. All baggage was loaded onto a pallet and strapped down by the Royal Air Force ground crew; we got on the aircraft and strapped ourselves in. After a quick security brief by the flight sergeant, the ramp came up, and off we went. A none eventful flight, thank God.

On landing at the APOD in Baghdad, we found ourselves in amongst both British and American soldiers who were going about their business, either waiting for flights to various parts of Iraq or coming in from various areas. We were soon picked up by a team of security men who were all armed to the teeth with 9 mm Browning pistols and AK-47 assault rifles. They guided us to the waiting security vehicles and spread us out among them. These vehicle were armoured Toyota 4 x 4s. We were driven out of the military side of Baghdad Airport, the APOD, and down dusty roads.

Finally we came across a large checkpoint, where we were ushered through by security men just like ourselves, men who worked for a different company. As we left the checkpoint, the team leader reminded us that we were now leaving the safe area and entering the Red Zone.

We sped down the motorway, which was called Route Irish. I looked out at the houses and immediate area, and I thought, 'What a shithole.' We could still see the remains of Iraqi armour that had been taken out in the war, tanks that littered the sandy area. Some had no turrets, and quite a few had their tracks missing or very badly damaged. What a dump! The civilian cars were much the same – rust buckets, some actually falling apart as they made their way along the road; some with no passenger or driver door; some with a bonnet or a boot missing. Nearly all of them had no windows at all. Dead donkeys and dogs littered the landscape everywhere, the smell at times was overpowering, and the stench of raw sewage was bad and made you hold your nose. What a mess the place was in! No war would make an area into such a shithole; this was purely a lack of commitment on the government's part to keeping the country clean and serviceable. This place was a complete shithole.

After about a twenty-minute drive, we found ourselves in a villa in the Mansoor area of Baghdad. In England, we would call such an area a slum, but in Baghdad, they called it an up-market area. Our villa was right in the middle of a huge housing estate which was bordered on three sides by main roads leading to the city centre. The villa was a large eight bedroom building with a sauna situated in the main shower area and a swimming pool, at the side of the building there was an annex which had a further four bedrooms, to the front and side garden were small in comparison to the building itself. At the front there was an entrance gate and further up was an exit gate however there was only enough room to park three to four vehicles. An eight foot high wall surrounded two sides of the garden which gave privacy. The villa belonged to Saddam's head of security prior to the war but when the war started turning in favour of the coalition the owner moved out, lock stock and barrel. Some Iraqi prospector who saw the potential took the villa over and rented it to our company. Directly across the main road was a Police station which was manned by four officers. Further up the side road was a large area of wasteland which backed onto some very impressive villa's which were all rented by foreign security companies or an NGO, None Government Organisation. I was escorted into the villa and given a quick tour of the inside before being given a bed space. There I dumped my kit before heading downstairs again for a security brief and a sort of welcome package. At that stage there were only about twenty guys in the villa but as time went by there was about fifty to fifty four men who slept there overnight.

The situation in Baghdad at the time was calm, with no major threats, and all the locals were happy to see the foreigners. The Iraqi Army was in disarray, and the police force was, at best of times, uninterested in anything other than what they could steal for themselves. The police had a good little trick up their sleeves – when they saw you approaching, they would try to stop you. The idea was that they would give you an on-the-spot fine for speeding; the unfortunate thing was that they never were able to stop you because that was a very big no-no for the teams. No team leader would have a job if he stopped for anyone on the road except a slow-moving person crossing in front of the vehicles, and that was supposed to occur only if there were no way around that person.

After the welcome package, we had to get our weapons, ammunition, and body armour. Unfortunately, there were not enough 9 mm Browning pistols to go around, so we had to do with the available guns, very bad-looking AK-47 assault rifles. The ammunition we had was Iraqi ammunition that some of the guys had scrounged off other security guys they knew from their Army days. Iraqi ammunition was worthless because when you fired it from your AK, the round didn't have enough charge to push the bullet out to the appropriate distance for the weapon. Sometimes you would see a puff of dust come up from the ground about fifty feet in front of you.

That was years ago, but I still remembered it as I sat at the Preston station while waiting for my train. I remembered when I had to go out on my own into the suburbs and find weapons – AK-47s, Brownings, and a pistol called the Tariq. To buy weapons from Iraqis, sometimes I would go out with twenty thousand dollars, sometimes as much as forty thousand, stuffed into a day sack on my back. After finding a source or gun runner, I would do a deal with him; when he brought the weapons to me at a venue, I would inspect the weapons. If they were good, I would pass the money over and place the weapons into my day sack and set off back to the villa. One of the main reasons why we had to buy weapons off street was because we couldn't buy them from overseas as no company had a license to buy weapons from abroad, anyway there were enough weapons on the market here in Baghdad. Another reason was to get them off the street and out of the hands of any terrorist.

These were the quiet days when there was not much trouble going on, but weapon-buying was still dangerous work. I met an Iraqi who said he could supply me with anything I wanted if I offered the right price. Here I was delving into the murky world of gun-running with Iraqi criminals. My contact for these deals was an Iraqi called Mohammad, a man in his late forties, who spoke perfect English. I would simply phone him up and tell him what I required. He would get back to me a couple of days later and inform me that he either had the guns and ammunition or did not, but mostly he would tell me he had what I needed. He would fix a time and night for him to pick me up from the villa in Mansoor. When Mohammad arrived, I would be waiting outside with my money in my day sack. I would get into his car. I would then inform him that the weapon pickup point had changed and tell him my preferred place. I took these precautions for reasons of trust, or rather the lack of it; carrying a single 9 mm Browning pistol, I did not trust him one bit. He could have had an ambush waiting for me. The most dangerous part of the deal was when other Iraqis turned up with the guns and ammo. Here I was, an Englishman with loads of money and a Browning pistol, amidst all these men with weapons galore, enough to carry out a good attack on anyone. To say I was not scared would have been untrue. I was scared, but I tried my best not to show it. I shivered at times even though it was hot, and my mouth was dry even though I had water.

Here I was in the murky, dark back streets of Baghdad, carrying out a deal with criminals. I was alone except for Mohammad and my trusted 9mm pistol, but I knew that if these men had bad intentions, Mohammad would have gone over to their side. There were four Iraqi gun runners who could not speak a word of English and never once smiled at me or took their eyes off me. I was in a house downtown Baghdad and needed weapons for the teams. This meeting had been set up by Mohammad so I could get those weapons so badly needed. I was sat on a chair while the gun runners sat on a sofa opposite. It was not the best of situations but I knew that if they started anything I would have no problems dispatching them. I was the first westerner they had seen and dealt with so they didn't really know what I could do and what I could not do so they were very hesitant of me. While they watched, I inspected each weapon to see if it was good or bad. The good ones went to one side; the bad ones went to the other side. An inspection could take an hour or two. When I had finished inspecting the weapons, I then had to get them to agree to take back the bad ones and sell me the good ones. Then came the tricky part, the price.

Difficulty arose once when there were serious quality issues with the weapons, and I had rejected many bad ones. Then the gun runners wanted more per weapon. We previously agreed on a price of four hundred dollars for each weapon prior to the meeting. I was not prepared to go higher because they had brought me inferior guns. Arab arguing started which is a fucking nightmare in itself because it could go on for hours. Here we all sat down on the ground, and I had to give a good reason why I was not going to pay more per gun, I must say that the reasons I gave were very good because the weapons were crap. Then they gave their reasons why I should pay more due to the dangers of their endeavor and because they were all poor. I gave my reasons of why the price should go down instead of up because I was only one man and had the dangers of getting caught by the Americans or Iraqi Police, I also told them that I really didn't give a fuck how poor they were and mentioned the BMW car which they drove to the meeting in. I told them my price was now three hundred and fifty dollars per weapon and that every time they put the price up I would drop it. Fucking hell you would have thought I wanted them for free because they went mad, it was quite laughable really because I didn't have a clue how to haggle and at times I would have to tell them to keep the noise down because they were working themselves towards a fucking heart attack. I would stick to the price of three hundred and fifty and never waver even though they became angry. In the end, after an hour of haggling I stopped everyone arguing and told them they had one minute to decide if they wanted to sell at my price or not and that I was ready to get the fuck out of here and deal with someone who could supply decent weapons instead of crap like they brought me, in an instant they agreed to my price, fucking hell I couldn't believe it, what a champ I am. The guns would come with five magazines, which was the normal practice, and the Iraqis never got uptight about that aspect of our deal.

Therefore, with the deal complete, all I had to do was load the weapons into the boot of the car and get back to the villa safely. Travel was not always easy, for the Americans had mobile patrols out, and there was a curfew in place. Anyone outside his house after 2200 hours would have been arrested or shot without question; here I was, with a car full of weapons, at 0200 hours in the morning. We left the venue and skirted round the back streets, heading for the villa. At times we would stop the car and turn the engine off and just sit and listen. Sometimes I would get out of the car and walk to the end of the alleyway and stand and look around for any foot patrols or any sort of vehicle movement. I would then signal for the car to move forward to me. After another check up and down the road to make sure all was clear, I would get into the car and leapfrog over to the other side of the street and carry out the same process again. I carried out this procedure all the way back to the villa.

Once at the villa, I unloaded the car and sent Mohammad on his way home. He didn't live very far from our villa, so I wasn't unduly worried. I thought the Americans would have been better at patrolling during the night, but this wasn't so; each time I went out to do my dodgy dealings, I would always get back safely. At times I would see American checkpoints and would always avoid them by boxing round and coming out further down the road behind them. If a patrol of humvees approached I would park up at the side of the road and let it pass by, once it was out of sight and there were no other humvees around I would slowly drive back onto the road and carry on my journey. No need to panic like the Iraqis did every time they saw an American, all I had to do was drive as normal as possible and not bring any attention to myself.

One pick up I carried out was in a hotel car park where I knew I would be safe because the security men were British so if anything went wrong I could always rely on them to give me back up. When I arrived at the car park I went over to the guys and told them exactly what I was doing, the only problem was it was three in the morning. I had a cup of tea whilst waiting for the Iraqis gun runners to turn up and passed half an hour or so chatting. The deal was very simple because it was only a couple of pistols and the guy who brought them only lived about fifty metres away. Mohammad and I then drove back to the villa avoiding all the checkpoints as we went. Driving down the road towards the villa was a different matter altogether. We were about seventy metres away from the villa when all we saw was an RPG rocket pass in front of us heading straight for the villa. Whoever fired the rocket must have been cock eyed because it missed the building and carried on right down the street hitting a building much further down the road. I parked up at the side of the road just in time to see another RPG fly passed, again heading for the villa, this one hit the ground and flew right up in the air and over the top of the villa. Some weeks previous to this we had a small guard room built onto the outside wall so the Iraqi guard we employed had somewhere to sit which kept them out of the sun. The third RPG to pass in front of us hit this small building and exploded on impact. The noise was terrific with dust and bricks flying everywhere. I knew someone was in the building because I had seen him a few seconds before the rocket found its mark so I got out of the car and ran down the road towards the building. As I got there I saw all the guys who lived there up on the roof and all armed and waiting for a target to fire at. Out of the rubble staggered one of the Iraqi guards who was called Raad. He was covered in dust from head to foot but didn't appear to be injured. He looked up at me, put his thumbs in the air and said "Mr. Jack, ok", that was a very funny sight and comment which brought a smile to my face. What a character this guy was, a pure genius. Fortunately that third rocket was the last one fired before the terrorists made their getaway. Mohammad and I quickly got behind the garden wall and into the villa. Because Mohammad was religious he was forbidden to look at a naked man or any woman. When we entered the villa we were met by the guys who had started to come down off the roof, a few of them were stark naked and a few of them, who had been on the piss all night, came down still carrying bottles of beer. When Mohammad saw the naked guys he gave a shriek before covering his eyes and trying to make it into another room, the problem was in his haste to get clear of the naked men he walked straight into the wall missing the doorway by miles, fucking hell that was so funny to see and everyone that witnessed it laughed like hyenas. After that little episode Mohammad was a lot more observant before he walked into the villa, what a sport he was because he really found the funny side of it and accepted that some of these guys liked walking round the villa naked, both inside and outside. One guy used to walk around the villa naked with half a football turned inside out on his head, must have thought he looked like a chicken or something.

Instead of adopting a complicated plan on how to move from one point to another, I would always keep it simple. During my military days, everything had to be planned right down to the finest detail so nothing would go wrong. If anything went wrong with a plan, there was always a backup plan to use. Here in Baghdad, my status was different. As far as the Americans were concerned, I was a civilian. British or

Iraqi, my status didn't matter to them. If they had ever caught me, I don't know what would have happened – an international incident? Who knows?

I remembered playing war games as a kid. I was pretty good at those games. Well, I adopted those tactics to get from one point to another. Kids will always get through a guarded position because they keep everything simple. I bet there were loads of kids moving round Baghdad right under the American patrols' noses, and I bet not one of them got caught. You find that ex-military men operate just as they did while in the Army when they plan an operation. I cannot remember any of them keeping things simple; they kept everything hard and complicated. I kept my methods as simple as I could, and kids' war games always got me through. Although my activity in Iraq could look like a big game, it was very dangerous and had the potential for fatal consequences.

One good talent that came with me to civilian life from the Army was the ability to talk my way out of situations when they went wrong. Unfortunately, the American soldier seems like a robot, a creature who cannot think outside the box. When he comes up against an ex-British soldier, the American soldier will always back down and takes what the ex-British soldier says as the truth. I have been stopped many times by the American mobile patrols and have always managed to concoct a story of why I am out after curfew, where I am going and why, why I have all these weapons and all this ammunition, and what I intend to do with them. I sometimes thought I was good at evading the American patrols but, hey, nobody's perfect.

One day Mohammad and I had to go to the green zone. Our normal route took us onto a wide intersection where we had to turn left. The Police Officer who controlled this intersection was the spitting image of Saddam Hussein; he was as good as a clone. He recognized our vehicle and nodded with a smile. Around these intersections drivers would get hassle off women and children who would knock at the vehicle window and ask for money, it did get quite annoying because they most probably had more money than half the people they asked. My eyes were all over the place, front sides and rear looking for anyone who thought we were an easy target when I saw this young woman approach our vehicle. My hand instinctively went for my pistol which

I took out of its holster and rested it between my legs. The woman simply came up to my window and pressed herself right up to the glass, she then took her top in both hands and parted her clothing showing the nicest tits I have ever seen, I nudged Mohammad in the ribs to get his attention from looking at shops to having a look at these lovely puppies. As he turned his head his eyes caught sight of the puppies and he shrieked with a look of horror on his face, fucking hell I roared with laughter at the sight of him trying to cover up his face and literally running round in the vehicle, it was hilarious. The woman stayed at the window waiting for some money while still showing her lovely pups, I slowly put my hand in my pocket and slowly took out some money and gave her 5,000ID, about four US Dollars. She then covered herself up, smiled at me and walked away. We then carried on towards the green zone in silence because Mohammad was disgusted in what he saw. As we got to checkpoint 12 we stopped and I got out of the vehicle and walked to the sentry to show my identity card. Just then shooting started right up the road and behind us. The American sentry told me in no uncertain terms that I couldn't come through the checkpoint as they had orders to lock down and take cover if shooting started. Well wasn't that just fucking great, the sentry took cover behind sandbags and there was I stood out in the open with no cover. Whatever was this guy thinking of?. Just over the road from the checkpoint was a tea stand. I signaled Mohammad to come with me and have a Iraqi tea which he was more than happy to do. We sat at the tea stand listening to the shooting going on further up the road and the American sentry shouting at me to get into cover. I shouted back to him "what fucking cover, there's none around". He shouted for me to get behind my vehicle so I shouted back that the vehicle was not armoured and a bullet would go straight through it. I ignored him from then on because he was boring me with tedious idea's, if he had of let me through none of this would be happening. I asked Mohammad why he couldn't look at women and he told me that the main reason was his wife. If she caught him looking at other women she would tell him off, I told him that it would be our secret and that I would never breathe a word of it to his wife. I then asked him if he liked what he saw; he looked around then whispered, "Yes they were very nice". I had to laugh at his actions because when he looked around it was as if he was looking for his wife, it was so funny.

The shooting stopped as quickly as it started and the American sentry shouted for me to get into my vehicle and get through the checkpoint. Having finished our tea and chat Mohammad and I slowly walked to the vehicle, got into it and drove the twenty metres to the barrier. The American sentry told me I was fucking mad and let me through into the green zone. Outside that checkpoint there is no cover whatsoever, only derelict buildings which had been bombed in the war and a grubby little tea stand with a man who looked about eighty who made it and served you. Who the fuck was mad, me for having a tea or the sentry for not letting me through the checkpoint and into cover with him and his mates?

I once designed an identity card on the same lines as a British Military identity card. I used this manufactured ID along with my American Department Of Defence card, which I found I could get anywhere. Not many Americans had encountered a serving British soldier, which gave me the edge, even though I was not a serving soldier the Americans did not have a not a clue what sort of person to expect.

Once I was stopped with about fifty AK rifles and loads of ammunition in the boot of my car. The American soldier wanted to arrest me on the spot, at least until I came out with a story of how I was part of a joint American/British operation to buy as many weapons and as much ammunition off the streets of Baghdad as I could and get them back to the Green Zone for the Intelligence people to look at them. After that, I told this American, the weapons would all be cut up and the ammunition destroyed. Well, everything was going great until the soldier asked me what part of the Green Zone I lived in. Thinking quickly, I showed him my fake British military identity card along with my DOD card. I told him I had just arrived in Baghdad from Basra two days earlier and wasn't sure of the name. However, I knew the directions to the location. I then started giving him directions to this villa inside the Green Zone. I didn't really know the inside of the Green Zone all that well because I had only been inside once or twice. I confused the hell out of this soldier, and finally he took one last good look at my fake British identity card and sent me on my way. Just before leaving him, I asked him if he could keep it quiet – we didn't want our agenda leaking out and every Iraqi learning what we were doing. On the rare occasions when an American soldier stopped me, I could always talk my way out of trouble.

I am not saying that the American soldier is useless. Far from it! They are brave men and women. I just believe that they need to be more alert and flexible, use their common sense, and think outside of the box instead of being blinkered. The American soldiers I did meet socially were extremely well mannered and very polite and a good bunch of guys to have a chat and laugh with. The Iraq conflict has not only damaged manly families in the U.S but stripped away so many young men who, in my opinion, died for a worthless cause. The soldiers I met much later when I was on my convoy duties were brave and always up for the fight.

Another time I had arranged to meet Mohammad and place a large order for guns. We had extra men coming into the country, and they all needed to be armed. Mohammad said he knew where we could get the quantity I needed without any problem. The price was $350.00 per gun, and they each came with five magazines. If I wanted more ammunition, he could supply that also; the ammunition came in sealed cartons. Each carton held 750 rounds of Russian 7.62 mm cartridges.

Mohammad picked me up from the villa at 2100 hours and drove out of Baghdad, heading north on the motorway towards a place called Taji. I had no money with me, but I had my trusted day sack. I asked him where we were going, and he said it was his secret place. I was very nervous and started fidgeting in my seat; he noticed and tried to assure me that all was well.

I pointed out to Mohammad that if he ever drove me into danger, I would kill him before anyone else ever got to me.

Mohammad smiled and said, 'Mr Jack, you are my friend and brother. I will never let anything bad happen to you. I would give my life first.' This statement did not reassure me at all and I reminded him that if he ever set me up he would get the first bullet, he just looked and smiled. I knew that these Iraqi gun runners stick together in any situation.

After driving for about twenty minutes, Mohammad turned left off the road and headed into the desert. He slowed down quite a lot and seemed to be looking for a marker. All of a sudden, he said,

'Yes, we are nearly there.' I looked out of the car windows and couldn't see anything that could be used to tell him where we were because we were in the fucking desert and all I could see was sand. After about five minutes more, he stopped the car and got out. I immediately got out of the car and pulled my pistol out of its holster and took up a position away from the car. If anything was going to happen, the car would be the target, attracting all the attention, while I dashed away further into the barren desert.

Mohammad walked to a spot in front of the car and bent down to look at something on the ground. He then straightened up and turned left, went a few more paces, and made a cross on the ground with the heel of his boot. He looked up at my position and said, with a smile, 'We dig here.' I was absolutely shocked when he said that, what the hell had he been looking at ? He got two shovels from the boot of his car, handed one to me, and without further ado, he started to dig. After about half an hour, he jumped out of the hole and told me to carry on.

I made my feeble attempt at digging; the ground was rock-hard with big stones. What a nightmare! After half an hour, with sweat pouring off me, I jumped out and told Mohammad to carry on. Mohammad jumped in and began digging again. Soon he popped his head up and indicated we had reached our goal. Five feet down, he had made contact with a wooden box. I grabbed a red filtered torch and shone it down the hole in the ground and sure enough there was the shape of a lid from a box. He cleared the sand and rubble off the top and grabbed a rope handle at the side; he heaved it out of the hole and placed it on the top. I looked at him as he took both clasps off and opened the lid. Inside were ten AK-47 assault rifles, still in their greaseproof paper. They were brand-new weapons.

After another hour, or so we had five boxes of new AK-47s laid out on the ground. I did not need to inspect these weapons, so we placed them in the boot of the car and buried the boxes. It would have been too dangerous to drive back into Baghdad with the weapons, so we just sat out in the desert next to the car. We sat looking at the night sky, sweat pouring off us, and began chatting.

I asked him how he had come across the weapons, and he told me that when the Americans reached the outskirts of Baghdad in the second war, the Iraqi Army deserted the camps and ran home. He and his friends went into the camps looking for anything of any value. He went into a building with metal doors and found boxes and boxes of weapons, ranging from pistols right up to anti tank weapons. He decided to take the boxes of AK-47s, AK-47 magazines, and pistols. In another part of the camp, they found the ammunition store; as with the weapons, they took all the boxes of ammunition. He told me it took him three days to get the weapons and ammunition out of the camp and into the desert. He said that during the war, the Iraqi Army personnel were terrified of the coalition forces. Most of the Iraqi soldiers knew that when the Americans reached Baghdad, they would lose, so they just took off their uniforms, put on their civilian clothes, and went home. He told me that his brother, Hassan, had been fighting up north near Tikrit. Hassan had been captured by the Kurdish Army. Hassan had his weapon and ammo taken off him; after that, he was questioned and then released. A bus brought all the prisoners back to Baghdad. When they arrived at their camp, they were all re-armed and sent back up north to fight again.

A week later, Hassan was captured, disarmed, questioned, and returned to Baghdad once again. This time, however, Hassan decided to go home instead of to the camp. It was the way Mohammad told me the story that made me laugh; his hand movements and facial expressions were quite funny. We stayed awake all night, talking about the war and what was going to happen to Iraq in the future, Mohammad's family, and a load of other crap.

It started to get light about five but for safety reasons six in the morning was a safe time to move, as the curfew was lifted. At about 6.30 we drove very slowly into the streets of Baghdad. The car was laden with weapons, and any speed would have had the two front wheels off the ground. The roads were full of cars now, a sort of Baghdad rush hour. We wound our way through the traffic and down back streets until I came out at the top end of our street and headed for the villa. At the villa I unloaded the car, and Mohammad drove home. He said he would call later for his money.

That afternoon Mohammad visited the villa, and I had all his money waiting for him. After he counted it, he put it in his jacket pocket. I told him I needed quite a lot of ammo, both 9 mm and 7.62

mm short, and I needed it tonight. He thought for a while, and then his eyes lit up as he remembered a man in Saduki Street who owned a watch shop. He told me he had five or six cartons of Russian 7.62 mm in the rear of his shop. However, it was very dangerous for me, a Westerner, to go to that part of Baghdad. Civilians were being abducted by that time, and any Westerner was fair game. The first kidnapped Westerner I saw on television was an American called Nick Berg. His end was not a good sight, and the idea of going out really worried me. Nick berg had been captured by insurgents and held captive. I don't know what he did for a living but he certainly had nothing to do with the Military or Security Firms, he most probably worked for a Logistics Company in support of the American's. He was held for a period of time and then decapitated in front of the camera. On the film, which was shown on Al Jezeera TV, he was seen knelt down, hands tied behind his back and dressed in orange coveralls. A huge guy stood behind him as Nick spoke to the camera about how we should not be there in Iraq and pleading for his life. The guy behind him started chanting, all of a sudden he pulls a huge knife out of his waste belt in his right hand and grabs hold of Nick's chin with his left hand, he pulls Nick's head backwards and starts cutting his head off, once he has finished his grizzly task he places the head on the small of Nick's back who is by then stretched out on the floor in a pool of blood. You could hear Nick pleading through gurgling speech as his head was being cut from his body. I decided there and then that nobody was going to cut my head off if I were caught, I would shoot myself in the head first – after taking out as many of those kidnappers as I could. They could do with me whatever they wanted after that.

I had to go with Mohammad because I was concerned about the type of ammo he might bring back. Iraqi ammo, though inferior, was abundant. The powder was not strong enough to force the bullet out of the barrel and caused many stoppages; it was absolutely terrible ammo.

I had a good tan; with a long-sleeved shirt and a *shamagh* on my head, nobody would know the difference between a native and me. Mohammad picked me up at six that night and drove me into the shittiest part of Baghdad; it was absolutely stinking. He found the watch shop and parked around the corner out of sight of the shop's front door. He told me that the man would walk out of his shop and take us to his friend, who had the ammo; I didn't like the idea of going round the back streets of this shithole with someone I didn't know. So, as we walked towards the shop, I devised my own plan. There were few people about.

As we walked to the shop, I saw the man coming out, about to lock the front door. I took out my pistol and stuck it into his ribs and marched him straight back into the shop. Mohammad had to follow me inside, as he didn't have a clue what was happening. Inside the shop, I told Mohammad to lock the door and leave the lights off, which he did. He gave me a puzzled look and didn't say a word. I spoke to the shop owner and asked him where the ammo was to which he replied it was with a friend across town, I was quite taken when he answered me in perfect English. I asked him again where the ammo was and who the contact was. His reply didn't mean fuck-all to me, so I strapped him to the chair where he sat and had a look in the back of the shop where Mohammad had said the man had the ammo. I first found the toilet because the smell was enough to make me sick; I turned the backroom light on and found a stash of ammo in the middle of the room. Looking at it, I knew something was seriously wrong, so I ran into the shop front room and untied the man. I dragged him into the back room and pointed at the ammo, I said if my ammo is across town who the fuck did this ammo belong too? Not surprisingly he did not answer but just put his head down.

Mohammad looked startled and then very afraid, for he knew something was wrong.

Mohammad started talking to the man very angrily in Arabic; from the look of the man, I knew he had other ideas for us. Without saying a word, I tied the man up and opened the back door of the shop, checked to see that the coast was clear then started moving the boxes of ammo to the boot of the car. Once all the ammo was in the car, I went into the back room and untied the man, gave him his money minus a thousand dollars, told him to stay in the shop for ten minutes, and left.

Mohammad got into the car, and we both drove off into the night. At the villa we sat and drank *chia*, Iraqi tea, and talked about what had happened. Mohammad agreed with me that we had been set up for something else. He was quite scared and wanted to get home. Just before he left, I gave him the thousand dollars, a sweetener to keep him on my side. I thanked him for what he had done, and with that, he got into his car and drove off.

That night I lay in bed and thought of what had happened; I thought of Nick Berg and what terror he suffered before his end. I realised that if I carried on with this wheeling and dealing, I might end up like him. To be honest, that incident gave me a reality check, and I decided to play the real bad bastard on every deal and see that anyone who fucked with me would end up dead.

Nothing happened for the next few days. I watched the news of kidnappings, which really put a strain on my work. I found myself wondering if the rewards really made the danger worthwhile. As with anything that scares me, I find that tackling it one more time it will either confirm or deny my fears. Take the job head on and get it done, regardless.

I remember one job that would have solved all our problems regarding weapons but the main problem was that I had to speak to a guy in downtown Baghdad. I agreed to go and see the person but deep down I wasn't happy, I was dressed in a long sleeve shirt, dirty trousers and wore sunglasses because of my blue eyes, most Middle East people have brown eyes. I was armed with a pistol which was pushed down in the small of my back under my trouser belt. Mohammad and I drove as far as we could into Baghdad, parked our car and set off on foot. I could not believe how many people were around shopping in this place; it looked like there were absolutely thousands. I felt very uncomfortable and said to Mohammad that we should go and that if the man wanted to sell us weapons he would have to come closer to the Green Zone. Just then Mohammad met a friend of his and after the normal greetings they started to talk, obviously I couldn't understand what they were going on about so ignored them preferring to look around for any possible attackers. The friend started talking to me but I just ignored him point blank, he then said something else to Mohammad before departing. I asked Mohammad what he was talking about and did he realise I was a white man, Mohammad said the talk was just idle chat but said the man did comment on me and asked why I hadn't spoken to him, Mohammad told the friend that I was deaf , dumb and not right in the head which the friend accepted. We left the area and returned back to the villa and safety.

Days in the villa passed quite quickly. The guys were up for anything when they knew they didn't have a job the following day. At night there might be a drinking party in one room or another, maybe two parties going on at the same time. Anyone who attended these parties was a brave man because squaddie humour really went wild, and anything could happen once you were drunk. Some of the antics that went on would have the normal civvie wondering what we were all about, whilst others would either have a laugh or just simply walk away. The food inside the villa was a personal thing. In other words, you catered for yourself from an American soldier's ten-man ration box. If you didn't like any of the menus, you simply went without food. Honestly the rations were quite good and very filling.

British Army banter (humour) has got to be the best in the world. Soldiers worked hard and played hard. Watching the lads drink and fool around brought back many good memories'. In my Military days drinking started at "happy hour" on a Friday afternoon in the "NAAFI" which was a soldier's social club and situated on the camp. The drinking would normally finish on a Sunday night. If the lads had a normal week on camp the drinks would flow and the horsing around would start, once everybody had had enough then they would hit the town. If the Battalion had just come off exercise then it would be a different matter in the NAAFI where old scores would be settled, often resulting in a fight. I have seen the place erupt on many occasions.

I got in touch with Mohammad a few days later and said I needed pistols. He said he would have a look around and call me back. Later that night I got a call. He said he had ten pistols, Browning 9 mm, five hundred dollars each; each weapon would come with two magazines, and I would have to pick them up that night. The thought of going out again, on my own, scared me shitless. I found myself trying to think of an excuse to tell my bosses, but I couldn't think of one, I am no coward by any stretch of the imagination but the thought of having your napper cut off if they caught you didn't do anything for my morale. I decided to go out and basically take the fight to whoever wanted it.

Mohammad picked me up at 2000 hours, and we drove off. He

wouldn't tell me where we were going, but assured me I would be very safe. Over the months I had worked with Mohammad, I had come to trust him more and more. All he wanted to do was help me and make some money for his family. The money he had made so far from me made him quite rich compared to other Iraqis, who were getting about ten dollars per day. Mohammad earned five hundred dollars per deal from me, plus his cut of the deal from the gun runners after he had dropped me off.

We arrived at the venue, a horrible area with different types and shapes of buildings. Raw sewage ran freely on the hard, dusty ground. It was dark, and I was taken to a mud brick building. Inside were four rooms, two at the back and two at the front. In one of the front rooms, I heard a television. I couldn't see into any of the rooms because they had blankets hanging where the doors should have been. I sat down by Mohammad and watched an old woman making *chia* on a fire. After about five minutes, three men entered the room.

I stood up almost immediately. They shook hands with Mohammad and me and gave the customary greeting, followed by kisses on either cheek. I declined the cheek kissing crap. We all sat down on the ground, as there were no chairs, and each one of us received a small glass of *chia*. While the others drank their *chia*, I pulled out my pistol and placed it on the floor in front of me between my legs. Each of the men looked at me, but I didn't change the look I gave them – *fuck with me, and you're dead*. The main man took out ten pistols from a bag and placed them on the floor in front of me, along with twenty magazines.

I began stripping the weapons down to inspect the working parts. Once done, I reassembled the weapon and, as before, put it to either the left for good and or right for bad.

As I was on my sixth weapon, an almighty gun battle started in the front street. I heard firing all over the place, from small weapons to fucking big weapons; it was that intense. I nearly shat myself. We all crawled on our stomachs to the walls and lay down completely still while waiting for the firing to stop. I crawled up to Mohammad and demanded to know where the fuck we were; he shouted back to me words that nearly made my blood freeze – Sadr City. This place was strictly out of bounds to anyone with an ounce of common sense; it housed nearly all the terrorists who fought and killed Americans.

That night, unbeknown to anyone, the Americans had decided to retake this small area to enable the Iraqi Police and Army to stabilise it and bring it under control. Here I was, a fucking idiot, right in the middle of World War fucking Three. For hours we lay there, waiting for the shooting to come to a halt so we could at least finish the deal or fuck off home. The firing was continuous, and I prayed that nothing would come through these walls because they were only mud brick. We all just lay there, listening to the gunfire and the shouting. A tank of some sort, possibly a Bradley, moved up and down the street outside. Someone took up a firing position right outside one of the windows and started to fire. We didn't know whether the gunner was friend or foe, and none of us were about to look to see who it was. I got more and more worried and didn't know how long this was going to go on. It could have gone on for days; that was normal out here. I was in the shit up to my knees and didn't have the boots for it.

About two in the morning, the shooting started to calm down quite a lot, but nobody was prepared to look out the window to see what was happening. At about three, all was quiet, and we listened only to the tanks moving back and forth. Humvees drove up and down the road outside the house. At four in the morning, you could have dropped a pin in the sand outside and heard it clang. It was deathly silent – no tanks, no humvees, and no soldiers shouting commands. All we heard was Arabic from somewhere outside, not the normal shouting from the Iraqis. This was just a normal speaking voice which was rare to hear.

Mohammad wanted to find out what was happening outside, so he got up off the dusty floor, went to the back door, and opened it. I watched as he took a gingerly step outside and looked left and right; he then got slightly braver and walked a couple of paces further out. Then, quite a bit braver, he walked out of sight. Two minutes later he was back inside to tell us that the Iraqi Police had put a small checkpoint up right outside the house – about forty meters away, actually. He couldn't see any Americans and told me we should hurry with the deal and get going as soon as possible.

I would not be pushed, so I took my time with the rest of the weapons. After I had done my quality check, I counted six good ones and four unacceptable ones. There were no arguments, and I handed over the money to them. They did a quick count and left after saying good-bye. Unfortunately Mohammad and I couldn't move until the sky became light, and any case, we didn't want to move anywhere until at least six. Later that morning we quietly walked out of the house and to the car, which was on the opposite side of the house from the checkpoint. The best way out of the area was to drive into Sadr City and exit somewhere else.

God, I was taking a serious risk, for if anyone had seen me, we'd have both been hung. If any westerner was caught within the city it would be lights out (Death), that's after being tortured for as long as they could or maybe they would sell you to other terrorist factions who operated outside of Baghdad, whatever happened they would always kill you in the end by the most barbaric way imaginable, cutting your head off. So it's no wonder I was slightly shitting myself. Mohammad managed to drive me back to the villa by back roads and back lanes, which he knew like the back of his hand. Was I glad that he used to be a taxi driver before the war! He knew every turn that would enable us to pass the Iraqi and American patrols. We eventually arrived at the villa, tired and sweaty, and I got out with my bag of weapons and said good-bye to him. I knew I would have to go back out again, for I was still four pistols short of my quota. I spoke to Mohammad about more pistols before he left, and he said he would look for some. I then went inside the villa, had a shower, and went straight to bed. Laying in bed and thinking of the night's activities I realized that all the fighting around the area I was holed up was more than likely Iraqi soldiers and not Americans.

As the days went on, more and more kidnappings were reported on the news, and it really got to me because I was always afraid of being caught. I had a wife and two sons to consider.

Mohammad called me and excitedly told me that he had found more pistols and was coming to the villa. When he arrived, he told me of a man who had twelve pistols to sell and lived not far from the villa. I told him to pick me up that night and to get the man to deliver the weapons in the car park next to the Al Hamra hotel. This place was not far from the 14 July Bridge checkpoint. If anything happened, I could fire a couple of rounds and run to the checkpoint. Mohammad called me and said the weapons were in downtown Baghdad; the man wouldn't move them for fear of being caught and was basically scared. I told Mohammad to pick me up and show me the place in daylight.

Arriving at the venue for the exchange, I had a good look around and did not like the area. It had too many shops, which meant too many people. Arabs love shopping at night, and the area was heaving with restaurants. Driving around, I saw roads leading off roads, back alleys, the fucking lot, and it sent a shudder down my spine. However, I knew this would be the last deal with these people, so I said we would do it. Later that night at the villa, I talked Mohammad through my plan. We would park the car in a side street and walk to a restaurant, and there we would do the deal outside, where there were many diners eating. Mohammad would go and get the man and bring him to me. Mohammad would carry the bag if necessary. If anything untoward happened, we would make a break for it and head for the railway line, cross over, and head in the direction of the villa. Once out of sight, we would walk instead of running, since running draws more attention. My favorite survival manual stresses that running draws more attention than walking, since a runner is likelier to be trying to escape something.

Mohammad picked me up, and we drove up to the main area. We drove up and down the very busy road, meanwhile watching for the man to appear at his given venue. An hour later Mohammad spotted the man at a table on the front street, I told him to drive up the road further and park up in a back street because I had spotted the restaurant where I wanted to do the deal. We walked to the restaurant and sat at a table. The waiter came, and Mohammad ordered two *chias*. Once the tea was in front of us, Mohammad left, and I watched as he walked towards the man on the opposite side of the road. I also looked up and down for anyone who might be taking any interest in him. Mohammad and the man headed back towards me, and when they arrived, they sat down. The man gave me the bag, which I placed between my legs on the floor. I opened the bag, and inside it I found a number of pistols and magazines.

When I looked back up at the man, I noticed that his attention was elsewhere and that his face was covered in a fine layer of sweat even though it was not very hot. I immediately cancelled the deal by whispering to Mohammad. We both stood up and walked away from the man, leaving him with the weapons. Whilst walking towards the car, I glanced back and noticed two men walking fast towards us from the direction of another restaurant, so I told Mohammad to quicken his pace just in case. As we got around the corner where the car was parked, I noticed a large garbage skip with a lid on top. I pulled Mohammad towards the skip and lifted the lid to find it half full with rotten vegetables and an absolutely disgusting smell. We both jumped inside and closed the lid, leaving a gap so we could see. I pulled my 9 mm pistol out and waited. The stench inside the skip was really overpowering and I could feel the water from the vegetables soaking into my boots and trousers; we had to take little breaths through our mouths to avoid being sick. The two men came round the corner and stopped and looked down the road, then looked at all the cars parked in the street. Then one of them said something in Arabic, and they both ran in the direction we would have gone. Once they were out of sight, we jumped out of the bin and into the car and, within minutes, were well out of harm's reach and laughing at ourselves. The car reeked of rotten food but I didn't mind because it wasn't my car.

At the villa I told Mohammad the bad news. My company had found ground inside the Green Zone, and we were moving in; this was the last deal we would do together. Mohammad was very sad and upset at this news but told me to keep in touch; he asked me, if the company had any jobs, to think of him first. I had known that my company was moving but did not want to tell him because I thought he may have gone bad on me, hence the reason for telling him after the job.

I was to go on leave for three weeks and was glad, even though I knew I would be back. Arriving at London Heathrow Airport I hurried through the crowds towards immigration. At immigration the queue was long and I thought it would take about an hour to get through. When I eventually reach the Asian immigration officer I handed her my passport and without even scanning it she asked me how long I intended to stay in the country, I asked her to repeat what she said which she did, I couldn't believe what I was hearing and promptly replied that I was a British Citizen and may I ask her how long she intended to stay in my country?. Within seconds a Police Officer escorted me to a small room and sat me down. He looked at my passport then looked at me and asked me what the hell I thought I was playing at. With a puzzled look I told him I was not clear as to what he meant and would he elaborate please. Wow, what an angry officer I had here. He asked me what I meant about the comment I made to the immigration officer and I replied 'nothing'. He said the comment could be taken as a racist comment. Here we go again a fucking jobs worth full of fucking love and harmony. Over the next hour I tried to explain that she only asked me the question because I was well tanned and therefore I had the right to ask her the same question but whatever way I tried to explain it away he turned everything around. In the end I was forced to apologise to the woman and was then escorted from the airport. This happened two more times when I was going home through London. On the third and last time it happened I was sat in the room with the officer who picked me up the first time. He asked me if I had been in trouble with the Police before to which I said 'no', he then told me he recognized me from somewhere but couldn't put his finger on where it was and was I sure I had not been in trouble with the Police, again I said 'no'. I looked at him and said that I know where we had met to which he looked quite amused with a smirk on his face. I said that it was about six months ago in another room where he and I were sat across the table having the same conversation. When the penny dropped with him he gave me a smile and reminded me that I couldn't say those sort of things or I would get myself arrested and charged with racist comments. After a little talk he again escorted me from the airport. One day I will learn to keep my thoughts to myself. When I arrived home, I hugged and kissed my wife, whom I had not seen for a long time. Trying to fit back into her routine was almost impossible. Many guys who do long stints away from home will tell you that whilst they are away, they get into a sort of military role. Meanwhile, the man's wife gets into her own private role. When back home, you find you are both living different roles, and the two of you may not meet in the middle. I even found myself calling my wife *mate* and asking, 'Do you want a brew, mate?' or 'Do you want a coffee, mate?' and so on. Anyway, she got used to it and never complained about it.

After about a week at home, I remember going to bed about midnight one night. Though I didn't feel at all tired, I fell asleep when my head hit the pillow. I woke up, sweating, about three or thereabouts in the morning; the room was dark, and I didn't have a clue where I was, I just lay there, listening for some sort of noise that I might recognize. After a while I turned round in bed to see who was next to me and luckily found my wife. God only knows what I would have done if I had found someone else. Joanne, my wife, woke up to find me sitting up in bed and looking at her. She asked what I was doing, and I told her I had just had the weirdest dream.

Some guys reading this may think I am being stupid or that I have lost the plot, but what I am about to relate is true. I am not religious by any stretch of the imagination. I never have been and never will be. If you believe in God, that is entirely up to you. As for me, well, I didn't. The only time I ever went to church in my adult life was on Remembrance Sunday, a twenty-minute service, a visit to the Cenotaph to pay your respects. As far as my religious observances were concerned, that was it for another year. I must admit I did go to midnight mass on a few occasions, but other than that, I wasn't interested. God had never helped me in any way, shape, or form; in fact, I don't even think God knew I was on the planet. I obviously went to Sunday school when I was a kid, though that was only so my parents could get a couple of hours of freedom from us terrors.

Getting back to this strange dream I had, I dreamt that I was in a very hot country with someone who was faceless. This was a human being, but for some reason, I couldn't see his face. I could breathe in the hot air; my mouth was dry. I could smell the dirt and a musky smell. I could also smell sweat from myself and my host. I was in a small room, and when I looked around the room, I found it to be a mud building. The door to this room was directly in front of me, and through the cracks I could see outside. As I looked slightly to the left, I saw a rickety old wooden bed in the corner. It had an old blanket on what appeared to be a straw mattress, and the pillow was just some rags; at least it looked like a pillow. Above this bed was a small window with a rag draped over it to keep out prying eyes and the harsh sunlight. So here I was. I stood in a room where I'd never been before, and I was with someone. I couldn't tell to whom this place might belong.

Sometime later I heard a light knock on the door in front of me. Neither I nor the faceless person with me said anything as the door opened and three men walked in. The first man stood right in front of me, about a foot away. This male was 5' 7 and had a slim build. He had shoulder-length dark hair that looked greasy, as though he hadn't washed it for a few days. He was also well-tanned. His clothing was a simple toga garment down to his knees, worn and grayish or brown in colour. I suppose he looked between thirty and forty years old, although I couldn't be sure. This man put both hands out and took my right hand and said something in a language I had never heard, a language somewhat like Arabic, but it was not Arabic. As he spoke to me, he was smiling, and he always looked me directly into my eyes. When he stopped talking, the man to my rear left, the man who had no face, told me in pure English that this was Jesus.

I went all numb and asked, 'Who?'

He said again, 'This man is Jesus.'

Well, you could have knocked me down with a feather. The faceless man who had just spoken to me added that Jesus had said he would look after me and was beside me always.

Well, that news just sent me ten paces left, and I honestly didn't have a clue what to think, so I again asked the faceless man who this man was.

Again, in the calmest voice you have ever heard, he said, 'This man is Jesus.'

Jesus! All the time I was speaking and getting answers, I never took my eyes off the man before me, and he never took his eyes off me. As we looked at each other, the man just kept smiling at me and still held my hand in both of his. For some reason, I really felt calm and relaxed. Again, this man, Jesus, spoke to the faceless man for what seemed ages but was no more than a couple of minutes.

Then the faceless man said, 'Jesus has to go, but he will always be next to you.' With that, this man, Jesus, still smiling, kept hold of my hand with one of his. With his other hand, he stroked my arm. He then turned and left the room. That was when I woke up.

As I said, I am in no way religious, so I wondered, 'Why am I dreaming a very powerful dream like this? Is someone trying to tell me something?' The mind boggles at such an experience. Anyway, my wife was quite intrigued by what I was telling her, but in the end it was decided that it was just a dream, and she went back to sleep, I couldn't settle that night and stayed awake till the early hours before eventually dropping off to sleep.

The next day, and for days after, I would recall the dream and try to make sense of it but couldn't, in the end I just accepted that it was a weird dream but just a dream nonetheless. I was to have the same dream twice more over the next year or so. Nothing ever changed in the dream and everything was exactly as it was in the first dream.

Well, my leave was over, and I returned to Iraq for yet another stint in a country that I knew God had left to its own devices.

I arrived at Baghdad International Airport and was picked up by a team and taken directly to the Green Zone where we had a camp. The camp accommodation was porta cabins which were in rows of five, each porta cabin housed eight men so to say we were not living on top of each other may be an understatement. If the insurgents ever got lucky and managed to drop a mortar round into the camp it would have killed many guys. Walking round the Green Zone was a pure eye opener because I saw many security companies, some very professional and some that just needed to be kicked out of the country for being a bunch of gung ho idiots. I remember a couple of vehicles driving at break neck speed along a road from the direction of checkpoint twelve with guys hanging out of their windows pointing weapons at everyone. I stopped to have a look and when they got level with me I had about three weapons pointed in my direction and being told to stay where I was and not move. The shamefull thing about this is that the security company doing this was a British security company. Everybody knew the American security companies did this sort of thing but nobody had ever said a British one did it, until now. I later found out that the team had come under fire on Route Irish travelling from the Airport to the Green Zone, one of the guys had been shot through the arm and the team were racing to get him to the Ibn Sina hospital inside the Green Zone. God only knows why they pointed weapons at everyone they saw and god only knows why they were hanging out of their windows cursing and abusing everyone, fucking idiots if you ask me.

The Americans had everything they needed inside the Green Zone which included a private swimming pool and take away cafes. When the Yanks do something they certainly know how to keep the morale of their troops at a high level.

Looking back on my escapades whilst we lived in Mansour, I knew I was very lucky to be here still. I could have been killed or kidnapped at any time. Arabs are very money-oriented and will do anything for a dollar, although that is not a bad thing in itself; everybody has to make a living. I was somewhat shocked at the depths some people would plumb to make that extra dollar. Kidnapping was the big money earner these days. The money they could make was substantial; all they had to do was kidnap a Westerner, and they had won the lottery. Westerners were sold on up the chain of criminals until they reached the bad guys who lopped off heads while chanting to a video camera.

As time went by and everyone settled into the Green Zone way of life, the television was reporting on the deaths of security contractors like me. The times had changed, and the numbers of American and British contractors killed rose day by day.

CRG had been able to maintain its operations because its men were very professional in what they did and how they did it. One day, however, we heard the very bad news that one of our men had been killed in an explosion. M C was the first CRG man to die in action; he left a wife and child. M C had spent twenty-two years in the Army and attained the rank of WO11, which in normal language means "Warrant Officer 2nd Class or Sergeant Major. His death really brought it home to the men that even CRG men could die. Another day we heard that another one of our guys had been hit by a suicide vehicle-borne IED, Improvised explosive Device. Both the driver and commander sustained bad injuries.

At this point, the men who thought that being a security contractor in Iraq was just a bit of harmless fun and were only in it for the ride soon began to go home, never to return. I really enjoyed my year with CRG; they were, without doubt, one of the best companies on the circuit, highly professional. CRG only employed very professional men to work on the ground.

The spider's hole, the entrance, was just in front of the small brick wall in the centre of the picture.

What was left of Saddam's money?

Saddam on his capture.

Saddam being paraded through the palace. Once this palace was home to him and
his family.

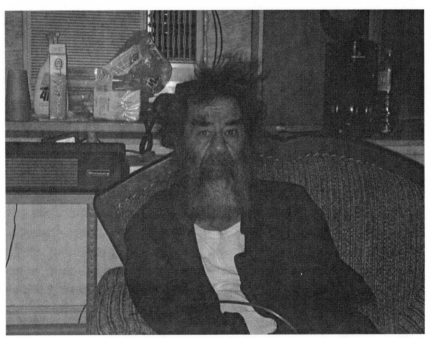

A bewildered-looking Saddam.

Chapter 2 (2004)

I left CRG after that year and went to work for Sabre International Security.

I started by helping them set up the company and began looking after their many accounts. I would also assist in PSD work when they lacked men. This meant going out of the Green Zone and escorting clients to and from meetings in the Red area.

I kept in touch with Mohammad every week as I carried out my work in the safe confines of the Green Zone. Then one day a vacancy came up for a guard position. All our guards were Iraqis. I phoned Mohammad straight away with the news, but got his brother on the other end. I spoke to his brother about the job and told him to get Mohammad to call me. His brother informed me that Sunni gunmen had kidnapped Mohammad the previous month and murdered him, along with many other Shi'ites.

This news devastated me. I had worked with Mohammad for four months when I lived out in Mansoor. I had been in the Green Zone for six months and kept in touch with him, and now he was dead. I will never forget the times and laughs we both had, the arguments and shouting matches we had or the times we fell out and didn't talk for a while.

Mohammad was a religious man who was married and had one son and two daughters; he was no threat to anyone at all. He lived in a small two-bed flat and was saving up to buy a nice house for his family. During the Christmas season of 2003–2004, he invited me to spend Eid with him and his immediate family and other members and relatives, and I told him I would be honoured. On Eid he collected me from the villa, and we spent all day with his entire family. After the huge meal, which was eaten on the floor on plastic matting, we sat and drank tea and laughed at my lack of Arabic. He would say Arabic words, and I would try to repeat them after him, much to the amusement of his family and their children. Mohammad spent four years in Carlisle, UK, training to be an airline pilot. When he passed his exams and returned to Iraq, he could not get a job because he was Shia. However, he enjoyed his time in England and loved the British people. His one wish was that the British Army, rather than the Americans, should be the ones patrolling Baghdad. That, in fact, was the wish of many Iraqi people.

One day I was told that Mohammad had been kidnapped while taking his children to school. He was missing for weeks when out of the blue his brother called me and told me they had found him, unfortunately he was dead with three bullet holes in the head. How could anyone kill a man like this and be able to sleep at night, it fucking amazes me what these people are capable of. The people who kidnapped him and shot him will, I hope, rot in hell for eternity as they are without doubt, the scum of the earth.

My only disaster while working with S.I.S was my kidnapping. The Green Zone was a hive of activity, with American Army and British and US security companies going about their daily business. Ever since the Zone was used, it was open to the insurgents, who would do anything to attack any westerner who worked inside the Zone. Kidnappings were high on the list for insurgents and Iraqis. To the normal, everyday Iraqi, a kidnapping was easy money; to the insurgent, kidnapping meant much more. Reports came in every week of attempted kidnappings of military and security men.

I had a good working relationship with a garage that all the security companies used on a daily basis until the day when it all went bad for me.

Statement taken from Jack regarding events on Saturday 26 Feb 2005

I had received a bill for $1400.00 for work that had not been carried out by STG Garage inside the Green Zone.

I went to the garage with Moneer, my assistant, to find out what was happening. I intended to query the invoice. I met up with Sharif, the manager of the garage. We shook hands and shared greetings as we had met several times before. Prior to the events that would follow, I believed that our relationship was quite amicable. We always had time to talk to each other and have a laugh and a joke together. We would sometimes sit outside and talk of things in general, nothing specific, just everyday things.

I was displaying my DOD badge and was not armed. I spoke to Sharif and complained about the amount the car was going to cost and asked him to bring the invoice into keeping with the size of the job required, almost immediately he began to get very agitated and began abusing and cursing say that we British think that all Arabs are thieves, he then seemed to work himself into a frenzy. I could not understand why he had reacted in this manner, as our relationship until that point had been mutually respectful and friendly.

At this point Sharif shouted something in Arabic, which I did not understand. Within seconds there were between fifteen and twenty people around me. They grabbed me and forced me into a building. I attempted to escape from them, but this proved futile. I was worried at this point. They continued to drag me into a building and across the floor to the furthest point from the door and held me in a corner. Some of them pinned me against the wall with my arms spread out, at which point I became slightly concerned. Sharif then came into the room and started screaming at me. He wanted to know why we British and Americans had come over and killed his people for no reason; he said that we were all scum and that he would not rest until our blood ran down the streets of Baghdad and Basra and our heads were on stakes. Screaming, he repeated this message. I was asking him to allow us to talk about the situation, but he would not listen to me. He then violently punched me several times in the face. I felt my bottom lip burst open at one of his punches; another couple of punches later, a fist to my eye made me see stars.

Then Sharif left the room. My arms were released, but I was still pinned in the corner. I tried to open my eye, but it wouldn't open. I could feel the blood trickle down my chin and taste the blood from my bottom lip. I knew this situation was going to get really nasty and that I had to act very fast.

I took my mobile phone out to call for help. Sharif reentered the room and saw me with my mobile phone in my hand. He started screaming, 'Give me your phone you fucking bastard.' I was not prepared to do this. One of the men grabbed the phone from me and gave it to Sharif while the other men beat me around my head and stomach. One punch connected with the side of my head, and I felt myself go slightly dizzy. I knew that if I went down, I would wake up somewhere other than the garage. He then grabbed hold of the badge holder around my neck, which contained my DOD badge and British Embassy pass, and tried to pull it off me.

I said, 'That's American and British property, and if you touch that, you'll be in deep shit.' God only knows why I said that, but it certainly did the trick; he let go of my badge holder. My arms were pinned again, and Sharif violently attacked me again. I tried to keep my head down to protect my face, so he continuously punched both sides of my head and the back of my neck and kicked me in the legs. Then Sharif reached behind his back and produced a huge fucking knife. He came closer to me and grabbed my hair and told me that he could, by law, cut my head off because I was a killer of Muslims. He put the sharp end of the blade against my throat so I could feel the cold steel blade. One thing I hate is knives but I did not want to show him this. This small action scared the fuck out of me because I knew this was the Arab way of treating prisoners. Fortunately it was only a threat, but it certainly woke me up completely.

I was in considerable pain by this point, bleeding from my nose and lower lip. My captors were quite overexcited and distracted and began talking between themselves; I decided it was time for retaliation. The man holding my left arm was the first; I hit him square on the nose with a head butt, and he immediately let my arm go as he bent forward to hold his broken nose. I managed to get my free hand around his throat and squeezed his windpipe as hard as I could and trying to rip it out. His eyes bulged out of the sockets as he gasped for air. Keeping my grip on his windpipe, I kicked the guy in front of me in the balls as hard as I could. He doubled up in pain and fell to the floor, and then I kicked him right in that fucking ugly face. The other one, the one I had by the throat, dropped to the floor. I thought he was dead.

By this time no one was holding me, and I made a dash for the door. There I had another two men to deal with, moving in to block my way. I punched the first in the throat and knocked him down immediately. As he gasped for breath, the second man took a kick to the stomach, which knocked the wind out of him. As he doubled up, I kicked him in the face from the side, and that kick knocked him off his feet and out of my path to the door.

Unfortunately, I couldn't gauge where the bloody door was because I could only see out of one eye, and the other eye was flowing with water. A scream sounded, and just as I got to the door, many hands grabbed me and began to drag me back inside.

I turned and went at the guys like a man deranged. I punched, kicked, and even bit one guy before they overpowered me. I still had my arm around the neck of one guy when they punched and kicked me to the floor again. I didn't mean to let go of this bastard until he was dead, but the punches and kicks got the better of me, and I had to let him go and curl up and protect my head from all the blows raining down on me. They dragged me up, put me up against the wall, and gave me a really severe beating. I cannot really remember much about this one because my pain perceptions just switched off.

If I was ever in deep trouble, it was then. I had failed to escape, and they were doing everything possible to me to make sure I didn't try it again. One of the men hit me on the side of the knee with what looked like a lump of wood, and the pain darted up and down my leg. The impact pitched me to my knees, though I was attempting to keep my damaged knee straight; pain shot up and down my leg when my knee was bent.

My attacker seemed out of control. He said, 'I have a thousand relatives in this country and could get you killed just like that!' while clicking his fingers. He then left the room again. My arms were then released again, and I fell to the floor on my knees. Then, because of the pain, I fell back and sat down, knowing it was going to be harder to get away. Throughout my ordeal, Moneer was held back away from me so he could not assist in protecting me in any way. He was distressed by everything that was happening, but they would not allow him to help me.

However, they then allowed Moneer to come over to me, and

he whispered 'Keys to the car.' I took the keys from my pocket and gave them to him without anyone seeing.

The others let Moneer leave the room. Sharif came back into the room, I was dragged up onto my feet, and he continued to attack me, punching me violently about my head and inflicting severe blows to my stomach. I was very concerned for my life, and it worried me that I was alone. I started to think that trying to get away might have been a bad idea. However, my effort showed that I was not going to lie down and take whatever they had in mind without a fight.

Sharif left the room again, and I was released from the corner and allowed to sit down before I fell down again. The door was blocked by about ten people, so I had no way of escape. One of the men gave me a glass of water and a cigarette. I was allowed to sit there for a few minutes. Whilst I sat, wondering what was to become of me, I was still looking for a way out and struggling to see one. The door was about ten feet away from me, and I decided to have another go at getting out into the fresh air. I leapt up and grabbed the first man I encountered by the back of his head and rammed his face straight into the wall. The second man got a kick in his bollocks, which sent him screaming to the ground. That last kick sent all the others into a panic, and for reasons only known to them, they parted and left a clear way to the door.

Then one of them jumped onto me from the side, which sent me off course and back to the ground, where I again took a beating. I was then dragged back up and placed back into the chair.

I remembered back to my Military days when I went on an escape and evasion course coupled with a resistance to interrogation course, in fact I had done a number of these courses in the Army and really enjoyed them. The course normally started off with the escape and evasion phase then when everyone was caught it progressed into the resistance to interrogation phase. Whatever anyone did to try and evade you were always caught in the end. The situation I was in did not include the second phase but certainly included the first phase. The best time to escape was when you were initially caught; this was because both you and the enemy would be in semi shock at having met each other, if you could keep your calm at all the commotion you would be able to get away. Unfortunately this didn't happen on this occasion. As

I sat in the chair my mind started to relive those courses. One course I did with a friend of mine in southern Germany culminated in us both being caught and taken back to an old Army camp for interrogation. Prior to you being interrogated the guards would try and wear you down with lack of sleep and making you stand for long periods in a stress position, a position that was not comfortable by any stretch of the imagination. Once they had worn you down enough they would put you in front of a panel of professional interrogators where you would be asked question after question for hours, sometimes they would try and trip you up by asking the same question but in a different way which meant you had to invent a story and stick with that story no matter what happened. Me and my friend were next to each other the a sand bag over our heads and both naked, hands were tied behind our backs and we were forced into a position where you're your feet were about fifteen inches away from the wall and your head was supporting your weight on the wall, after a while stood like this it gets extremely uncomfortable and your forehead goes numb. My friend whispered to me that he was in trouble. I asked him if he had taken a kicking from the guard when he got captured to which he replied 'no he hadn't', the problem was, he told me, was that he had a hard on. That was one of the funniest comments I have heard and the only reaction he got from me was immediate laughter, I was nearly crying with laughter. The guards immediately grabbed me from the wall, pushed me down to the ground and started shouting and pushing me around the floor with their boots until I had to tell them why I was laughing. Unfortunately everyone else started laughing and the whole course had to start again. My mate was taken out of the room and given the bollocking of his life. Fun times back then but this was a different matter altogether.

Sharif and another man entered the room. I had seen this man on previous occasions. He was wearing a DOD badge, which made me feel safer, as I thought he was there to help me. I did not realize it at the time but the man with the DOD badge worked for Sharif and was from the Lebanon and was the interpreter for the Americans on one of the entry/exit checkpoints which protected the access of people who came into the Green Zone. I stood up, and he immediately punched me hard across the face. The force made me fall back onto the chair, the chair went right back, and I ended up on the floor. The punch didn't register because my pain barrier was still locked down. I was then lifted back up onto my feet by three or four people and punched hard again, this time I did not move because I had guys holding me up. The punches kept coming in and even though I kept my head down some of them were connecting and hurting.

The Lebanese man with the DOD badge then said, 'Get down on the fucking ground.' He sounded loud and aggressive. I said I would not and asked him who he was.

He said, "Never mind who I am. I'm the security manager.' He then told me that I had attacked these people, broken the nose of one, and the other was finding it hard to breathe because I had nearly ripped his throat out. While he waffled on, I thought to myself that I hadn't really done a bad job so far.

I looked around at the other guys and realised these guys were scared of this man, the men holding my arms let go of them and backed away from me. Without any warning I punched this man straight in the face and made a dash for the door but again I was caught and dragged back inside. There were just too many men in the room. Again I took another beating before being paraded in front of this man again.

He then said, 'Get down on the fucking ground or I'll shoot you.' Meanwhile, he unsheathed his pistol and pointed it at me. His pistol was a Colt .45, a huge silver gun.

I lifted the sides of my shirt up and said, 'I'm unarmed, and I'm a DOD badge holder.' I asked him to get the Iraqi police and the American Military Police.

He then put his pistol away again and walked off into a side room, looking angry. While he was there, not one of the men in the room said anything. Their silence made me very concerned, and at the same time, I was thinking how I was going to handle the guy. He came back out seconds later with a pair of handcuffs and an electric shock baton. He instructed the men to hold me, which they did; he then punched me repeatedly around the face, head, and stomach. Still my pain barrier was locked down, and all I felt was a fist hitting me. The punches in the stomach made me want to be sick as I tried desperately to get air back into my lungs. He then stood about four feet in front of me, his hands on his hips and his legs slightly open, and I thought this was another good time to try and get away because all the others had congregated to watch what he was going to do with the baton. By coming together in a cluster, they had left the door unguarded.

Without thinking, I kicked him straight in the bollocks. He doubled over almost immediately and dropped to his knees, and the sight of him sent shock waves throughout the rest. They all just froze, and the two men holding me loosened their grip on my arms for a split second, which gave me ample time to free my arms and run for the door.

As I exited into fresh air and freedom, a huge Iraqi man I had never seen stood right in front of me and punched me straight in the face. The blow knocked me right back onto my arse inside the room again, and the pain was excruciating. I thought my face had exploded. Three or four men then jumped on me and started punching me, and it took all my strength to curl up into a ball. They dragged me to my feet and placed me in front of the guy with the electric shock baton. He pointed the baton at me and held it on my chest, then pulled the trigger. The shock of it must have had my hair pointing to the sky. I have never known such pain, and I don't even know if I yelped or whatever. My body just gave in, and I fell to the ground; I had no control over anything my brain was telling parts of my body to do. I just convulsed on the floor like a piece of jelly. I don't know how long I was on the floor, but whatever length of time it was, the pain never subsided. Eventually I was lifted back to my feet by a number of hands. I made a point of keeping my head up, although I could have just left my chin on my chest. I thought, though, that I was not going to let this bastard beat me.

He took some silver metal handcuffs out of his back pocket and told me to put them on whilst threatening me with the baton again. I declined his offer by telling him to fuck off. He told two Iraqis to hold me tight, which they did. He then put the baton back onto my chest and pressed the button again, and this time it had me wriggling on the ground in severe pain. I couldn't see anything other than a black haze. I was pleased that the two men holding me also got a shock – I heard them scream like little girls as they let me go. Two men jumped me again and turned me onto my front, then grabbed hold of my arms and held them behind my back. They then attempted to clip the cuffs around one of my wrists. I twisted my wrist so the cuff would not go on properly, doing all that I could to avoid letting them cuff me behind my back. They lifted me up onto my feet, gave me a couple of slaps across the face, and told me in no uncertain terms that the handcuffs were going on, and whatever I did wouldn't make the slightest difference. They then forced my arms around to my front and put the cuffs on both wrists. I was extremely worried about his intent to use the baton again, as the pain was excruciating, something I had never felt before and never want to feel again. He spoke to some of the men, and eight or ten men dragged me outside, punching and kicking me on the way. I was forced towards a car, a silver Golf, parked in the car park.

He opened the rear passenger door of the car and told me to get in. I refused and said, 'Who the fucking hell do you think you are? I'm not getting in the car.' I put my foot against the side of the car as several people tried to push me in. As they tried to push me, I pushed back on them. I felt the muscles in my back tighten and start to go hot and thought, 'If they keep pushing, my back will go.'

He then put his hand on his pistol again and said, 'Get in the car or I'll shoot you where you stand.' I told him to fuck off again and that there was no way I was getting into the car.

I was a bit worried at this point and was not thinking clearly, and I said, 'The only way you will get me in this car is if you shoot me.'

He said something in Arabic to the men, and they punched and kicked me around the stomach and head, and I went to the ground and felt the boot going into me. By this point, I was worried that one more good kick might knock me out cold. I felt a hard kick to my jaw and instantly tasted blood in my mouth, which I quickly swallowed. I didn't want these bastards to think they had hurt me in any way, shape, or form because that would have sent them into a frenzy.

Really, it was like a cartoon fight! I was in the middle of all these smelly, sweaty guys and each one wanted to punch or kick me. I looked up at one stage and saw one of them punch his friend in the back of the head – a little funny, I thought. They then dragged me back into the room again. I was forced back into the chair and beaten again around the face, neck, and head. They also kicked my legs, mainly on my shins, until they eventually got bored and left me alone. I didn't see the guy who had shocked me, which was a relief.

I looked up and saw the door was blocked again and that I was surrounded by men. I sat still and contemplated another rush for the door, but my head was buzzing, I could now taste quite a lot of blood in my mouth, and my eye was closing fast. The punches had hurt, but my knee hurt worst.

All of a sudden, a guy called John, one of our company's team members, appeared in the doorway. He looked at me, then looked at all the men in the room, and then back at me.

His first words to me were, 'Hi, Jack, how are you feeling?'

I looked at him and said I had felt better. Just seeing a friendly face lifted my spirits. He told me to get up and go towards him at the door. I could hardly stand, but made a huge effort and eventually got to my feet and stumbled over towards him. John was very calm and never left the area of the door. He looked at my handcuffs and then at all the men, who just stood stock-still. As I got to him, he grabbed my arm and told me to walk slowly with him. I told him that not all the guys were there and that some of them might be in another room or elsewhere in the compound. We then walked together towards the main gate at the opposite side of the car park. There were a number of Iraqis in the car park, and as we walked towards the gate, they backed away. As we wanted the situation from here to remain calm, we attempted to talk to them whilst still approaching the gate. There was a gap between two hesco barriers and we were able to get through this gap. I then saw Mark, another of our employees, coming out of another building, where he had been searching for me. A hesco barrier is a wire mesh frame with a heavy duty liner inside, when full with earth it protects from explosions and small arms fire.

One of the Iraqi men shouted something, and the rest of them then ran towards the main gate to prevent us escaping. They managed to close the gate before we could get there. As we got there, they were trying to padlock the gate to see that we could not leave. John let go of me and ran to the gate and managed to get the padlocks away from the Iraqis before they could secure the gates while Mark and I tried to hold the others back away from us. A fight started between us three and a whole load of Iraqis. Fists flew and connected with heads and faces, and all I could do was kick. I was lucky to grab a man round the neck with my handcuffs, and I just squeezed the life out of him. The others saw this and started to back away from us, but I kept hold of this unfortunate bastard.

We managed to force the gate open by about one foot, at which point I could see H and Neil, other employees. I shouted to them to help us. They were armed and came over to help us. They pushed the gates wide open and drew their weapons on the men. These men then backed right away and ran off.

Neil and H dragged me to safety onto the street. I was still handcuffed at this point. The silver Golf then approached us, followed by an Iraqi police car. Both vehicles stopped, and that is when I saw Sharif and the guy who gave me the two shocks. The Iraqi police officer got out and walked over to us while Sharif and the other man stayed by the car. H requested of the police officer that the handcuffs be removed and that I be released. The police officer walked back to his car and spoke to Sharif and managed to get the keys off him, under protest, and removed the cuffs.

An Iraqi National Guard (ING) patrol arrived with an American military officer and Military Police. The American officer came over to us and was briefed about what had happened by me. He appeared quite shocked and immediately told his soldiers to arrest everyone. The Military Police carried out his order to the letter by rounding up all the garage staff and putting them up against the wall. A little fat guy came over to me and whispered to me that some Americans where being kept locked up in a room at the back of the compound. I informed the Iraqi police, and they, along with John and Mark, went back into the buildings and searched for them. After about six or seven minutes, they emerged from one of the buildings with three people, all white. Each person looked as though he had received the same treatment that I had, and all three were in handcuffs. The sight of this outraged the American officer, and he got on his radio and requested more men. Ten minutes later, about thirty military policemen came round the corner in humvees. They were then ordered to arrest all the staff at the garage, which they did, handcuffing and searching them and putting them into a humvee. While this was going on, the garage staff protested their innocence, but their pleas fell on deaf ears.

We all then went to the police station. At the police station, we were requested to go and see the chief. His office was quite small and crowded with the group, which consisted of me, John, Sharif, Mahesh, and another man, plus the three other men whom John and Mark had found. The Iraqi Police tried to get a deal going, but I was not having any of it; I wanted these men charged with kidnapping and assault. Sharif had the audacity to turn up, holding a Koran, in an attempt to hoodwink the chief. Fortunately, however, the chief was a sly old guy and knew all the tricks. Sharif made matters worse for himself by flashing the Koran because the chief asked him to swear on it before he was allowed to tell everyone what happened. Sharif did this and then lied very freely, and I protested his lies. The chief told me to be quiet and listen.

After Sharif told his story, the chief reminded him that a member of the coalition forces had been severely beaten for nothing more than asking about an overpriced invoice... He then made Sharif and the other man look at my face, the blood, my closed eye, the marks on my shin, and the two burn marks on my chest. The chief then quoted something from the Koran and went absolutely mad, shouting in Arabic at Sharif and the other man. He then instructed some police officers to cuff them and take them to the cells to join the others. The chief was very compassionate towards me and said he was sorry for what had happened. He agreed that what I did was good and that what had occurred was not the way of the Iraqi people. He then informed me that the case officer was a captain whom he trusted and that I should give him a statement so they could charge all these men. I pointed out that not all the men were involved with what went on, and he asked me if I could identify those who were involved. I said that I could.

Ten minutes later the chief took me to a large cell with some other officers and ordered all the detainees to stand against the far wall. Once they were all in position, he and I went inside the cell and started with the man on the left. As we walked along the line, I pointed out men who were involved and those who were not. The uninvolved ones were set free, and the others remained inside. As we were leaving the cell, I noticed a little fat guy who was really sweating and looking very nervous, and I thought to myself that I hadn't ever seen this man other than when he informed me about the Americans and told the chief. The chief looked back and forth between me and this man and asked if I was sure.

I replied, 'Yes, I am sure." The chief then instructed an officer to release the little fat man. Over the next hour or so, I managed to give the captain a full statement, and he thanked me and told me that charges of kidnapping and assault would be brought against these men.

Over the next few days, I gave statements to the British Embassy security manager, the American Embassy security manager, British Police, Canadian Police, and American Intelligence officers. The American Intelligence had me for three full days. They told me that they were aware of a cell inside the Green Zone but had never been able to locate them. They showed me hundreds of mug shots of suspected insurgents.

The man who held the weapon and threatened me was Adam, and he was the interpreter on Checkpoint Two. He was taken to court on attempted kidnapping and assault charges and sentenced to six years in prison.

Sharif went on the run and, as yet, has not been found. He has dual nationality and has a Canadian passport. If I were ever to come across Sharif in the UK, I would kill him without a second thought. If I ever had the misfortune of bumping into him while in Iraq, I would shoot him dead, again without giving it a second thought. Others involved received sentences of between one and three years in prison. I was assured that prisons in Iraq were nothing like prisons elsewhere in the world and that these people had a slim chance of surviving. Adam was Lebanese and would not survive six years. In Iraqi prisons, a prisoner's family had to bring food and water in for the prisoner, and his family lived in Lebanon. I remained working inside the Green Zone for a further three to four weeks but my nerves were shot to hell. Every time I left the villa I made sure I was armed with a pistol. It got to the stage where I did not trust anyone at all and I felt I was becoming paranoid and that I had to move away from Baghdad and the Green Zone to another project somewhere else in Iraq.

One day a mate invited me to the Green Zone café for a bite to eat and a bit of time out of the villa, from there we would visit the local bazaar and have a look round before heading back to the villa. We decided to walk to the café so I armed myself with a pistol and off we went. The Green Zone café was owned by an Iraqi and was very popular with security guys and American soldiers, the bazaar was all Iraqi owned and quite worrying because nobody really gave any of these people a security background check. As we neared the café, about 100 metres away, I saw a friend on the other side of the road who I had not seen for a few years, I quickly dashed over and grabbed him by the arm which made him jump. A conversation started and I introduced him to my mate and told him we were planning to go to the café then down to the bazaar and asked if he was heading that way. Bloody hell he didn't even get the reply out when all of a sudden the café exploded and caught fire, what a bang. the three of us dived for cover thinking it was a mortar attack, heads down and arse's up. When the dust settled and no more explosions we lifted our heads up to see what the problem was when we saw the Americans who were there within a minute or so getting all the wounded out and into the hospital which was right next door. We ran down to see if we could be any assistance and tried to find out what had happened. An American soldier told us to keep going and move out of the area and that he didn't have a clue what had happened. We decided to get back to the villa the shortest route which took us past the bazaar and headed off in that direction. At the top of the road from the bazaar we heard two massive explosions, one after the other and further down the street which was right in the middle of all the shops. Both Americans and security men ran towards us trying to get away from the blast, loads of the guys running had been injured and blood was all over them. The three of us went into action and detailed uninjured men to help the injured to Ibn Sina hospital about 50 metres further up the road. The dust had settled and the sight we saw was utter carnage. Bodies lay strewn all over, parts of bodies, an arm, a leg, a head, a torso with blood and guts all over the place. We saw the point of impact, hard not to really, but what puzzled us and everyone else who had turned up was the lack of a hole in the ground, another puzzling thing was we didn't hear the mortar round whizz through the air or no alarm of incoming mortars. The only other option was suicide bombers. The carnage was left for the Americans to sort out and the three of us left the scene. Later that day we were told that three suicide bombers had infiltrated the Green Zone and targeted the café and bazaar knowing full well that soldiers and security men mingled in both places. Across the road from the café the bombers had planted a bomb in the wall as a secondary device but luckily it failed to go off, it was meant to explode when the soldiers had maximum people in the area tending to the dying, dead and wounded. One thing that crossed everyone's mind and was the topic of conversation for a good few days was, how did they know where to go and how did they know when to set their bombs off. I think everyone knew that there were Iraqis inside the Green Zone who were reporting back to the insurgents on a daily basis. This would also confirm how the enemy mortars were quite accurate in where they landed. A mortar is an area weapon and designed to cause maximum confusion and carnage over a vast area, these mortars always landed on the Palace car park. From that day on the trust of any Iraqi dwindled and every Iraqi was given a wide berth, nobody went to anything in any part of the Green Zone that was Iraqi owned. A café up by the four soldiers roundabout was immediately put out of bounds after the bombings because like the café and bazaar it was also a haunt of security men. All security companies up scaled their security to the point that nobody without an appointment got passed the guards on the front gates. Iraqi security guards then came under the direct supervision of an ex pat security man from the company he worked for, the days of employing an Iraqi guard supervisor was now over. From now on anything that an Iraqi used to do on his own was now in complete control of an ex pat supervisor.

Chapter 3

After my year with S.I.S and a month's leave, I went back to CRG and was posted down to Basra. Basra was the main Tactical Area of Responsibility for the British Army. Basra is a huge city housing millions of Muslims. The main airport was outside the city limits on the opposite side of the Tigris River, and the streets of Basra were filthy, with carcasses of dead animals left to rot by the roadside. Men wandered the streets looking for work. Women stayed at home, looking after children, because that was the traditional arrangement there. Women are not allowed a voice in anything that occurs in Iraq.

Basra's streets are very dangerous for both foreign military and PSD teams, even though these personnel are there to help reconstruct the city and bring life back to it. The Iraqi people did everything in their power to make the job hard. The British Army carried out operations from within the confines of the airport because it was far enough away from the dangers of Basra, or so everyone thought. The main problem was the incoming mortar attacks, which happened nearly every night, plus the added fact that the Army used Iraqi labourers from the city. Nobody knew who was friend and who was foe. Nobody trusted the Iraqi Police or the Iraqi Army because most of them moonlighted for the militia at night, meanwhile functioning as policemen or soldiers during the day shift. Many abortive kidnappings occurred, but there were successful abductions, and the men who were taken are either still captive or, sadly, dead.

I was the security manager at a small camp within the airport. I was in charge of forty Iraqis who guarded the camp. The actual guard force lived in Basra and traveled to and from work on local transport, which turned out to be very dangerous for all concerned because the local militia hated anyone who worked for the British Army.

I formed a good relationship with the Royal Air Force Counter Intelligence team and got snippets of information from them. Whatever my Iraqi guard force told me about anything happening inside Basra I would pass the information onto the Intelligence team. Gathering Intelligence from various sources either confirms or denies previous Intelligence or brings new information to the table. You cannot get enough Intelligence and quite honestly it didn't really matter where it came from.

With both of my sons serving in the British Army it was only a matter of time before I met up with one of them in Iraq. My eldest son John was carrying out his six month tour in Basra at the time I was there while Andrew, my other son, was serving in Germany. John was a corporal serving with the British Special Forces based in Hereford and I knew this year was not going to be an easy tour for me down in Basra. It took me a couple of days to locate my son but we eventually found each other and from that moment my worries escalated. I would go to great lengths to meet with John but never questioned him about anything to do with his work as I knew it was secret and he wouldn't tell me anyway, all I wanted to know was that he was safe and unharmed. Because the food in his camp was below standard I invited him to my camp each evening to have a decent meal with different company, when he turned up the first time he brought his mate Tom with him as a bit of support I think. The guys I worked alongside made both John and Tom feel welcome and after the evening meal we all remained at the table and had a good laugh, mostly at John and Tom. I am very protective of my sons and therefore the pressure in Basra was greater than I realised. Anyone stupid enough to harm either of my sons would soon realise that he fucked up big time because I would hunt him down and stick him in intensive care. I hated thinking about what I would do if John was fatally wounded because I knew deep down that he joined the Army because he wanted to and would be able to look after himself but those thoughts would creep into my head and it was hard to get them out. In reality anything could happen in and around Basra which was out of everyone's control. It is hard to say how I felt about being in the same theatre of war as my son, my thoughts, feelings and worries were all over the place.

The threat was greater in Basra because the Army had only a limited amount of ground where they could accommodate the troops. Nightly mortar fire was not helping the troops' morale. Each night the enclave was mortared, and each morning we would hear of the injuries sustained by the Army. Walking round the enclave during the day, I was shocked to see how few armoured vehicles the Army had. Their Land Rovers were very similar to those I had used in Northern Ireland in the 'eighties and 'nineties vehicles of poor quality. Some of the soldiers told me some horror stories about having to borrow kit, equipment such as body armour from their friends to go out on the streets of Basra.

Others told me about being afraid to fire their weapons if they got into a contact with the insurgents because the Military Police would need an accurate statement of exactly what happened and why. I know from past experience how the Military Police worked and nothing would stop them from reaching their aim and charging a soldier. I was told of the witch hunt in progress against the troops. If any Iraqi made a complaint about a soldier, the soldier was immediately charged. It's no wonder that the soldiers felt as though the whole world was against them. I know that any soldier who was charged would be made an example of, just to show the Iraqi people that whatever they said would be believed. The list went on and on. I can honestly believe all that was told to me because I knew how the Army operated. Days went quickly as we ramped up with teams that would take the Parsons oilmen out to the oil fields to carry out the work programme.

Each day that the team went out with the client, a new problem occurred. For some reason, the Iraqi guards at the various oilfields changed the rules regarding who could come in and what they were allowed to carry; some wanted the team to disarm prior to going through the gate, while others wanted paperwork. Some even had the nerve to ask for a bribe. I often wondered why the Iraqis made it so hard for the teams to get through the gate into the oil field. Parsons came from the USA and was a huge oil company. The oil fields were in a mess, so it seemed appropriate to put the right people in to fix them and bring these facilities into the twenty-first century. Iraq was, without doubt, a complete shambles, and how it had survived for so long puzzled me.

The corruption in Basra was such that without bribery, you didn't or couldn't get what you wanted. Bribery just made the situation worse, though. The Iraqis got very creative in extortion, and those who didn't bribe them didn't get what they needed. The Iraqis soon demanded that anyone coming from the UK had to pay an airport tax of $180 to get a passport stamped; it was necessary to go into Basra City to get the stamp. They then demanded that we had to have a blood test. Coming off leave once, I was informed that I needed to have a blood test and that I would have to go into Basra to get my passport stamped. The blood test was done inside the airport so I naturally thought there was some sort of clinic inside the building. I and a mate went across to the airport and told the Iraqi guard that we were here for our blood test, he escorted us inside the building and handed us both over to another Iraqi guy. We were told to sit outside a room and from there I was escorted into a dark room which was getting light from a window because the power was off, I rolled up my shirt sleeve and waited until I heard footsteps from another doorway inside the room a female nurse appeared (I think it was female) who wanted to take blood from me. I took a close look at this woman, who wore a grubby white doctor's coat and was holding a needle that I was sure had already been used. This needle was out of the protective cover and on a dirty dusty table. Needless to say, I declined the offer and left very quickly. On my way out I grabbed hold of my mate and told him to follow me, while walking towards the main exit I told him exactly what happened, we left the building never to return. The main problem about all these rules was security, since nobody trusted the Iraqis one iota. If you gave your details to the airport security police, you did not know if they would sell your information to the local militia. It was and is still is common knowledge that nearly all Police and Army personnel in Iraq belong to some militia. Nobody knew exactly how far the terrorist grubby web extended across the world but everyone knew we had hundreds of thousands of Middle Eastern people living in the United Kingdom. The last thing I wanted was some terrorist knocking on my front door. Due to the security in downtown Basra being what it was there would be no way on earth that we would venture into the city to get our passport stamped because you may have ended up in some sort of ambush or attack. What I learned was that you gave your passport to a local guy who worked with the company and he would take the passports into the city and get them stamped. Call me what you like but I had no intentions at all of giving my passport over to some fucking guy that I didn't know from Adam and let him wander off down town with it. Why we needed a visa in the first place confused me because we flew out on either a Military flight or a chartered flight. Needless to say I went the whole year in Basra without a visa.

My meetings kept up with my son but each night it got harder and harder to sleep. During the day everything was ok because I was working but of an evening when I was alone and knew John was out in Basra, my mind wondered off into a different pane so to speak and I just wished he wasn't in country but back home. God only knows what my wife Joanne thought because she was home alone most of the time.

Daily intelligence briefs warned every one of the dangers of everyday life in a confined area. Iraqi workers were working all over inside the enclave. Soldiers and civilian contractors were often told not to walk anywhere alone; everyone had to walk in pairs or groups. It was not a good place to walk alone, as the kidnapping saga was hitting everywhere, not just Baghdad.

Teams from different companies were being stopped by militia in police uniforms, who demanded to search all vehicles. If you let them do that, you were vulnerable to attack and capture. The best thing to do was hold your ground or reverse out of the checkpoint. All Iraqis know who we are in the big armoured SUVs and that we are armed to the teeth, so why do they still stop us and expect to search one's vehicle?

Well, there are only two motivations driving that scenario, and they are *capture* and *money*. If they capture you, they will sell you on very quickly to other militia, who in turn will sell you on higher up the chain. At the top of the chain, a ransom will be delivered for your release, and if it is not paid, you will die a very nasty death and be left out in the desert for the wildlife to feed on, if the ransom is paid, you will still die a nasty death and be left out in the desert. A no win situation.

Due to the ever-increasing threat from inside the enclave, I decided to get myself a dog. My interpreter was a twenty-five-year-old lad called Jawad, who spoke very good English. One day I asked him to get me a dog from Basra. He agreed, and the very next day, he brought in a black puppy. One of the Iraqi guards called him 'Black Jack.' I made a little sleeping box for him, and he soon settled down. The Iraqi guards would go nowhere near him, and if he wandered over to them, they would scream, curse, and run.

Black Jack at one month old.

Black Jack

For some reason, as he grew, Black Jack came to hate Iraqis. All the Iraqi guards knew this and would give him a very wide berth when I took him for a walk to check the security; I had to use a chain to keep him under control. One night I decided to check the guard and to see if there were any problems. As I walked round to where Black Jack slept, I could hear laughing and a few yelps. As I turned the corner, I saw the guards kicking the dog. They knew he couldn't get loose from the chain, and they all stayed just out of reach of his teeth. They all saw me and acted as if what had just gone on had nothing to do with them. The dog saw me and wagged his tail and jumped around with excitement.

As I got to him, I decided to teach all those present a hard lesson and released the dog. I have never seen a bunch of grown men run so fast in all different directions in my life! Grown men made for the highest point to evade his gnashing teeth, running and screaming like little girls! It was, without doubt, the funniest sight I have ever seen. Needless to say, I had to take Black Jack to my cabin at night because I couldn't trust the guards.

As the dog got bigger, the guards would have nothing to do with him. They also knew that if they got too close to him, he would draw blood from them; he had done just that to quite a few of them. They tolerated the dog out of respect for me. I would take the dog wherever I went, and I didn't get stopped by any Iraqi. The Iraqis gave the dog a new name, 'Little Jack,' even though he was a year old and huge. Little Jack was a threat to all Iraqis; he also took a dislike to some of the American oilmen in camp. I was the only one who could fight with him and get away without a scratch, but I always knew that if I went too far, he could rip my arm or leg open.

When feeding him, I made sure he got a really good meal before he settled down for the night. While he ate his meal, I would sit next to him and look out across the desert at the oil fields burning off excess gas, and the entire place would be lit up. Little Jack never bothered about me being next to him. One night, as I sat next to him while he was gulping food down, one of the oilmen came from round one of the offices. He startled the dog and gave me a jump also. Although the dog was on a chain about twelve feet long, he would still have a go at you if you came within range. I told the oilman to stay back out of range while the dog was eating.

Well, I got the usual bollocks, a story of how this guy was an ex-US Army dog handler and knew how to treat dogs. What a load of crap! I reminded him that the dog didn't like anyone around him when he was eating because he thought the person might steal his food. This idiot boasted that he could make Little Jack do whatever he wanted the dog to do. While he was talking, I kept reminding him about not getting too close. However, the guy came one step too close, and the dog had his leg. As far as I was concerned, it wasn't the dog's fault but the fault of this idiot, who was by that time hopping around and yelping like a stuck pig while holding his leg.

The guy informed the boss of the camp, my boss, and I thought it would be curtains for the dog. When the boss spoke to me about the incident, I told him exactly what happened, he told me that he had heard it differently. The boss got the guy out and put my story to him, and he admitted sheepishly that mine was the correct version. The boss was happy, no more was said on the subject, and that guy never came near the dog again.

I would take the dog around the back of the camp, where I would throw a ball for him, mainly to give him a run around. I was in an enclosed area, and when I entered, I made sure the gate was secured behind me. Once, though, I did not know that an Iraqi guy was in one of the cabins inside the fence. As I threw the ball for the dog, this guy emerged from one of the cabins. He took one look at this huge dog running past him, and I swear that he went white and nearly passed out. I had to grab the dog and hold him, and then tell this guy to get out quickly before the dog got free; he was off like a shot out of the gate.

Another time I decided to take the dog for a walk into the enclave where all the British soldiers were based. The soldiers made the dog the centre of attention. Quite surprisingly, he never even barked or showed his teeth to any of them. He looked very relaxed with all who petted him, even to the point of having play fights with some of the guys. I met up with a guy from the dog section, and this man enquired about where I had gotten my dog and how I used him. I told the guy that he was brought in from Basra in a sand bag and that I kept him as a sort of guard dog, and the soldier seemed quite intrigued. He arranged for the dog to have vaccinations and a check-over by the military vet. I was over the moon with this because I never hinted that he hadn't had his vaccinations. I arranged to get the dog there the following day to have his check-over and vaccinations.

To return to my camp, I had to go through the military checkpoint and walk about a kilometer. The road was long and lonely. About five hundred meters along the road, I noticed four Iraqi men chatting by the cement factory where they made T walls for the British military. As we got closer to them, with the sentry well behind us, I noticed that they had all started taking an interest in me. Although I was armed with a Glock pistol, I was still very apprehensive. About thirty to forty feet away from them, I decided that if any of them made a move in my direction, I would let the dog go. The ones the dog didn't get, I would. I drew the dog back towards me on the chain and decided to let him go; he would at least scatter them in all directions, which would make it easier for me to pass. I got the end of the chain, which was connected to his collar, and just flicked the latch up with my thumb.

The dog immediately ran for the Iraqis, barking his head off. The Iraqis gave out screams, ran for the highest point, and clambered up as if the devil were after them. I found them very funny to watch. I pretended that the dog had slipped his lead and said I was sincerely sorry, though I wasn't. Then I got the dog back on to his chain and walked away; the Iraqis stayed up where they were until I was well out of range before I saw them getting back down to ground level. On entering my camp, I had no problems with the Iraqi guards, who knew who I was and that Little Jack didn't like them. They opened the gate and made sure they were behind the mesh fencing and let us both through. Once in my cabin Jack settled down on his carpet and dropped off to sleep. I showered and got into bed, read, and dozed off.

The next day I took Little Jack back into the enclave and met up with the military dog handler, who took me to the kennels. The vet, a captain, gave him the once-over and said he was in good health. He then told me to hold the dog as he gave him two or three shots. The dog didn't like this one bit, and so he could get his own back on me for bringing him, he bit me on the arm. He didn't draw blood, but it bloody hurt.

As my year in Basra was coming to an end, I learnt that Jawad had been kidnapped by militia. Jawad was no threat to anyone; he was engaged and had just partly finished building a house. All Jawad wanted to do was earn some decent money, finish building his house, and get married. They found him two days later with three bullet holes in his head; he had been left in a ditch. This sent shock waves around the rest of the guard. It was a worrying time for everyone concerned. I was told by another member of the guard that a certain person working on guard duty had Jawad set up and that this person thought Jawad was getting too big for his boots. I knew that Jawad was only doing his duty as my right-hand man and never really saw anything untoward in his behavior.

The tribal system is rough in the Middle East, and for a small price you could have someone killed for the slightest reason – what a way to live.

One of the guards approached me and asked if he could take Little Jack home with him. I knew that if I let this happen, the dog would not last a month. He would never be fed the way he was used to being fed, so I declined the request. In the enclave one night, I met up with the dog handler again and told him my problem – that I was leaving Basra. He suggested that I get the dog to the kennels tomorrow, and they would put him through a little test to see if he was good enough to be a guard dog. Next day I was straight up to the kennels with the dog and handed him over to the soldiers. I was asked to wait in the NAAFI and told that they would give me a call when they had finished.

A couple of hours later, I got a call to get back to the kennels. When I arrived, I was greeted by Little Jack, who was wagging his tail and jumping around the place. I honestly thought the dog had failed or had bitten one of the guys. The dog handler told me he had passed the test and if I wanted to give him up, all I had to do was sign him over to them and that would be it; he was still young enough to train with a handler. I asked them if I could be alone with Little Jack for five minutes, which they agreed to. I sat on the ground next to him and thought about the situation that now faced me; I was heading back up to Baghdad, and then onto a base called Taji. I had a dog that I adored and who had the chance of a better life as a guard dog with guys who would look after him. I didn't want to lose him, but due to the work I do and the places I go, I knew I had to give him over.

Little Jack just sat watching me while I pondered. I think

he knew that he was going somewhere else without me. I called the handler back and told him to make the paperwork out, and I would sign it. He returned about ten minutes later, and I signed the dog over to him. I looked at Little Jack as I signed the papers and told him that he was going to be in a far better place than I could give him. I gave him a hug, ruffled his hair, and walked away. At the gate, I looked back and still saw the dog sitting with his ears pointing up and his tongue hanging out the corner of his mouth, panting, I think he was waiting for me to call him. I turned and walked away from the kennels.

Even to this day, I still think of Little Jack and all the fun we had, how he came to me as a little bundle of fur, how he grew up to be a lovely dog, and how he protected me from whatever stood in my way, friend or foe. I think of some of the guys he bit – as they jumped around, screaming, he would give me that puppy dog look as if to get my approval for what he had done. I know giving him over to the military was the right thing to do, and it also gave him a far better life than I could ever hope to give him. He was a lovely dog and is sadly missed.

Little Jack in the shade.

Little Jack at one month old

The Government should be ashamed of themselves for putting our soldiers' lives at risk just to please the Americans. Everyone knew the Iraqi nation was no threat to the outside world in a military sense; they could, however, be a small threat when it came to oil. Saddam Hussain used to make threats, which everyone knew he could never carry out. The coalition forces went to war with Saddam for oil.

I learned from an Army officer that after WW2 the British gave quite a lot of Iraq over to the Kuwaitis, basically because Kuwait was a very small country. The part that was given over had Iraq's oil pipes underground. When the Kuwaitis found out about this, they tapped into the oil and sold it on the oil market. Years went by, and nobody gave Iraq or Kuwait a second thought until Saddam Hussain came to power. Saddam, I am told, tried many ways to get paid for the oil which the Kuwaitis had taken – which, in reality, they had stolen. The Kuwaiti royal family knew they had friends in the West who would come to their aid if requested, so they basically told Saddam to go to hell. This obviously got Saddam into a frenzy, and that dispute was basically the onset of the first Gulf War. That is what I was told, and I honestly don't know if it was true or not, but if you look at it logically,

I could be swayed into believing it.

In Gulf One and Two, the British soldier was let down by the government he served. The Americans called the British soldier the desert gypsy because the British would pick up and use anything the American soldier threw away.

I believe that any war, big or small, should have no input from a civilian government; nobody in government has any idea about war or how to run one. Brigadiers and generals should be left to sort out and execute plans with limited guidance from the Government. At the end of the day you don't become a General because you are a duck egg, you become a General because you are intelligent and educated and you know what the hell you are talking about, unlike politicians who would shit themselves at the sight of an angry terrorist. When you get an army like the British Army, you know you have one of the best-trained armies in the world, even though it is small and doesn't have the right equipment to sustain itself for long. You basically get what you see. However, the men fight for pride and the pride of the regiment they are serving in – nothing more, nothing less. So when government officials say the fight is going the way they planned, it isn't; it is going the way the troops on the ground want it to go so their regiment can get noticed. The government is under the illusion that the Army belongs to them, and in reality, that is correct. However, ask any soldier who he fights for, and he will tell you he fights for his regiment. If you put it to him that he is fighting for his government, he will most probably tell you to fuck off and then throw out a stream of abuse directed at the heads of the party in power. The Labour party that was in power at the time had many internal fights going on with Blair and Brown. Brown wanted to be the boss, and Blair stood his ground as boss. Brown even had the audacity to stop funds reaching the troops to teach Blair a lesson. What sort of government does that to its forces? Only the British Government could do that.

During my years in Iraq as a civilian security advisor, I was far better armed and fed than any British soldier, and my armoured vehicle was far superior to any the British Army had on the ground. My welfare was better; in fact, everything about my situation was better. You would have thought it would be the other way around, but it wasn't. Civilian companies have to make a profit, but they would always look after their men first. Most companies were run by ex-British Army officers who knew how to treat men. These ex-officers left the Army because of all the crap they were expected to do for a government that didn't care for them or their soldiers.

One thing I will mention is that Security guys are in more danger than the Soldier because we did not have the back up those Soldiers have. In other words if we got into trouble nobody would come to your aid, you had to get yourself out of it as best you could.

Incidents that occurred while I was in Basra summed everything up for me of what these people were really like, although, unlike everywhere else in Iraq, I was not involved.

A good friend of mine took his team, with client, to one oilfield just east of Basra. When the team arrived the Iraqi guard opened the gates and let them straight in before securing the gates when the last vehicle was through. About two hundred metre's further on the Iraqi's had set a road block up with huge boulders strewn across the narrow road. As all the vehicles came to a halt my friend saw three vehicles come through the gate they had just come through, on the open backs of the vehicles were Iraqi Policemen. My mate was the only one to get out of his vehicle to try and find out what was going on. He was told in no uncertain terms that he and his team had to give all their weapons over and would be escorted to the nearest Police station. An argument started about weapons being handed over and the exact reason for the team to be taken to the Police station to which the Iraq commander could not give any reasonable excuse. As the hours went by and with no way out of the oilfield things started to deteriorate rapidly. Fortunately another PSD team from the same company parked up at the other side of the main gates and communications were made with the team inside the oilfield. Weapons were drawn and targets identified by the team outside the gates which was passed on verbally by my mate to the Iraqi commander. The Iraqi commander saw that he was in a sticky situation because he was in the middle of two teams who had armoured vehicles and would fight their way out if necessary and decided to release my mate and his team. Within minutes my mate and his team were heading back to their camp with a shocked client.

Another incident occurred on the border road between Iraq and Kuwait. A PSD travelling to pick up a client from Basra Palace were stopped by Iraqi Police at a road block. The Police demanded the team get out of the vehicles and give their weapons over to them. Unfortunately the team leader was not experienced in these situations and as one of the Policemen approached the vehicle thee team leader wound the armoured window down. This was without doubt the worst mistake he ever made and one that cost him his life. The Policeman approached the vehicle on the side where the team leader was sat; he immediately took his pistol out of its holster and shot the Gurkha driver straight in the head then shot the team leader in the head killing both instantly. Other Police men fired at thee tyres of the vehicles immobilizing them. The team members, a total of four men, decided to get out and fight their way out of trouble, unfortunately they didn't assess the situation properly and didn't see the other Police men to the right or left of the road. As they got out doing a fighting withdrawal they were hit by bullets from the sides of the road. All team members were killed instantly. One guy managed to escape and ran hell for leather towards some buildings further back along the road with bullets whizzing all around him. As luck would have it a Danish Army patrol were driving towards him, stopped and picked him up. After telling the Danish commander what had happened they drove to the roadblock. The Danish commander informed the Military by radio of the situation and a QRF force was dispatched. The story the Iraqi commander gave was that the team opened fire on them for no reason and that they were just protecting themselves by shooting back. To save the situation from getting any further out of control the Iraqi Policemen were let go. The QRF turned up, put the bodies into body bags and pushed the immobilized vehicles to the side of the road and torched them.

The incident of when a PSD team got hit by an IED which killed the two men in the front vehicle. While the shooting was going on between the insurgents and the two men from the rear vehicle, children (yes children) robbed the dead men of clothing, watches and anything else close at hand. One of these guys was a close friend of mine which only strengthens my feelings for the people who did this as the scum of the fucking earth.

Driving along a ring road around one part of Basra I saw a crowd ahead of me. On reaching the crowd I saw a dead man halfway out of a car with a youngster, about nine years old, hitting the body with a stick holding hands with his father, what the fuck is that all about, sick bastards.

Many incidents involving private security men happened like this in and around Basra but never made the news back in the UK which in itself is a shame. A theory I have come up with is the less you tell the people back in the UK the less they will worry. When they don't hear any news at all everyone thinks it's all settled, next thing they know is that our troops are returning home, the only problem is that nothing has really changed.

John left Basra after completing his six month tour unscathed and safe save for a major problem when two SAS guys ended up in the care of the Iraqi Police. The story I heard, and there have been many stories, was that they were out on a job in Basra watching a particular person. The car that they were in came under the attention of the Iraqi Police. As the two man team sat and watched their target two undercover Iraqi Police dressed in civilian clothing approached their car. One of the Police Officers pulled a pistol out of his waistband as they neared the car, the two operatives fearing their lives were in danger opened fire on the Iraqis killing one. A car chase ensued but eventually both soldiers were arrested and taken to a nearby Police station. This is where my son came into the problem because at the time of the incident he was on the ops desk. He controlled everything from the start to the finish. The end result was both soldiers were taken by force away from the Iraqi Police and flown straight out of the country back to Hereford. The pair of them had been beaten and all their equipment had been taken from them and has never been returned. I knew exactly how those two guys felt and what they went through.

Chapter 4 (2006)

Well, my year in Basra with CRG was up, and it was time for me to depart. I left and went home. Whilst at home I decided that enough was enough and I would not go back out to Iraq. I had completed just less than three years. All I wanted to do was to settle back into civilian life again, something ex-soldiers find hard to do. A big problem for me was I hated civilian life because it was fucking mundane to say the least with a Government who were only interested in how much tax they could rob off the general public and also stuff the forces over for everything they could. I had no idea what job I wanted to do. I decided to take my wife away on holiday abroad and just chill out. When we got back home from a very relaxing time away, a time when I never even thought of checking e-mails, I fired up my computer and saw I had an e-mail from a friend who needed help on the convoys. I carried out a bit of research on convoys in Iraq and spoke to quite a few guys who all told me to stay away from them as they were very dangerous and not worth the risk. I had seen convoys travelling up and down motorways in Iraq and I had also seen burnt out trucks from convoys which had been attacked. I thought about the risks and the challenge and decided that this was something right up my street.

Those days in Basra passed into my own history. Now I was going back out to start a new contract, carrying out convoy work for the Multi National Force Iraq (MNFI). It was work for the American Army – which, even though they had substantial numbers of men on the ground, could not release any to carry out this work. These were very dangerous times, and they needed everyone on the ground to fight the insurgents.

I started with a company called R.G.S, Rover Global Services, in August 2006. It was owned by an ex-British Army officer called R. R. This person had reached the rank of major in the British Army. The operations manager was a large person called A. W, an ex-corporal from the R.L.C, the Royal Logistic Corps. The business development guy was a Frenchman called Richard; the mechanic was some fucking window licker from Croatia, a real nutter with a haircut that made him look like Adolf Hitler when Hitler was in the trenches in world war one. The mad Croatian always walked around the camp while talking to his imaginary friend, which at times was quite amusing. The camp was an absolute shithole. There was no organisation or anything to the camp itself just a hard building where everyone lived, a total of 60 guys. The head shed lived in porta cabins next to the building. What a fucking nightmare of a camp.

Convoy work is very dangerous. It is slow and predictable to the enemy. Convoys could be long or short, but all of them were dangerous. Anyone doing convoy work had to have balls. When the firing started, it was up to the expats in the team to deal with it and get the firefight won with the assistance of the security team. Success in convoy work meant getting out of your vehicle and standing face to face with the insurgent and fighting him round for round. Success meant getting out when the firing was going on all around you and getting the damaged trucks hooked up and towed out of the kill zone; it meant getting out and changing flat tyres; it meant going back into the kill zone for a fallen comrade if necessary. In this work, you have to be prepared to do the unthinkable when the shit hits the fan and hope to God you survive. I have known loads of guys to get a one-way ticket to the funeral parlour.

All convoy guys have my utmost respect because I know firsthand what they experience each day just to be able to get a vehicle or weapons or ammunition to a Forward Operating Base. Any expat who bottled it on a contact would be asked to leave on the return to camp. It's no disgrace at all to bottle it; some people do, and some people don't. Some people like the shooting and the fight, but at the end of the day, it's not everyone's cup of tea, so to speak. In all my time out on convoy work, I witnessed quite a few guys who said it wasn't for them and that they didn't know it was so dangerous; at least they tried.

A team leader from one of the teams was a person called M.H, and the other team leader was a person called P.C. I got on well with M.H and P.C and would often go out on convoy with their separate teams. My first task was as a 2i/c (2nd in command) of M.H convoy. This was purely for me to familiarize myself with the ground. We had to go to Basra and drop off a fire engine. Two hours south of Baghdad on Route Tampa South, we had to stop at a staging yard called Scania. This place was situated right on the motorway, and everyone passing through and heading south had to book in and book out of Scania. It was designed to track convoys and PSD's moving south to other destinations. All went well on the trip down, but that soon changed on the trip back because we got hit by insurgents. After passing through Scania and refueling, we headed off out of the northern checkpoint on our way to the outskirts of Baghdad.

About half an hour north of Scania, the shooting started. In the ensuing gun battle, we managed to keep the small convoy moving, but the rear gun truck was taking a beating. I informed M.H that I would drop back and assist the rear protection vehicle until we broke contact. When I got back to the rear gun truck, I heard a fearsome rattle of automatic fire from the machine gun on the back of the gun truck. I told my top gunner to watch for the fall of tracer and fire, and no sooner than I had said that, my top gunner was firing.

I jumped into the back of the vehicle to see where and who they were shooting at. Watching the fall of tracer from my gunner, I saw three figures firing at us from the reeds. I ordered both drivers to keep driving. Once we broke contact with the insurgents, I radioed M.H and told him I needed to stop to check a knocking sound coming from the engine. I jumped out of the vehicle and opened the bonnet of the vehicle to see what the noise was; as I was looking inside, I heard and saw two American humvees come out of the desert and onto the motorway alongside us. I went over and spoke to an American sergeant in the front vehicle and told him what had happened and where the bad guys were shooting from.

The sergeant told me to get my vehicle fixed and get going and that he would take care of those motherfuckers. With that, they left us and headed back toward the place where the insurgents had fired on us. I carried on and found the knocking noise to be a plank of wood. God only knows where that came from. As I walked to the passenger door, I heard the noise of fifty-caliber weapons being fired, and we got going.

We rejoined the convoy, and I gave M.H a heads-up on what had happened; we then carried on towards Baghdad without further incident.

After two weeks, M.H was promoted to assistant operations manager, a position that I thought took him well out of his depth. I took over his team as team leader. My team consisted of four expats and twenty Gurkhas from Nepal. I only had one British Army Gurkha, Rabi; the rest were Nepalese and Indian Army Gurkhas. I found a lifelong friend in Rabi and relied on him to keep the men in check and good order. He was well-respected throughout the camp purely because he was an ex-British Army Gurkha. Rabi was married with two small children; his wife and kids lived in Nepal while he served in Iraq as a civilian contractor. Also in my team were a couple of Fijians, huge men with hands like shovels. Mind you, they need hands that big because they eat like lions. What a normal human eats in a full day, they would eat at one sitting, and then go back for more. I have never seen anyone put away so much food at one sitting than a Fijian.

I decided to start off with a training programme for a two-week period just to get everyone singing from the same song sheet. On Monday morning we got the gun trucks, and I went through everything with the entire team. I got the vehicle mechanic, the window licking Hitler lookalike, to go through the engine compartment with us and tell us what to look for if they broke down. I then went through wheel-changing drills, contact drills, and stop drills including contact drills left, right, rear and head on, I also covered what to do in the event of another gun truck breaking down and a gun truck being shot up so badly that we would have to cross deck people from one vehicle to another. I made them go through the various drills morning, noon, and night until they could do those drills blindfolded. I taught them basic medical skills and how to stop the bleeding from a gunshot wound. I taught them how to insert an Intravenous drip and even let them try that skill on me – my bloody arms were black and blue. Letting them use me as a human guinea pig earned me more respect from them.

Convoy drills were practiced daily; in fact, every spare moment we had, we would practice the drills. The idea was for the convoy to stay in the middle of the road with a front vehicle which the team leader occupied. Range work, shooting, kept me and the ex pats very busy because even though these guys were all ex military their shooting was fucking hopeless and I often thought that if we ever get into a contact these guys wouldn't hit a thing, very worrying. Rabi was an excellent shot and the key man here; he was the same breed as these guys and I knew they all had the utmost respect for him and did not want to embarrass him in front of us. When on the range the ex pats with me attempted to zero the weapons to the guys. First time at this the firers were shooting the ground in front of the targets. Patience is a virtue. We struggled on with the shooting until everyone was competent although some of the guys couldn't hit a barn door even if they were sat on the door handle; these guys were given tasks that didn't involve much shooting, more administration.

The convoys drove down the middle of the road because the insurgents planted their IEDs in the sand at the sides of the road. If they detonated the device when the convoy passed, driving in the middle of the road, the blast would go over the heads of the top gunners. If the device was detonated while the convoy drove next to the verge, the blast would blow the vehicle over, killing the top gunners. In front of my lead vehicle, I had a point vehicle that I used as a reconnaissance vehicle. That vehicle's main task was to clear the route for the convoy and report back to me any problems they saw on the road ahead. The rear of the convoy was protected by a gun truck with two machine guns. The last two vehicles protected the centre of the convoy and also functioned as sweep vehicles. The main task of a sweep vehicle is to keep the truck drivers going and not let the convoy split; they also stayed wide of the convoy and headed off any problems coming in from the sides. Sweep vehicles also drive up and down the convoy, blocking roads left and right and enabling the convoy to keep moving. The convoy sweep is very dangerous because they drive next to the verge and could be blown up at any time.

Each morning I took the team out for a run. We started with short runs first, then built up to longer runs. I was quite shocked at how many of the men were unfit. Half of them could not even make it through the first runs, which were only about a kilometre. The others came across the finishing line knackered.

As the days went by, the men perked up quite a bit. The fitness programme was coming together, and each man felt a lot better about himself. The training was going great, and all the men enjoyed what they were doing. At times, when I saw them standing around, I would make them change a tyre against the clock or pick two teams of four men and make them race against each other. At times we had good laughs, and I honestly think they liked what I was doing.

Short programme for convoy training teams. Basics 1.

1) Weapons training, full training and familiarization with the weapons available to the team. Stoppage drills, safe handling, stripping and cleaning, zeroing.

2) Range time with weapons, 25m zeroing, 100 m fire exercises (firing positions) 25 m automatic fire multiple targets.

3) Convoy layout, positions within convoy. Familiarization with different vehicles and their jobs within the convoy.

4) Contact drills, IEDs, VBIEDs, SAF, FRONTAL, REAR, AND BOTH SIDES.

5) Static drills for immobilized vehicles, cross decking, evacuation of injured personnel, pushing vehicle out of kill zone.

6) Radio drills. Contacting OPS, medical evacuation awareness.

7) Route awareness, areas that you are in. Safe havens available, nearest medical facilities.

8) Warning shot drills (when to and when not to fire warning shots).

9) Sustained fighting drills (static and mobile).

10) Threat assessment, identification of possible threats on the route, i.e., IEDs, PAX, possible high-level threat villages and towns.

11) Knowledge of the ground situation, the route being traveled, hot spots on route.

12) Top cover drills. Vehicle control from behind, sides, or front.

13) Casualty evacuation / cross decking from immobilized vehicle, drill listed below in appendix A.

Appendix A

Medical evacuation / Cross decking from immobilized vehicle.

1) Threat assessment of area – IEDs, VBIEDs, and POSSIBLE AMBUSH.

2) Secure disabled vehicle(s) with all-round defense.

3) DESIGNATED personnel to deal with injured.

4) Vehicle to be stripped of all essential equipment (only if unrecoverable).

5) Quick assessment of safest route out of the kill area. Nearest medical facility or safe haven (coalition camp).

6) Nothing enters or leaves the area without the permission of the TL or his 2i/c. This includes the Iraqi Army and Police.

7) 7 Top cover should stay in place unless told otherwise by TL or 2IC or MEDIC.

ALWAYS BE AWARE OF SECONDARY ATTACK WHILE PERFORMING EVACUATION.

Static convoy drills.

1) On going static, choose an area with no obvious obstructions, i.e., no static vehicles, culverts, razor wire, boxes, oil drums, or crowds.

2) Position vehicle correctly, facing direction of travel at an angle and ready to move quickly if necessary.

3) Top cover should stay in position (unless told to do otherwise by TL). There should be 360 degrees all-around cover.

4) One person to exit vehicle and do 5 m clearance check; the 20 m check is at the TL's discretion.

5) Personnel on the ground should have their weapon butt in place and the weapon correctly placed on their shoulder and carried correctly.

6) Personnel on the ground should, at all times, remain mobile. (Static targets are easier to hit.) Always remain vigilant, maintaining 100% concentration.

7) Only vehicle doors of those on the ground to remain open. This is for quick access and to avoid openings for insurgent snipers.

8) Top cover in rear protection and front sweep may be called upon to do traffic control. Stay vigilant for the threat of VBIEDs.

9) Cover may be required around the convoy; this is at the discretion of the TL. If needed, continue to be mobile.

10) Remain vigilant at all times while static, expect an attack, stay mobile, and handle weapons professionally. Work as a team at all times.

Civilian vehicle drills.

1) On approaching a civilian vehicle (same direction as travel), the driver will flash lights and sound horn.

2) Stay on the left-hand side of the vehicle; this will allow the driver a better chance to see you in his rearview mirror.

3) The top cover must wave their arms or flag to gain the driver's attention; they must indicate the direction they want the driver to go.

4) Push the driver to the right-hand side hard shoulder and make sure he goes static.

5) One of the top cover is to watch the driver at all times so that he does not try to rejoin the convoy. Do so until the next vehicle takes control of it.

6) The static vehicle is to be watched until the convoy is clear.

7) If a vehicle is proving hard to move, take a position to the left and alongside it. Gesture to the right. If necessary, shepherd the driver to the hard shoulder. The civilian vehicle must go static.

8) Do everything you can to move the vehicle before you have to use force. Try to minimize the use of force.

9) Warning shots are a last resort.

10) Vehicles which are in front of you are to be escorted to the right-hand hard shoulder with the use of lights and vehicle positioning.

IF IN DOUBT, ASK.

Team Gun Truck

All the gun trucks were ex-British Army Land Rovers, so all the expats had plenty of experience with them. The Land Rover was the workhorse of the Army, and we had used them extensively in Northern Ireland. The tyres were supposed to be run flats, but every time we went out, we would have a flat.

Gun truck, old British Army vehicles

Because our company lacked enough gun trucks, only two teams at a time could go on a task, so the third team left in camp would either train or be on guard duties. Taskings would come in for trips as far up the country as Mosul and Al Kasik and as far down south as Basra and the Kuwait border. Each team had to have four expats, and one of them had to be a qualified trauma medic. I was very lucky in that I had a medic who was worth his weight in gold. That was G.H, the best medic I had ever come across. I did not worry about where I had to go because I knew if anything happened to any of the team, G.H would be able to help them. He was a god.

I had five Land Rover armoured gun trucks, and each gun truck had one expat vehicle commander. The only vehicle that didn't have an expat commander was the fifth vehicle, and the gun truck was made up entirely of Gurkhas. I had a Gurkha driver and two top cover men with each expat vehicle. Inside the vehicle I had enough water, rations, and ammunition to last forty-eight hours. Spare parts for the vehicle were nonexistent. If we broke down and couldn't fix the vehicle, we would cross all the guys and stores from the damaged vehicle across to a serviceable vehicle and burn the vehicle that is damaged. If we could tow it, however, we would.

Our camp was a derelict camp inside an old Iraqi military base called Taji. Taji got bombed quite extensively in the second Gulf War and was just a camp full of rubble, bombed tanks and signals vehicles. There were open sewer pits at the side of the main hard building, and everyone was either stuffed tightly into small rooms or in porta-cabins that leaked when it rained. What a state. The camp was really untidy, to say the least, but it was somewhere to work out of, at least if one could ignore its two open sewers, its lack of water, and a generator that looked like it was going to blow up. During the winter months the sewers would fill up and then overflow spewing out piss, shit and whatever else was down there up to ground level and into the accommodation. The unfortunate thing was we couldn't do anything about it and just had to live with walking around in shitty water for a couple of months but of an evening we would sleep outside up on the fence line where it was dry. During the summer the sewers would dry up. When a wind kicked up, dust and dried shit would come out of the sewer and float around the camp, basically we were breathing in flakes of human shit. All year round the place stank.

Open sewer

The cookhouse.

All the food was cooked by the Gurkhas, and they made some of the best curries I have ever tasted, and some of the hottest. These men could make a curry out of anything.

Each convoy was supposed to include twenty-one trucks carrying the cargo with seven gun trucks full of armed security. Weapons used were the trusted AK-47 rifles and light machine guns, PKCs or PKMs, both types belt-fed.

The places we visited were not for the faint-hearted; I don't even think that the devil himself ever ventured into some of them. I was hoping that every man had the nerve to stand and fight if it came to that point, but nobody really knows how he will react until the bullets start flying. Then it's too late to start thinking of how you ever got into this game. Many of the American camps we visited were in built-up areas, and many were out in the desert with one route in and one route out. The desert was an insurgent's paradise, full of deadly ambush areas.

We carried out a lot of ammunition convoys from a camp called Buckmaster, which was up north by Tikrit, home of Saddam Hussain, to Al Kasik, which was further north, through Mosul. Mosul was very dangerous, and all convoys that went through Mosul normally got hit. We transported vehicles to Fallujah and Ramadi, which is west of Baghdad; trucks and uniforms to Numanijah, which is south of Baghdad; trucks to Rustanamiyh, which is opposite Sadr City; and kitchen containers to Kirkush and Baquba. In all, we delivered to quite a few places, including Basra, that were all very dangerous.

The team's first run was into the Green Zone, I told the men that I was classing this one as a training run. If anything went wrong, we would iron everything out when we got back to Taji. All went well and without incident. I knew in my own heart that things would change as we carried on taking convoys out.

A.W tasked us to take stores down to the B.I.A.P for the Americans. The problem was we had to go through the rear gates which were near to Abu Ghraib. As we drove along route sword heading out of Baghdad we had to negotiate a very large Iraqi Police checkpoint. About two hundred metres from the checkpoint we got fired on from a house on our right. The top gunners opened fire direct onto the house where the insurgents were firing at us from the bedroom windows. As I was calling in a contact report into the ops room I was looking at all the bullets hitting the wall next to the windows when I saw the front door open, an insurgent ran out of the building and took cover behind a telegraph pole and almost immediately was shot dead by my gunners. Next thing I saw was another insurgent run from the building and take cover behind the same telegraph pole next to his dead mate. Again my gunners got a bead on him and shot him dead also, he slumped over next to the first dead insurgent and as quickly as the firing started it stopped. They obviously didn't have the stomach for it because they had already seen two of their men die.

As we neared the Iraqi Police checkpoint we got the usual angry stare but not one person said anything to any of us. The convoy got through the checkpoint and into the B.I.A.P without further incident.

It did not surprise me that the Iraqi Police didn't assist us because as the convoys continued in the months ahead I realised that instead of assisting they became the problem.

That was my first major incident on the convoys and I knew life would get harder and more dangerous in the oncoming weeks and months. Back at camp that night I sat down and realised for the first time that this convoy lark was very dangerous because not only where we out day and night but we were out all on our own, without any form of back up. On the same road a few nights later we got a job to head to Scania and escort trucks back to Baghdad which were full of uniforms for the Iraqi Army. It was about 2100hrs when we turned onto route sword and saw a convoy that had been attacked. A few miles up the road my top gunners had reported hearing shooting and explosions ahead of us but I never expected to come into something that looked like a movie set. Because we were running free, without trucks, I decided to stop and assist. There was a long line of trucks which were obviously a convoy heading into Baghdad static on the other side of the dual carriageway. Quite a few of the trucks were on fire with men running in all directions. I got my convoy to move to the trucks and gave a quick set of battle orders. My last vehicles were to go static at the front of the convoy and then equally spaced out between the trucks until my first vehicle went static at the last truck in the convoy. As I jumped out I grabbed hold of a guy who was running from one truck to another, when he turned to face me I saw he was in a bad way, his eyes were the size of saucers and he was screaming at the top of his voice and babbling all kinds of things to me which I could not make any sense of. In the end I had to punch this guy to keep him from trying grab me in a sort of bear hug. Two of my men kept hold of him on the ground and I ran further down to see if there was anyone else I could speak to. In the end I found a man huddled up close to a wall and shaking uncontrollably, I touched his arm and he nearly jumped out of his skin. I calmed the guy down and asked him what had happened. In a shaky voice he told me they were supposed to be delivering fuel to the Green Zone, as they came along this stretch of road they came under attack from RPG's and small arms fire from the houses on the side of the road. I could see three trucks which were ablaze and saw four men laid out on the road who had been shot dead. The guy I was talking to was an American and he said that the convoy security were from an Iraqi company, when the firing started the security drove away and left the convoy. The large Police checkpoint further down the road just looked on and didn't assist. We got all the truck drivers together and put them into the back of two of the guntrucks while we went and recovered the dead men. We wrapped the dead in blankets secured them to stretchers which we secured to the back of our gun trucks, once completed I told the drivers to get into their trucks and follow me to the Green Zone. We arrived at checkpoint 18 where I left the truckers in the safe hands of the Americans. I decided not to go on the job and called the ops room to cancel the job until the following night. With this done I and my very quiet team returned to Taji.

In August 2006 we were tasked to pick up Iraqi Police cars from a place called Al Hateem. This place was not a nice place, and all the people in the village were against the coalition. A few months prior to our trip, an American patrol had fought a battle in or around the area. After the gun battle, two American soldiers caught two females and raped them. In retribution, the insurgents captured two American soldiers and tortured them in the most hideous way before beheading them and dumping the bodies. That was the story, and I am not sure if it was true, but nobody could take chances. The trip down there was a nightmare because we had to go through a small town on a road that was just wide enough to take the trucks. As we entered the small town, I knew we would have trouble because the electric cables and telephone lines were hanging right down between the telegraph poles and across the road. Each of the wires had to be lifted up to enable the trucks to get through; dealing with those wires took hours and grew more and more dangerous as the hours passed. We eventually made it through to the other side without upsetting any of the town's people.

One factor that really got my attention was the fact that there were quite a few Iraqi military and Iraqi Police. Although they neither bothered us nor helped us, I wondered why so many men in uniform were in this very small town. On the outskirts of the town, I noticed hundreds of men, women, and children walking in the same direction. When I enquired why all these people went in one direction, I was told that it was a religious day and they were all going to pay their respects. This made my blood run cold because these were Sunni, and these people whip their backs with metal chains, which obviously made their backs bleed. Some of the hardened ones hit their foreheads with metal bars and anything that would draw blood. Their territory was not the ideal place for us to be.

As we neared Al Hateem, everyone went on very high alert. This was a very dangerous place, and we didn't want to get caught out by anything, least of all a full-scale gun battle. The place was very quiet, with only a few people roaming the streets. The pavements were quite high, and I thought, 'If we do get into any bother, it's going to be a real problem trying to turn these vehicles around.'

Oddly, when we drove into the village, the minaret, which usually calls people to prayer, started broadcasting music and what sounded like preaching. This noise, quite eerie, went on all through the night. It took ages for us to get these long trucks through some tiny back lanes and around some very tight bends. Most of the time, all the expats were out on foot, directing the trucks while the Gurkha top cover guys watched for anything suspicious. Eventually we got all the trucks through to the other side. Whilst doing this, many of the locals walked past us, and even trying to say hello met with an angry face. Some people even spat on the ground in front of us.

Well, if that was what got them off, I was happy. I didn't plan to spit at the first person who pointed a weapon at us. However, their spitting and hostility were indicators that I really didn't want to see. What a godforsaken place. All the streets we went down had rubbish strewn all over; dead dogs had been left where they fell, and you could see where the rats and possibly other dogs had chewed the meat off various parts of the bodies.

Al Hateem Report

Contact 28th August 2006   Time 1250 hours

GTR T0063 USAMET539427#76309

Grid 38S MD 29738634

RGS C/S 20a MOVEMENT FROM AL HATEEM TO TAJI

On 27 August, I was tasked to command a team to pick up twelve trucks from the paint factory at Al Hateem and deliver them to Taji. Al Hateem is situated south of Baghdad, approximately fifty miles. The trip down was not a problem; however, we did not encounter any coalition checkpoints because at that time all checkpoints where either Iraqi Army or Iraqi Police.

My team arrived at the paint factory at approximately 1830 hours; the area was secured, and sentries were positioned. The compound we controlled was by no means secure, as I had been led to believe in my intelligence brief.

An old Iraqi military camp, which had been destroyed in either Gulf 1 or Gulf 2, was close by but afforded no protection. We had a visit from an Iraqi Police patrol at 0145 hours in the morning.

During the night, the guard woke me and informed me that they had seen lights coming from the disused Iraqi camp. My 2i/c and I decided to go over and investigate. I woke everyone up and informed them of what was happening and what I was going to do about it; in other words, I and my 2i/c would move over to the camp on foot and investigate where the lights were coming from. I informed everyone that if any shooting took place, they were to light the whole place up. Mickey, who was my 2i/c, was ex-Foreign Legion of nine years; he was a real hard case, small in stature but absolutely fearless. We both made our way over to the buildings. It was a slow tactical move, and by the time we got there, we were soaked with sweat. The camp was huge and stretched for hundreds of metres in all directions. We decided to check the nearest buildings because, if anyone were trying to get close to us, they would certainly have reached this point. As we slowly crept around the buildings, all I could hear was buzzing from my ears; the sweat was pouring out of me and down my face, stinging my eyes. Every time I wiped the sweat from my face, another waterfall cascaded down over it again.

After about thirty minutes of creeping around these buildings and great efforts not to make a noise or trip any wires, we concluded that the guard might have mistaken lights from the main road, which was about two kilometres away, for lights inside the buildings. After standing still in a doorway for a further ten minutes and just listening, we decided to head back to the team. Just as we were about to move, we heard a very loud clang of metal on metal that made me freeze to the spot. My hair rose all over my body, and I very slowly turned my head to see what it was. I scanned the whole area but saw nothing and certainly did not hear any more noises, thank God. We had both moved off towards the team when the radio crackled to life with a message from one of the guys, informing us that an Iraqi Police patrol was slowly making its way in our direction.

With that, we moved quickly forward and found a depression in the sand, where we both huddled. We watched the patrol drive along a track then turn about fifty metres in front of us. The rear gunner had a huge searchlight on the rear of the vehicle and was scanning the whole area. I told Mickey that if he spotted us and opened fire, we would just brass the vehicle up; I informed the guys what was happening and what they were to do, should the Iraqi Police discover us. They were to fire onto the vehicle. The gods obviously favoured us because the patrol drove straight past us and away from us. Mickey and I got up and made a short, sharp exit from the area and back to the vehicles and team.

At approximately 1215 hours, we again had a visit from the Iraqi Police on a pretext to see if everything was fine. Unfortunately we were preparing to leave the factory, and the police saw this. Neither I nor anyone else trusted the Iraqi Police, as we all knew they would be militia, and it just seemed wrong that they kept visiting us. Their behaviour was not normal.

We left the factory shortly after the police visit and headed out onto the main road, where we took a right, heading south down Route Jackson. At the main crossroads, we turned left on a road that would link us up with Route Tampa (heading east); this road was approximately three kilometres long. I noticed at the crossroads that there were quite a lot of IP and IA in vehicles. As my rear protection vehicle passed the IA and IP, he observed one of the police officers using his radio briefly.

At that, my alarm bells started ringing, and I knew something was going to happen. I got on the radio and told all the security vehicle commanders to watch for anything suspicious and, if need be, fire warning shots at anyone who seemed out of place. The area was open and flat .Although animals were grazing, I saw no shepherds. This absence was not right; every other time I had seen sheep and cattle, they had always had a shepherd with them. The mud huts where the farmers lived with their families were deserted. Nobody was around anywhere, and this lack of normal human traffic did not look good.

At 1250 hours and approximately 1.5 kilometres along the country road, the enemy made contact with us by detonating an explosive device on our left, right in the centre of the convoy. The device exploded next to a truck; the truck made a sharp turn to the left and stopped. Automatic fire came from three positions – two enemy positions to my right (south) and one enemy position to my left (north). We engaged all three positions at the same time. The position on my left (north) was very quickly silenced, therefore letting all three of my gunners concentrate on the positions to my right (south). Both enemy positions were situated behind a bank, with a cornfield behind them, in the middle of a farm complex. The gun battle lasted approximately five to six minutes before all firing ceased.

As I was sending my contact report to my operations officer, the IP and IA from the crossroads approached my position. I instructed my rear protection not to let them through, but they could not hear me well. Although I told them to let only the senior police officer into the kill zone, they let all the Iraqi Police and Army through. I could sense that the situation was getting very hostile.

On meeting an officer, I expressed my thoughts to him and told him that I felt that someone in his group had known what was going to happen; he obviously disagreed with my statement. I told him, in no uncertain terms, that the only thing they had achieved was to kill an Iraqi. I then instructed him and the rest of his men to leave the area, and as he was on his way out of the area, one member of my team saw him talk to one of the drivers briefly. This conversation was duly noted, and I told all vehicle commanders to be aware of a possible secondary device.

My team medic, Glen, tried for nearly half an hour to save the Iraqi driver, but he died. He had both of his legs shattered below the knee, a large hole in his thigh, a large hole in his throat, and two holes in his head. He was, as they say, riddled. Blood was everywhere.

At 1340 hours, the American QRF arrived on the scene from the Route Tampa direction. A US medic pronounced the Iraqi driver dead and assisted in putting the body into a body bag. I took the American team commander on a tour of the positions, and he instructed the team photographer to take pictures. The Iraqi's body was now sealed in a body bag and put into one of the vehicles on the back of the flat-bed trucks. The Iraqi drivers were going mad, crying, slapping their chests, and punching the side of their heads. Their responses all looked rather weird to me, as I had never seen anyone do this sort of thing before. Unfortunately, while all this was going on, seven of the trucks made a run for it and headed back towards the factory, a development that we didn't try to stop.

The US team commander told me that, due to the current situation, we should all leave together. I gathered all the remaining five trucks and informed my team about what was going to happen. I placed the remaining trucks in the centre and gave the order to move. Just as we were about to leave the area the five Iraqi drivers stopped and got out of their vehicles. I immediately gave the order to abandon the trucks; we did so and headed east towards Route Tampa. Approximately 500 metres along the road, we were attacked again by another IED. My gunners immediately opened fire on likely enemy positions, and we fought through the potential ambush. On Route Tampa, I stopped and was informed that we had a casualty, so I ordered my medic to administer first aid. One of my top cover had shrapnel in the side of his face. However, he was fine, and he was the first guy of the group to have a war wound that he could eventually tell his children about.

The American commander told me that the area we had been in was out of bounds. I told him I had nothing in my intelligence reports about this area other than a note that it was a nasty place. I had read all the intelligence reports for this area and saw nothing about it being out of bounds. I thanked the commander for helping us and wished them a safe journey back to their camp, and we left the area, heading back towards Taji.

Conclusion

The Iraqi Army and the Iraqi Police, from the crossroads, initiated the attack. I could not trust them inside my cordon. Therefore, I held them out, only letting the most senior member inside. I believe the senior police officer warned the Iraqi drivers not to continue. The ammunition, 1,000 rounds per gun, was not enough; we had approximately 100 to 150 rounds per gun left after the attack. This was made clear to the RGS operations officer, A. W., on my return.

I was informed by the US team commander that the area we had driven into the previous day was so hot that nobody had ever ventured down that far.

J. Heron, Team Commander

On returning to Camp Taji, I looked at the ROC intelligence report, and nothing in it gave me any doubt that Al Hateem was just a sleepy town. A. W., who was the "In Country Manager" and who gave the intelligence brief, never mentioned the area being out of bounds or anything else for that matter. I had a friend inside the ROC intelligence cell and phoned him that afternoon. I asked him about Al Hateem, and as soon as I said the town's name, he told me not to go anywhere near the place, as it was as hot as hell. I told him we had already been there and that we got a good kicking. I asked him if he would send the ROC intelligence report directly to my mailing address. Later that afternoon I checked my mail and found the ROC intelligence report. I printed a copy off and read it. This report looked different from the one I had read. I got an old copy of the report and compared it with the one I had received from my friend and was shocked to see that the part about Al Hateem had been cut out. I kept this quiet and did not tell anyone; however, I made discreet enquiries and found that the intelligence report went direct to A. W.'s laptop. Again I said nothing. One Iraqi driver had died, and someone was doctoring the intelligence.

In camp that night, we got all the guys together and talked through the incidents of the last couple of days and the lessons we had learnt. All the guys were fine about everything, and nobody was worried about further jobs. I spoke to Mick about the paint factory in detail, and we began asking each other questions, why were there so many Iraqi Army and police in the small village just north of Al Hateem? Why did the Iraqi Police carry out a patrol inside the paint factory nearly every hour or so? Why did they check on us in the morning? Why wouldn't the guard on the front gate allow us to put two of our men on the gate with their sentry? It was decided that the Iraqi Police were keeping checks on us throughout the night just in case we moved out while it was dark. The last straw was when the Iraqi Police made another surprise visit to us when we were packing up to leave; that is when they must have formulated a plan and set up the ambush. That day we had learned never to trust any Iraqi military person or policeman.

We had a simple job of taking F350 vehicles from Taji to the BIAP, very simple job that should have taken a couple of hours. I went down to the loading point in the camp and checked each vehicle over, what I was looking for were holes, dents and scratches. All vehicles were in a very good condition and so I signed the paperwork for them. The trip down to the BIAP went without any problems and all the team were happy that nothing happened. When an American Major, who I was to hand the vehicles over to, inspected them we found all the vehicles had holes in the sides, burst tyres and shattered windows. I had to tell the Major that we got into a small gun battle on route; he accepted this and signed for the vehicles. Later on and back at camp I asked all the guys if they heard any firing to which they all looked quite bemused and said nobody had fired on the convoy. I know deep down that if anyone had of fired on us the top gunners would have fired back but nobody fired a round. I think we got lucky that day that nobody got hurt. I would love to have seen the insurgents faces when no rounds were returned in their direction, I wonder what went through their heads?.

Our next job was to take a convoy down to Habbinayah. The route was south from Taji into the outskirts of Baghdad and then west towards Fallujah and Ramadi. This area was known as the Fallujah/ Ramadi corridor, and it was very dangerous. Ramadi and Fallujah are known for being very much against the coalition and for having the highest number of VBIEDs. A few kilometers passed Ramadi we would take a left and get onto the desert route called, Long Island. The road here was about 4 meters across and any deviation left or right onto the sand could be fatal as the insurgents planted mines which were hidden by bushes. About an hour out in the desert on route Long Island we would again take a left and head for about a further ten kilometers before we hit Habbinayah.

I realised that if someone wanted to drive a car packed with explosives into the convoy, there was not much that anyone could do about it. To keep us clear of these suicide bombers, I told the team that our convoy had an imaginary bubble all the way around it and that the bubble extended for a hundred metres in all directions. Any vehicle that entered the bubble would be warned by the top cover man, who would wave an orange-coloured flag. If the driver ignored the warning, then the top cover man would fire a warning shot across the driver's bows. If he still ignored the warning, the top cover men would brass the car up. Normally, when a driver saw the waving orange flag, he would slow down and back off. Unfortunately, some drivers who were intent on getting into our convoy to kill us fell foul of the warnings and paid the price. I don't think it was the shots that killed the driver of these cars but the explosives that went off when the shooting started.

My bubble excluded both vehicles and pedestrians. We had known for some time that innocent-looking people standing by the roadside might be suicide bombers. They would amble up to the convoy and blow themselves before any of the top cover men could react. All that would be left of the bomber would be her shoulders and head and her hips and legs. I saw the after effects of two such attacks. Not one of the security team were harmed, but when I looked at the body, it was a mess – the glazed stare from the eyes, the intestines, a mass of blood spread out over a large area, and blood, guts, and bone splattered on the side or front of a vehicle – such a waste of a life. I made my team look at the bodies and reminded them that if anyone got this close to my convoy, whoever was at fault would be in deep shit, whether he was dead or alive. One time on route sword we got stuck in traffic and had to come to a halt. I reminded the top gunners to keep low and to keep their eyes peeled for any problems. As I finished my sentence I watched as a young woman walked over towards the convoy, at first I thought she just wanted to cross the road but when she got to the front of my armoured vehicle she just exploded. Fucking hell what's that all about, here I am in an armoured vehicle and she is trying to kill us. What sort of mentality have these people got?. The blood and guts were everywhere, all over the road and all up the side of my vehicle and window screen. I couldn't see a thing out of any window so I had to grab a few bottles of water, get out of my vehicle and wash the windows down of blood, guts and bone. If some half wit wants to blow themselves up next to me as I sit in my armoured vehicle and really think I give a fuck they are mistaken. After cleaning the windows we carried on with our task.

The other time a woman ran from the side of the road and as she hit the side of the gun truck in front of me she disappeared in a cloud of dust and blood, as my vehicle passed where she detonated herself I just saw parts of her body. What a fucking waste of life.

Well, all the best planning can go wrong, and tonight it was going to go wrong.

The company took on extra Gurkhas from some other company. As they were new guys, they needed to be trained in convoy work and had to complete live firing training. However, that night we had to go to Habbinayah to deliver stores for the Americans. One of the team drivers reported sick and was taken off the task. Short of a driver, A. W. decided to ask one of the new guys to drive. Not wanting to let the team down, the guy said he would do it. The gun trucks are top-heavy, and you need a good few days to get used to them; this new guy had not even unpacked his kit. When A.W told me of the plan for the new hire to drive, I argued strongly against the idea of the new man driving the gun truck.

After half an hour of argument, I was overruled, A. W. was the In Country Manager, and I was a mere team leader. What did I know about the ground that Andy did not know? Basically everything, although A. W. spouted off stories of racing with his team all over Baghdad he had never ever been on the ground or left the safety of any camp he worked in; he was a fat, useless bastard of a coward.

As we left Camp Taji, we turned left on Route Tampa and headed for Baghdad. About three kilometres down the road, I heard over the radio that one of the gun trucks had flipped over onto its side and there were injured people. I immediately stopped the convoy and arranged the security trucks as best I could before heading back to the scene. There the two top cover men had been thrown clear but had suffered one broken arm and one badly twisted leg and back injuries. The worst was the new driver, who had five tons of gun truck on his head that made his head oval-shaped, was dead.

The American QRF came out and assisted by taking the injured and dead persons back to camp for us. We quickly stripped the vehicle of all radio kit, cross decked all other kit over to another gun truck, and torched the wrecked truck at the side of the road. Then we headed off towards Baghdad to complete the task. I made a phone call to A.W and told him not to be in camp when I returned because I was going to punch the living daylights out of him. The next day, when we returned,

A.W was nowhere to be seen – good job for him.

Three weeks after the incident, one of the Gurkha's told me he had received a phone call from the dead Gurkha's father, asking when his son would be out of intensive care. This puzzled me because everyone knew the lad was dead. I went straight into see the company clerk and asked him straight out if someone had told the family their son was in hospital. The clerk looked at me and said yes. I asked who had started this sick rumour, and was told it was A. W.

I walked straight into A. W.'s office and told him that either he stopped his deception now or I would inform the Americans of what he had done. I would then put him into intensive care and tell *his* parents *he* was dead. Within an hour, a phone call was made to the dead driver's family, and they were informed that their son was dead. A .W. is one of the sickest bastards I have ever had the misfortune of meeting. I still cannot understand why he didn't inform the lad's family promptly of his death. His action really puzzles me to this day.

As the weeks went by the team started to come together very well. While we were on the road, everyone was in good spirits. At least, they were in good spirits until we had time in camp. Nobody liked it in the camp because A. W. had no personnel management skills and did not know how to talk to people. A. W. used to make people feel that they were not doing enough, especially my Gurkha team. When I appeared, he would skulk back into his ops room and be a nice In Country Manager – the fat, useless, spineless bastard.

A.W was 5' 8 tall, dark-haired, and almost clean shaven. I say *almost* because on some parts of his chin, you could see a tuft of bristle, and on other parts, he managed to shave the bristle off. He is about eighteen stone in weight, and he always wore baggy shirts and shorts that came just below his knees. On his shins he had what looked like red boils, which he had burst. When the sun was at its highest, he would sweat buckets, and his tee shirt always smelled of vinegar. Now I don't know if that is the smell of sweat or if he washed his clothes in vinegar, but whatever he did, he reeked. I don't know anyone who was brave enough to stand next to him for a long time. He wore sandals and had what I can only describe as hobbit feet, big and hairy. If you asked him a question, he would tell you what he thought you wanted to hear. Then, whatever he told you, he would do the opposite. He had no connection with any of the guys and thought he could use and abuse them whenever he wanted. The team guys were humble guys and very polite. A. W. thought that humility and politeness were weaknesses and used to revel in using and abusing these men as a bully would do. One thing nobody ever saw him do was eat. He never ate with any of the expats or the guys and always gave the excuse that he was on a diet.

I followed him to the American PX one day and watched him eat. The PX has everything a soldier would want for morale purposes, including Kentucky Fried Chicken. These places, PX's, follow the American Army all over the world and are far superior to anything the British Army has. This guy ate two large cartons of the stuff, an amount that would have made anyone else sick. That is the description of this fat bastard who was supposed to be our operations manager. I have met blokes like this before and know exactly how to pull them down and put them back onto their soapboxes. Play along with what a man of this type wants and then, out of the blue, remark on how much weight he has lost. Surprised, he will give you all the details of how he is on a diet, and so on.

Then, reliably, he will say, 'Do you think so?'

Then, just say, 'No, I was joking,' and comment that he really seems to have put on some weight.

This lure is a killer, a conversation stopper; your target will normally make some excuse up and wobble away out of sight. It always works. This guy was no different, but I couldn't get it out of my head how he thought he had the God-given right to send a guy out on the ground. He used to brag and boast how he and his mate used to dart around the airport in Baghdad, strapped into a vehicle without doors and secured with a bungee. What a fucking dickhead! That detail didn't show me how big and hard he was, quite the opposite, It showed me how unprofessional he was. He really shouldn't play with the big boys out here because one day he may just find himself getting hurt.

One day, while relaxing with a book and a cup of tea in my room, I heard him shouting at someone. I went out to see what all the commotion was about and found Fatty shouting at one of my Gurkhas. I walked up behind Fatty and stood there, listening to him abuse this Gurkha. When I had heard enough, I slapped him on the back of the head. A. W. spun his head round, ready to take on whoever slapped his head. He nearly shit himself when he saw me. He tried to come out with some feeble excuse of why he was telling this Gurkha off, but I was having none of it. I told him to shut the fuck up and listen to what I said. I told him that he was never to speak to one of my Gurkhas like that again and if I ever caught him at it, I would knock him out, period. I then told him that if he wanted to get back into his ops room in one piece, he had better apologise to the Gurkha. Which he did, then scurried back into his hole. Unfortunately for him, A. W. lost face with all the Gurkhas because, unbeknownst to him, all the other Gurkhas had watched all that happened. The team hated him and gave him his nickname, 'The fat controller.' Whenever anyone referred to A. W., from that day on, they would call him *the fat controller.* If I had the choice of saving a suicidal, criminally insane rat with rabies or A. W. from the firing squad, I would pick the rat.

My team was issued orders to take a convoy north to Al Kasik, via Mosul, and the cargo was ammunition. The expat medic that I had was G.H. G.H looked after the rear of the convoy. Even though he was a medic, he was also a good scrapper.

Mosul was an absolute hole. The drains all spilled out onto the road, spreading dirty water and human waste. Dead dogs were everywhere and in different stages of rot. Rubbish and mounds of earth were all over, and the traffic seemed to go wherever it wanted to go. In other words, Mosul was in a lawless state; the Iraqi Police or Army had no control over anything that went on in the city. The curfew ran from 1800 hours in the evening to 0600 hours in the morning, but that did not stop the insurgents from coming out of their holes to have a go at us.

I gave the usual orders to my vehicle commanders and then had an 'O' group for all the guys in the team. One of the points I stressed was the curfew. If anyone was out after the curfew began, the top cover was to fire a warning shot. If it turned into a gun battle we would use a vehicle as a firebase and hose the entire place with fire. Some gun battles may require you to ask one or two vehicle's to go static (Firebase) and open fire on the enemy positions, this then gives the trucks time to get out of the area, once they are safely out of harm's way the static vehicle's rejoin the convoy. The term "hose the place with fire" is quite basically firing at the enemy positions.

We left camp at 1500 hours with fifteen trucks laden with various sorts of ammunition and seven gun trucks as armed protection. Each gun truck had four men inside – one driver, one vehicle commander, and two top cover men. About twenty kilometres north of Taji, we came across a permanent vehicle checkpoint manned by Iraqi Police.

Nobody in his right mind stops at these checkpoints for any reason. Sometimes the Iraqis on the checkpoints liked to stop you and try to search the vehicles, which is not allowed and is basically a show of strength and power by the Iraqis manning the checkpoints.

As I passed through the checkpoint, I looked over to my left and saw a white car parked inside the perimeter of the blast walls. Oddly enough, this car faced north instead of south. Also oddly, two men sat in the driver's seat and passenger seat and watched us drive through. I immediately got onto the radio and warned all vehicle commanders to be aware of these two.

Approximately eight hundred metres further up the road, we were hit by two IEDs. The first one went off without causing any damage, but the second one damaged a truck by blowing out one of the tyres. I was forced to halt the convoy, and as I did, we came under machine gun fire from the left. My first reaction was to set the alarms off on our trackers and infoerm the ops room by phone that we were under contact, I gave them an update then told them I had to go and sort this out. My top cover men returned fire almost immediately. As I looked left, I could see two buildings in the middle distance, about 500 metres away. Enemy fire was coming from the upstairs rooms and from the flat roofs of these two buildings. Trying to direct my top cover gunners onto these targets over the radio was impossible, so I had only one option open to me; I had to get out of a perfectly good armoured vehicle and run to each gun truck and direct the gunner onto the target. The main problem was the language barrier because we had Nepalese men who spoke limited English and although they could understand you if you spoke slow they couldn't understand you when the shit was flying and I spoke faster because I needed people to react quicker and get fire down. Making sure I was on the other side of the gun truck to where the rounds were hitting, I ran about seventy metres to the first one, I directed the gunner to fire on the first building. Next I ran about another seventy to eighty metres and directed that gunner to fire on the second building. I also dragged every driver out of his truck and made him crouch down by the front wheel and told him not to move, which was the only protection I could offer the drivers; the trucks' cabs were not armoured.

From behind the second gun truck, I had a look at the area where the shots originated and assessed the impact of my gunners. Then I noticed the bull rushes on the other side of the motorway moving quite a lot. I jumped back up onto the gun truck and told my gunner to aim at the bull rushes, and just as I finished telling him, we saw four men with AK-47 assault rifles taking position to engage us from a distance of about 50 metres. My gunner let loose with about a hundred rounds straight into their midst. I could hear the screams of the men who had been hit and wounded, but couldn't see them. The gunner carried on firing; the screams and yells died away to nothing. He then carried on firing at the buildings. Doing a stupid thing like getting up on a vehicle to direct-fire in full view gave the insurgent a golden opportunity to kill or wound you, but it had to be done because the noise was deafening; nobody could hear any words of command because of machine guns going off, AK-47 rifles going off, commanders shouting orders to their riflemen, and the crack and whizz of incoming rounds. In such a racket, there is also a sort of buzz in the ears. To be heard over all that noise was impossible.

When I was in the Army I was a section commander with the rank of Corporal. A section commander is in charge of eight men out of the platoon of thirty men. For me to assist the platoon commander in any given gun battle it was down to me to move around the section, who would be spread out, and make sure they were firing at the right targets. It meant me getting up when the shots were coming in to my position and co-ordinate the battle in my area. It was these principles that I used every time we had a contact and I am glad to say they always worked with effect.

Some people reading this may think I was stupid, but others who have been in a gun battle like that will understand my position. I know that some security men in the same situation would have done exactly the same. It's either you react with aggression or they overrun you and kill you on the way through. It's as simple as that.

Was I scared? I don't really know because I never even thought about it at the time. Later, when I did think about it, I realized how lucky I was not to be hit. One thing I was well aware of was the helmet. A major problem with the helmet was the sides of the helmet came down to about half way down the ear, making it hard to hear what people were saying even without all the extra noise of weapons being fired. Once I was happy that the gunner knew exactly what to look for, I got down and made off towards the back.

Eventually I reached the rear of the convoy, covered in sweat and panting as if I had run ten miles. I was exhausted even though I stopped at each vehicle to lend a hand by firing at the enemy. I spoke to G.H and told him to keep a good watch on the rear, as I thought the two men in the white car in the checkpoint had something to do with this.

Just as I turned around, I saw Rabi, my Gurkha driver, behind me. Rabi had followed me all the way down the convoy.

I asked him what the problem was, and almost immediately, he said, 'You, big problem.'

I looked into his sweaty face and asked why.

He lifted his right hand, and it was then that I noticed my helmet. He jabbed the helmet towards me and said, 'On head.' Then he turned and ran back towards our vehicle. My face must have been a picture; when I looked at G.H he was laughing his head off. I am not saying we were brave or anything, and I am not saying our minds had run off the map or that we had cracked up, but when something like that happens, you cannot do anything other than laugh. In a situation like that, it is funny.

Anyway, I never put the helmet on. I hated wearing it, and I just slung it over my shoulder and headed back to the front of the convoy. Again I made a point of stopping at each security vehicle to make sure everything was going as planned and that we had put more rounds down than the insurgents and not forgetting to change my empty magazines for full ones One thing I did know was that if you outgunned the insurgent, he would back off and disappear back down the rat hole he crawled out of. It was vital that we win this firefight.

All this time we had been exchanging shots with the enemy.

Halfway up the convoy, I stopped to take stock. Then I saw this old Iraqi man of about seventy years; with a walking stick in his right hand, he was walking slowly through the gunfire. Quite a few rounds whizzed off the road in front and behind him, but he kept on walking. I thought that any minute now, one round would connect with him, and it would be lights out for him. I could not do a thing to help him. There was no way I was going out there to drag him to cover because he was over the other side of the motorway.

I watched in utter disbelief as he kept walking along as if he on a Sunday stroll down to the corner shop, the only difference being the cracks and whizzes of the rounds going to and fro. One round did hit him in the arm and knocked him down to the ground, and after a little while, he got up and kept walking in the same direction, holding his arm. He eventually walked through the hail of gunfire and out the other side and sat down on the hard shoulder and nursed his arm. He then got back up and waddled away down the road.

I stood there and thought to myself that he must be deaf and blind or completely stupid to walk right through all that gunfire, I preferred the first option.

The tempo of the shooting went out of control by the insurgents and they unleashed a tremendous amount of fire down on us to the point that my gunners had to get there heads right down, all I could do was crouch down behind a vehicle and listen to the huge amount of fire cracking and whizzing past us, the sound of a round when it hit armour is a sort of splat and this went on for what seemed like eternity. I heard the firing slow down and thought I was in for some sort of a frontal attack so I ran to each gun truck and banged on the side shouting for the gunners to get up and fire, I grabbed each vehicle commander and told him to keep the guy up and firing because I thought they would send in an attach force. The gunners got up and unleashed a torrent of fire back into the insurgents positions while I ran back up to the front of the convoy. As I was running up the convoy I heard the unmistakable sound of a rocket fly over and explode the other side of the convoy next to some trees. As I reached one gun truck one of the top gunners shouted "what the fuck was that" I shouted back at the top of my voice "what the fuck did you think it was, it's a fucking RPG, now get firing for fucks sake". I reached the front of the convoy where my gun truck was and slumped into the front seat, I then got on the phone and informed the ops room that we had been fired at by an RPG and gave them an update on what was happening. The firing kept going and I was dreading hearing the words "man down", words that meant we were outgunned and in trouble.

Then to my utter relief as quickly as the shooting started, the gunmen stopped firing; we had obviously won the firefight, I told everyone to stay in position in case they started again or decided to mount some sort of attack. One of my top gunners told me he had seen movement from the bull rushes across the road in the direction of where the other were shot. This was getting out of hand so I grabbed Rabi and another guy and quickly told everyone that I was going across the road to intercept the insurgents before they could mount any form of attack. We all ran across the road where I saw the dead guys when I noticed the bull rushes a little further down moving. Making sure I had a full magazine on I ran towards the moving bull rushes and saw two men with weapons, I opened fire immediately into them at the same time as Rabi and the other guy I was with, it was then that I felt pain in my foot. With the two insurgents now dead we ran back to our vehicles. I hopped most of the way because every time I put my foot down I got a shock of pain in the top of my foot, my first thoughts were that I had been shot. At my vehicle I sat down on the ground behind my gun truck and looked at my foot and saw that I didn't even have my ankle boot on anymore, "where the hell is that" I asked Rabi to which he gave a puzzled look. Sticking out of my foot was a piece of wood about six inches long. G.H, our team medic, arrived and slowly took the wood out, luckily it was only in about an inch. G.H laughed at me saying he didn't realise the insurgents fired wood as well as bullets. I told Rabi to get everyone stood to just in case the insurgents had other ideas. I then got my bergan from the back of the vehicle and got my spare boots out, pointless going round with one boot on because I didn't know where the other one was.

While the gunners kept watching, I gathered up the drivers and told them they had better be very fucking quick at changing the flat tyres. I made a point of telling them we did not have long and that the enemy might be back for a second attempt. As the drivers set about their task, I got on the radio and asked for ammunition and casualty stats. I feared the worst because of the amount of fire coming into our position. I thought we must have lost one or two men and would find that they were either dead or wounded.

Each gun truck replied in order, and although the ammunition stats did not look too good, we had absolutely no casualties, not one. None of us even got a scratch. I looked at Rabi, who was holding a pencil and paper, ready to take names and jot down ammunition stats, and told him that the gods had looked after us. Rabi could not believe it either. I quickly told Rabi to spread out the ammunition we had left evenly among the gun trucks.

Whilst he was doing this, I ran with my head down across the motorway with another man and looked down into the ditch by the bull rushes and saw the four bodies in various positions. Each one of them was dead and was covered in blood, with pools of blood around them. The weapons I saw were AK-47 assault rifles. I saw the path we took to get the other two and saw no movement from that area.

I decided to leave the bodies where they lay for the dogs to munch and ran back to the convoy across the motorway. Everything was sorted, and each gunner had enough ammunition for another fight, if there were another fight. As the convoy moved off, G.H told me over the radio that the white car had started to move in our direction, and I told him to keep an eye on it.

It must have been about three minutes later when I heard the machine gun fire. I thought it was all going to happen again when G.H got me on the radio and gave me a situation report on exactly what was happening at his location. The white car moved out of the checkpoint perimeter and stopped, and two men got out and started to fire at the rear gun truck. G.H ordered his gunner to open fire on them, which he did. One man dropped almost immediately, dead and spurting blood. The second man was obviously hit and fell to the ground; he was just wounded and dragged himself into the nearest cover and out of sight. We moved away from the contact site and headed north towards Mosul.

About one kilometre up the road, I brought the convoy to a halt. I spoke with the medic and told him we had to go back and help the old man out. I told all the other vehicle commanders what was happening, and the medic and my gun truck headed back towards where the old man had fallen. On nearing the site, I noticed two Iraqi policemen in the area where the IEDs had gone off. One sat on a motorbike, and the other was kneeling down at the side of the road, where he appeared to be digging.

I got my binoculars out and had a better look, unsurprised at what I saw. The kneeling policeman was digging in an IED. I told Rabi to take his foot off the accelerator and just cruise down. When we got nearer, the guy on the motorbike saw us and made a dash for the checkpoint, which was about 200 metres away. I immediately ordered the top gunner to fire, which he did, sending about a hundred rounds at the man on the motorbike and hitting him.

When we got to the motorbike, the man was riddled with holes, and blood was seeping out of every hole and trickling down the road. I then noticed the other policeman making a run for the checkpoint and immediately shouted for him to stop. He took no notice of me, so I got my pistol out and shot him in the leg. That brought him down with a scream. I received a phone call from my operations room, stating that the American Quick Reaction Force was soon to be with me. Whilst I had the ops room on the phone I gave them an update on everything that had happened.

The policeman whom I had just shot was on the ground, holding his leg and moaning. Oddly enough, there wasn't really that much blood coming out of the wound. One good thing I did know was that it certainly hurt him.

I looked down at him with a smile. He spoke to me in English and started to swear and curse. I told him to save all his complaints for the Americans, and at that, his eyes opened wide. I told him the Americans would soon be here, and he could explain to them about what he and his friend had been doing. I told one of the guys to watch him, and the medic and I went to where they had been digging.

I saw a satchel on the ground and opened it with the barrel of my weapon. Inside there was quite a bit of bomb-making equipment. I shouted over to another guy and told him to keep an eye on the satchel. Looking down towards the checkpoint, I saw five policemen coming towards us with guns at the ready. I told my men that if they shot first, we would be within our rights to shoot them.

I walked over to the group and told them they had no business here and to return to the checkpoint. They tried to draw me into an argument, but I just turned and walked back to the dead body. To their credit, they stayed where I left them. If they had ventured any closer, they might have ended up like the guy on the ground with a hole in his leg.

About fifteen minutes later, the American QRF turned up. I spoke to the
Sergeant who was in charge and told him exactly what had happened. I pointed out various locations and showed him the satchel of bomb-making equipment.

The policeman with the hole in his leg started to beg me to shoot him and not let the Americans take him.

'No deal,' was my answer.

The sergeant got one of his men to take pictures of the satchel, the dead body, and the policeman with the hole in his leg.

Whilst he did that, I took the sergeant on a tour of the site and showed him the four dead bodies with all their weapons, then took him further into the bull rushes and showed him the other two we had shot dead, then on to the car where there was only one body and a blood trail leading to the willows. Following the blood trail, we ended up at the checkpoint, and after a quick search, we found nothing. They had obviously gotten the wounded man out of the area, and how long he would last was anyone's guess, but from the amount of blood I had seen, I knew he wouldn't last too long.

The American sergeant told one of his men to treat the injured policeman and put him in the back of a humvee; the dead man was to be handed over to the police at the checkpoint, as were the six other dead men. I remember him saying that if they didn't want them, the dogs could have them – a good call, as far as I was concerned.

Eventually the sergeant said we could go and carry on with our task. Rejoining the convoy, I found everything to be shipshape and ready to go, so we headed off north again towards Mosul. This part of the trip was quite uneventful until we reached a big checkpoint just outside Mosul. Inside the checkpoint was a T-62 tank with its barrel pointing in our direction. I looked both left and right and saw between forty and fifty policemen spread out all over the place.

I stopped next to an officer with three stars on his shoulders.

This guy was waving his arms all over the place and appeared to be speaking, although I couldn't hear a word he was saying. Appearing very angry, the officer came up to my window. He stood about 5'6ʊ and was thin, with a stupid-looking moustache above his top lip. I told the lads over the radio to be very careful and watch that this encounter did not get out of control and to fire only if the Iraqi policemen fired first.

My plan was to get out of the vehicle and confront this guy face to face. After leaving the safety of the gun truck I stood directly in front of this small man. He was going mad; obviously the other checkpoint had informed this idiot about what happened earlier on. The officer told me to get everyone out and hand all weapons over to his officers.

I cut his orders short by saying, "you are having a giraffe, mate.' In other words "you're having a laugh".

He carried on, saying that I then had to open all the containers so his men could search them. I told him in a calm tone that he knew as well as I did that his request would never be fulfilled; he had more chance of watching me chew my own head off! I reminded him that all the equipment on these trucks was the property of the United States Army and he had no authority to search any of it. Then I asked him to move the tank so we could be on our way.

I don't know what I said to cause his response, but this small man went absolutely crackers, screaming and shouting and waving his arms all over. I think the phrase *chewing my own head off* may have hit a nerve. He then repeated his request, and again I turned him down. I told him he either got the tank out of the way or we would just drive around it. He again went mad, and I knew he was on some sort of power rush, and if I didn't start to get tough with him and make him look foolish in front of his men, the situation could get out of control. I told him again that the equipment was US Army equipment, and he had no authority to search any of it, and that if he didn't get his tank out of the way, we would drive around. He went all quiet and then said that if we moved an inch he would order his men to fire. That quote was enough for me and I was not taking anymore fucking bullshit from this little twat.

I looked directly into his eyes and said to him in as firm a voice as possible that if his men opened fire on any of my men, I would kill him first. Then all his men would die, and if he thought I was fucking around, he had better try me. I then pointed out that he wouldn't be able to see the end result because he would be dead, and it was his call from here on.

After he thought about it for a minute or so, he decided to let us through. He ordered the tank to move and then told me to go. I stayed where I was and got on my handheld radio and ordered the convoy to move. I made sure all the vehicles got through the checkpoint before I got into mine and headed off, and meanwhile I didn't take my eyes off this fucking upstart for one moment.

What an absolute nightmare! The sweat was dripping off me, and I could feel that all my clothing under my body armour was soaking wet.

The main problem security men have with this sort of scenario is trust. Finding the courage to trust the police or military was very hard. It was possible if you decided to take them at their word you could end up in an orange jumpsuit and be sold to insurgents. Alternatively, the police may be genuine.

Nine times out of ten, though, you would end up in some Iraqi police station, waiting to be sold to the highest bidder. Police and military are connected to different militias, and the militias are always looking out for an easy target from which they can obtain money. Anyone who would stop at a police or military checkpoint and give weapons and ammunition up should not be in Iraq because, sooner or later, he will get people killed – including himself.

Driving through Mosul, I found it hard to comprehend why anyone would like to live in that hole. Nearly all the buildings were down or partly down. Water was all over the road, and heaps of rubbish was everywhere – rotten food and God knows what else. As you pass through Mosul, you have to take a motorway which heads east towards Tal Afar. This road is very lonely, and if you come into contact with any insurgents, you had better be ready to fight because nobody is going to come to your aid. The potholes caused by IEDs were everywhere; the burnt-out cars along the side of the highway testified to the number of VBIEDs set off along this road. Hundreds of cars were strewn all over.

In some places, barbed wire was dragged over the road in an attempt to get someone to stop and move it. Whoever did stop may have set himself up for some sort of attack. We never stopped for minor things like wire despite what anyone thought about it. We eventually reached our destination, Al Kasik, without any further problems. After we got unloaded, I spoke to the American sergeant and told him of the problem we had on the drive up. I asked him if he could give us some ammunition for the drive back, and he said he would see what he could do.

Half an hour later, the sergeant was back with about ten thousand rounds per vehicle. I thanked him, and he left. Anyone who messed with us on the route back was in for a rude awakening; everyone was fired up for another gun battle. Fortunately the drive back was uneventful – over 380 kilometres, not a thing happened. We arrived back in camp and were met by the guys who had remained there and who were all eager to hear about what had happened.

Well to be honest, I was hungry, sweaty, and tired, and the last thing I wanted to do was to sit with these guys and tell them anything. I made my usual report out and left them to ponder it. I left the office and went to my cabin, had a shower, got something to eat, and got my head down. I was wakened after about four hours and told I had to see A. W. about my report. I told the Gurkha to tell A. W. to fuck off, I then turned over and went back to sleep.

Later on that day I went over to see A.W in the operations room. He told me that I was heading off to Al Kasik again the following afternoon and that the trucks were being loaded as we speak, the cargo was humvees. This really didn't give me any time to plan for the long drive. Even though we had just come from there and had up to date intelligence on the route it did not mean that an incident had not occurred on the route. I got the team together and gave orders for a move the following day at two in the afternoon.

I knew A.W didn't like me and quite honestly the feeling was mutual because I fucking hated him with a vengeance, I also realised that he could, and would, send me on the dodgy jobs just to prove a point.

We got all the gun trucks separated amongst the trucks loaded with the vehicles and left camp approx one thirty and headed north up route Tampa.

About twenty kilometres north, J.S who was looking after my

point, and the first vehicle in the convoy, got hit from the front by a hail of bullets. One of his front tyres blew out which made him stop dead in his tracks. J.S immediately got on the radio to me and told me what had happened and that he was static due to his tyre being shot out. I got on the radio and told everyone to remain inside their gun trucks, it was just as well that I did because about a minute or so later two IED's were set off. The first blew up next to my vehicle which made it wobble from left to right but there was no lasting damage other than everybody's ears ringing, the second IED blew up about half way down the convoy and managed to blow a tyre on one of the trucks. Almost immediately after the explosions all hell broke loose from my right with bullets hitting the sides of nearly every vehicle. I couldn't see where the insurgents were because a large sand bank, about five feet high, which blocked my view. I knew I had to get out and get things moving or we would be sitting ducks. I immediately called in a contact report by phone to my operations room and told them exactly what had happened and what I was doing about it, basically the usual shit, I then called J.S on the radio and asked him if he was coping or did he need back up to assist him, he replied that he was alright for the moment. I then told all vehicle commanders to get their top gunners up and to get as much fire down as possible to keep the insurgents heads down. I got out of my vehicle and ran to the sand bank and then crawled up it on my stomach, once at the top I slowly popped my head over to see where the insurgents were firing from. All I saw was a small patch of trees with what looked like a trench in front of them, it was here that the insurgents had taken up a position to attack us. I then scramble back down and ran to the truck behind me to get the driver out of his vehicle and into the back of my armoured vehicle, when I opened the driver's door I saw that the driver was frozen rigid with both hands still on the steering wheel with wide open eyes. I grabbed his arm and pulled him out of his vehicle, which seemed to snap him out of his trance, and pointed at my vehicle shouting to him to get in the back, bloody hell he didn't know what to do so I ran him over to my vehicle, opened the door and literally threw him inside before slamming the door behind him. I told each commander to get the truck drivers inside the gun trucks as they were in the direct line of fire from the insurgents. We still had bullets flying around from the front of the convoy but for some reason they seemed to be going high.

Just then I felt a tap on my shoulder and with a jump turned to see J.S. who had ran about one hundred metre's from his gun truck to mine, how he made it to my position without being hit amazed me, we both got down onto one knee and I asked him what the problem was and very calmly he asked for more ammo. I handed him two boxes and off he ran back to his vehicle with his head down below the sand bank. It was soon after that when my medic called me on his radio and told me they had a gun battle going on at the rear. I honestly thought this was going to be curtains for all of us because here I was fighting three groups from the front, the side and the rear. Could it get any worse...?

About half an hour later we got bullets coming in from the left which meant that we were completely surrounded. Could it get any worse, yes it just had. This could have serious consequences for us because we were nearly surrounded and I had heard and read on intreps that the insurgents had ambushed a convoy on this same road, surrounded it and had killed everyone, including the Iraqi drivers.

I had to get my skates on and get down to each vehicle and get them to return fire onto insurgent positions over to the left. I was quite glad that the convoy was not all that long, about four hundred metres in total, because I had to get to every gun truck and get one top gunner to keep firing to the right and one to fire to the left, the front would have to be held by J.S and the same would have to be done at the rear by the medic. Any support for the front or rear would certainly not happen now as I needed everyone firing to protect my flanks. The rounds were coming in thick and fast and all you could hear was the crack and whizz of the bullet as it went over your head. The position that the insurgents had picked was very inferior because they could not fire directly at us but had to fire over us, the only holes in the trucks would be on the top of the drivers cab, this made me wonder why they had picked such a bad position. I heard over the radio that we had our first casualty; one of the top gunners had been shot in the upper arm. I raced to the gun truck firing as I ran after stopping at the rear of each truck, once there I dived inside. The bullet had passed straight through and broke his arm in the process, god he was in pain. Putting my head above the gunners parapet I realised the vehicle was in full view of the insurgents position and had taken a bit of a hammering. I called the medic on the radio and told him to wait until I got to his position before he moved and that I would look after the rear until he had sorted out the guy who had been shot. At the rear I got guys firing at three insurgents positions even firing six full magazines myself. Soon after I got to the rear I heard another guy had been shot in the lower leg by a ricochet. The medic was still busy with the first gunshot so I told the guys who were with me to keep the tempo up at the insurgents firing positions and that I was going to assist the guy with the leg wound, if they saw anything like an attack they were to inform me as soon as possible How much of that statement any of them understood I don't know because it came out of me pretty quick. When I eventually jumped into the injured guys vehicle I looked at the his leg, there was a gash from just below his knee running down his shin and a hole in the top of his boot which came out of the sole of his foot, the round had followed his leg down and entered the top of his foot and exited from the bottom of his foot. I left his boot on and set up an intravenous drip for him because the blood was everywhere and he was going into shock pretty dam quick. I grabbed a knife and cut his trousers right up his leg and grabbed a first field dressing and slapped it onto his leg and shouted at him to hold it firm in position to try and stem the flow of blood. Just then the medic jumped inside the gun truck and, as calm as you like, he told me to go and that he would sort the guy out.

I left the casualty with the medic and called my operations room and gave them an update on the situation and that I had two casualties, the operations room told me in no uncertain terms that I was by myself and that the Americans would not assist me with the QRF or the Helivac until the area was safe for them to approach. I fully appreciate the problems for the Americans coming into a hot area like this one but even if they had of let the insurgents see a distant helicopter it would have all been over and they would have buggered off back to their rat holes.

The main thing with having to stand and fight like this was ammunition, although we carried about 10 thousand rounds for each gun and 50 thousand rounds for the AK47 rifles it would still not be enough to sustain a prolonged fight like this, I had to think of getting the upper hand here because rounds were still coming in from all sides, literally.

I decided to move things up a few notches. When the medic had finished with the second casualty he returned and took control of the rear from me. I grabbed his arm and told him that I was going up to J.S and get his tyre sorted then we would be heading back to Taji. I ran as fast as I could up to my vehicle and jumped inside, before we moved I threw my empty magazines into the back and grabbed another ten full magazines, it was then I realised that I had gone through fifteen magazines in total, each magazine held thirty rounds.

I got hold of J.S on the radio and told him what I was going to do and to make sure his top gunner stopped firing when he saw us at the side of his vehicle. Eventually I got my vehicle in front of J.S's and told his top gunner to move into my vehicle next to my top gunner. With this done and two machine guns now firing at the insurgents firing positions J.S and me set about changing his flat tyre. The sweat was pouring out of us but we managed to get things going. Four minutes later everything was sorted and we were roadworthy again. I told my medic over the radio to get the drivers back into the trucks, turn them around and head south back to Taji. The rate of fire from us stepped up and the noise was deafening but it seemed to work because the fire from the insurgents eased off quite considerably. While the trucks turned around two of the drivers got shot, one through his wrist and the other through the top of his head, I didn't realise he was shot in the head until he fell down on the ground because what happened was he got out of his truck and ran round in circles before dropping. When we got over to him we saw a circle of blood which had obviously been spraying out of the hole in his head, he was the driver of the truck which had a blown tyre. Fortunately the guy who got shot in the wrist was still able to drive so he jumped into his cab and got going pretty dam quick and white faced. The dead driver was thrown into one of the gun trucks unceremoniously and landed in a heap. I grabbed a grenade out of my gun truck and threw it into the cab of the dead driver's truck and waited inside my vehicle for it to explode which seemed like ages. Eventually the grenade exploded and the cab of the truck caught fire but still I couldn't move until the Humvees on the back caught fire.

With all three Humvees now alight I told the driver to get the fuck out of here and as we passed the last insurgent firing position I gave a sigh of utter relief before I again heard both top gunners firing again. "Fucking hell what now" I shouted as loud as I could and asked them what the problem was to which one answered that four insurgents had come onto the road and fired at them in the open, all he did was return the fire, I wouldn't swear to it but he claimed he hit one. It still puzzled me why they picked such a bad position for an ambush and to this day I have never came out with an answer other than w caught them on the hop.

J.S and me eventually reach the rear of the convoy and told the front gun truck to slow down and stop. We had to get ourselves sorted before we went any further. Static at the side of the road I went to check on the wounded truck driver to assess his condition, he said he was fine and would carry on. The two wounded security guys also said they were fine but from the look on their faces I knew this was not the case.

I informed the operations room of what was going on and told them we were returning to camp and that I needed and ambulance at the American checkpoint to receive the wounded. We put the body in a body bag and secured it to the rear of a gun truck before setting off again.

Half an hour later we were inside the American checkpoint and static. Two U.S Army ambulances were there to meet us and the medics took charge of the three wounded guys and took them off to the Military hospital. The dead Iraqi guy was transferred over into the medics vehicle and was taken to the mortuary were his family were able to pick him up later that night.

Back at our little camp I felt exhausted, as if I had just taken a load of my shoulders. I sat on the pavement still in my body armour and assault vest and just thought through everything that had happened and came to the conclusion that the insurgents had planned the attack very well indeed but in the wrong position.

The shooting of the point vehicle making it stop dead then waiting for the security men to get out to see what the problem was which would initiate the two IED's then the attack from the right. When they thought we were low on ammo they hit us from the left. I don't think the person who initiated the two IED's could see us and think he did it on time or a signal, normally what happens with some companies is when a vehicle goes down quite a few guys jump out and assist the driver to change the tyre. We didn't do this but remained in our vehicles, hence the reason I don't think he saw us and that it was detonated on time. Time from when we stopped, to when he thought the maximum amount of people were on the ground, three to four minutes.

Burnt out humvees with the sand bank behind.

Now it was the paperwork to get through, what a pain that was. When I had finished the report with all the incidents and timings it was only then that I realised that we had been fighting for two hours and fifty minutes and had expended well over one hundred thousand rounds of ammunition. A.W didn't seem to give a shit because even before he enquired about the wounded guys he asked if the gun trucks were alright. That little comment said it all, for me he was definitely a grade one bastard. I also realised that everytime I had been out lately I had been contacted.

The guys were elated that we had got through that major gun battle without any serious injuries other than the three wounded however, they were sad that we lost one of the Iraqi drivers. Singing and dancing went on well into the early hours.

J.S, Mick and I sat up well into the early hours and talked about what had happened and how it happened, we discussed how to beat it if it occurred again. Mick went as far as producing an intelligence report from the year previous and showed how the insurgents in that area carried out a similar attack on a convoy very much the same size as ours, the only difference was that the security guys, all Fijians, were all killed as were the Iraqi drivers.

As the old saying goes, all plans can go wrong. I think to beat the insurgents is to do something out of the ordinary, something they are not expecting. I don't know, and nobody ever will, what those Fijians did in that gun battle which cost each one his life but obviously what we did sent the insurgents off on a tangent, in other words we didn't do what they thought we should have done.

Insurgents will watch different convoys to see what they will do when confronted by various incidents, when they think they know everything they will throw in what we call a spectacular and think they are on a winner. We obviously did something that wasn't supposed to happen and therefore got away with it. I still have to comment on their position because if it had of been another 100 metres further up the road it may have been a different story, for them and for us.

Camp routine was both boring and mundane with head shed everywhere you went. If you trained in the morning, you obviously hoped to get the afternoon off or even play a little sport, such as basketball or a game of touch rugby. No, though – as soon as the head shed saw you, they accused you of getting money for doing nothing. Then they would ask about the training. Money for nothing – they didn't go out and get shot at. Even though it was my decision to be there, I hated all of them.

The sun in the summer is at its highest at around midday, seething hot. That is why the Arabs have a siesta. Not the daft British, though – we worked through the day. Who is stupid? I hated being in camp even for a little time! I would rather be out on the ground where I was more comfortable. I decided to spend more time on the firing range and doing dry training with the guys, contact drills very much the same as we had encountered in the last few days, this enabled us to iron out any major problems.

Well, the days went by quickly until we got another task. The task was to take weapons from J4 at Taji to Al Kasik. *Al Kasik again,*

I thought. We were going to this place much too often. I made my observations to the ops room staff and A. W., but they fell on deaf ears. A. W. said he would check the intelligence for us and let me know if there were any problems with the route. The only route we could take was straight up Route Tampa and into Mosul and then west towards Al Kasik.

I knew this route was dangerous and tried every way I could think of to minimize its danger. I did not trust A.W one iota; as far as I was concerned, he was a coward and a liar.

I knew we would get hit again like all the other times but we ramped up for the job and got all the stores and kit ready to do the trip, including extra ammunition. I worked out a plan to get us there without the hassle of gun battles, but I needed the intelligence to be correct: no lies, just the truth.

I sat down with A. W., and we went through the intelligence on the area in fine detail. My plan was to leave Taji at 2359 hours; this would still enable us to get through Mosul at about 0500 hours, an hour before the curfew was lifted.

All was set, so the lads went to bed and had an early night; I, in the meantime, kept looking at the intelligence for windows of opportunity to get through any trouble that might be brewing up in Mosul. I eventually got to lie on the top of my bed at around 2000 hours.

I drifted off to sleep only to be wakened a couple of hours later because I was needed in the ops room. Arriving at the ops room, I saw A. W. at his desk. I asked him what was going on, and he told me that, due to the weapons we would be carrying, we had to have air cover from the USAF. Unfortunately, however, they could not give us the cover required that night. They could assist us in the early morning at about 0400 hours. I told him to postpone the job until the air cover could be provided at the time I specified on my orders sheet. He told me that they could not give me the time I wanted, and the troops in Al Kasik were in dire need of the weapons. I had to think of another way to get there, but there was no other, and I had to go at the time he said, 0400 hours.

This schedule would get me into Mosul during the day, and Mosul was very dangerous during the daylight hours. The insurgents did not give two hoots about who was around when they set something up; as far as they were concerned, any civilian killed in the attack was killed for the cause and martyred.

Bollocks to that crap; they just did not care.

I decided that J.S should stand down for this trip and I would take another ex pat in his place.

Among my team of Gurkhas I had an expat called A.O. A.O would take point for me, and G.H, the medic, would look after my rear protection. We had fifteen trucks laden with weapons and other stores, all covered up in their boxes. I had nine gun trucks and a total of thirty-five men, including all three expats, and enough firepower to take on a sizable attack if need be.

I gave orders at 0300 hours, and we set off at 0345 hours for the long haul north up Route Tampa. We got as far as the outskirts of Tikrit when A.O radioed to me that there was a lone humvee in the middle of the motorway. I immediately looked left and right for the other humvees but could not see any, and this one in the road struck me as odd because the Americans never ventured out alone. There would always be a few humvees in any patrol. As we got closer, I called the convoy to halt about a hundred metres away from the humvee.

It was prudent to halt. Americans are very jumpy, and even though we British were on their side, they would still brass you up if you did not stop well away from them. The drill was for you to stop then one man had to walk to the humvee on foot with his weapon slung over his shoulder.

A.O set off to the humvee and was met by an American soldier. They chatted for a while before he made his way back. I got out and met him by his vehicle and asked him what was happening. He told me that the soldier said we could go closer and that he wanted to speak to me, the team leader. When I arrived at his vehicle, he enquired where I was heading. I told him I was going to Al Kasik. He said that the road was out of bounds because the Americans had a very big operation on in the area and that I couldn't pass, I told him my orders were to get these weapons to Al Kasik and that the Americans there were in dire need of them. He again said the road was out of bounds. He then took me to his captain and had a chat with him before introducing me to him.

The captain took me out onto the road, pointed towards Tikrit, and told me there was a gun battle going on there. He then pointed into the desert and told me that the Army had insurgents on the run and that they were heading north. He pointed up the motorway in the direction we were supposed to be going and told me there was fighting up there. Then, to my horror, he pointed down the motorway in the direction we had just come from and told me that there was also fighting in that direction, and I had obviously driven through it.

I told him we hadn't driven through anything and that all was quiet down there. This news sort of shocked him; he went back into his vehicle and pondered over some paperwork before coming back out and telling me he had reports of heavy fighting in the area I had just came through. He then asked if I had any sort of intelligence briefing before I left Taji, and I told him I did have an update of intelligence.

I went to my vehicle and got my folder out and returned to his vehicle. In my folder I had brought along a scaled-down, handwritten intelligence summary of the area I was travelling through. It contained absolutely nothing about out-of-bounds areas or gun battles. The officer had a look at it and said this report was not up to date, and immediately I thought of fat boy A.W. and his cutting and pasting crap on the reports.

After the officer gave me the paperwork back, he told me to return to my vehicle and wait for further instructions from him. I asked him what sort of instructions he meant, and the answer shocked me somewhat because he said he would need to get an escort for me to see that I didn't come to any harm. I pointed out to him that I had platoon strength of security with me and that I wouldn't come to any harm whatsoever. He looked a little shocked at my answer, but I think he knew what I was about. The officer went back to his vehicle, and I returned to mine. I informed everyone what was happening and said they should brew up, as we might be here for a couple of hours. I noticed the officer looking over at the lads getting their gas stoves out and preparing a cup of tea. I then saw a soldier walking over to us.

When the soldier reached us, he told us to stay in the vehicle because there was a sniper operating in this area. He didn't need to repeat that message. As soon as he said it, everyone jumped back in their vehicles. I sat thinking of what the officer had said – tank battles, humvees chasing insurgents, and bloody snipers! What had I driven into?

I decided to phone up the fat boy, but every time it started to ring, he would cut me off. I then called M.H on the mobile and got straight through to him. I asked him to put the fat boy on the line, but after a second or so, he told me A. W. was in a meeting.

'A meeting, my fucking arse!' I shouted down the phone. I told M.H to pass on a message that when I got back to camp, Fatty should be elsewhere, and that if I saw him, I was going to shoot him. I then gave him a situation report on where we were and of what we had encountered. As far as I was concerned, the fat boy was going to get a punch in the fucking nose when I got back. He would have known what was going on up here in Tikrit, and he also knew that if he had told me, I wouldn't have put so many lives at risk by doing the job. His greed for money knew no bounds, and he wouldn't think twice about sending anyone into a very hot area to make money.

After about an hour, the officer returned to my vehicle and told me that I might be with him until the following day. I told him that was impossible because the troops in Al Kasik needed the stores badly. I asked him to get onto his commanding officer and get me authority to pass through, as I really had to get going. He told me to wait again, and off he went. Half an hour later, he returned and said it was my call if I wanted to go on and that if I got into any difficult situations, I would be by myself. Time was against us, and I knew we would have to go through Mosul in daylight – not a good move, as we would have every idiot waiting for us.

I told the officer we would go through their lines and carry on with our task. He was fine with my answer, called me mad, shook my hand, and said I should be careful, bloody careful. That was an understatement. I got the guys sorted, gave a quick set of orders, and left the area, heading north.

We got about five kilometres north of where we had been stopped, and all hell broke loose. I couldn't believe how many tanks, humvees, and soldiers there were. We had just driven, *slap bang*, into the middle of an almighty gun battle, and it was no joke. We had to lay down a terrific rate of fire to keep the insurgents heads right down to enable us to get all the trucks through safely. Further up the road we got stopped again by a group of soldiers who wanted to know where the hell we were going. I told them we were going to Al Kasik. They all looked puzzled by my answer, so I told them exactly where it was. One of the soldiers laughed and said we would never get through because there were insurgents everywhere. I told them I had to get through because the troops up there needed the stores I was carrying, that I didn't have time to make small talk, and that I had to be off.

The soldiers tried to talk me into staying with them until everything had calmed down, but I told them that I had to go. If they were still around the area tomorrow, I would see them and maybe take up the offer of a coffee.

We headed north again, and to say I was worried was an understatement. I knew that if we met up with any insurgents, we would get into some serious trouble. However, I also knew that the guys with me wouldn't let me down. They would fight until we won.

We seemed to get out of the battle into a semi-quiet area when, all of a sudden, the firing started. The incoming rounds were horrendous; my top gunners had to get their heads down below the parapet of the vehicle or risk getting their heads shot off. The incoming rounds eased off a little, which gave my top gunners time to get up and start firing at the enemy or likely enemy positions. This seemed to work; the incoming rounds stopped. I ordered the top gunners to stop firing and just to stand by for the next salvo, no other firing occurred. I quickly asked all vehicles for casualty and ammunition states, and all the vehicle commanders answered that they had no casualties, but ammo was getting low.

Coming up to Baji, which is out of bounds, we had to take a left and head along a route that was called the Hershey Bypass. The initial road went for about two kilometres in a built-up area, then went out into the desert and came out at the other side of Baji on the same road. As we got to the start of the desert area, I noticed a brown cardboard box right in the middle of the road. I immediately stopped the convoy. I sat in my vehicle for a moment while observing the box through my binoculars, looking for any wires. After a while, I told my top gunner to put a few rounds into the box.

A couple of seconds later, the gunner fired the first burst. Lo and behold, he missed then fired a second burst. Again he bloody missed the damned thing! How hard can it be to hit a huge fucking box in the middle of the road? Although the machine gun is an area weapon, he should still have hit the bloody thing. I told my gunner to stop and jumped out of my vehicle, got my AK-47 out, and fired two shots at the box. The shots hit the box and moved it, so I fired another three rounds. Again I hit the box, but nothing happened.

Normally the insurgents would leave their explosives at the side of the road. However, some insurgents knew that soldiers are very nosy and will pick up anything that looks good and worthwhile. No such luck with this call sign. A couple more shots into the box turned it over so I could see what was inside. I looked again through my binoculars and confirmed the box was indeed empty. I got on the radio and gave everyone a sitrep, and we moved on and passed the box. About five hundred metres down the road, we were stopped by some guys from another security company; their team leader asked me if everything was okay.

I told him all was well and enquired why he asked.

He asked me if I had heard any shots. The penny dropped with me. I bluffed him and said I had heard shots from way behind my convoy, and with that, he thanked me, got back into his vehicle, and drove off, looking for someone who had fired the rounds. We quickly made off before he came looking for us. We left the desert road and hit the main highway the other side of Baji and continued north towards Mosul.

As we reached the outskirts of Mosul, we again had to pass through the dreaded checkpoint where the guy with the Small Man Syndrome was stationed. I, for one, was dreading it. As we neared the checkpoint, I looked all over and saw nobody around. I gave the order to speed up and told everyone that I would peel off to the right and remain behind just in case the guard had any ideas of trying to split us up. As I waited just outside the checkpoint, watching all the trucks and security vehicles pass through, a few Iraqis emerged from inside a hut that they used for resting and sleeping. Each one had a good look at what was passing through, and each one had a good look at my vehicle parked up and my gunner trained on the checkpoint. Not one of them made any sort of move to stop us. They just looked, took it all in, and then went back into their hut. God only knows what they thought. Normally Iraqi Army or Police checkpoints would take note of how many vehicles a convoy was escorting and what protection they had which they would phone up ahead to another checkpoint or militia. If a convoy had ten fully laden trucks with three gun trucks as protection this far up country they would most certainly get attacked.

When we reached Mosul, we took the left off a small roundabout and then a sharp right, just as we normally did. The area was full of shoppers, and all looked very normal. Just as we followed the road around to the right, a huge explosion came from the left. Debris and shipyard confetti blasted right in front of the point vehicle, I saw a huge boulder fly right across the bonnet of the first vehicle, and then everything went into slow motion. The point vehicle seemed to stop, then move forward again. It disappeared into the cloud of dust thrown up by the blast. I didn't know if everyone was okay or not, so I immediately got onto the radio to A.O. A very calm voice replied that everyone was okay and nobody had been hurt.

At the same time, I had noticed a woman browsing at one of the stalls. She was about forty years old, with long dark hair and a beautiful face. She wore a long dark coat and held a bag over her right arm. After the explosion, I saw her on the ground and minus her legs, both severed just below the knee. She wasn't the only one to get hurt. Many had been hurt. All over the area, people were screaming. Some lay where they fell. Some were badly hurt, and many dead. What a mess it was – blood everywhere, parts of bodies strewn all over the place!

We couldn't do anything to help even though we had a medic. People must realize that the insurgent is after the white man. The insurgent will kill or injure anyone just to get anyone connected with the coalition forces. If it means killing innocent people to get what he desires, then that is what he will do. I personally didn't care because the insurgents are from the local militia.

Some do-gooders will disagree with me, but these are people who have never even seen an angry terrorist, and if they did, they would most probably mess their pants. Such people really make me sick. I had my men to look after, and that is what I was more concerned about. I ordered the convoy to keep going. Up at the next roundabout, we came to a sudden stop. An Iraqi soldier stood right in front of the point vehicle with his arm up. I noticed a few other Iraqi soldiers milling around the roundabout and gave the order to keep alert.

A.O told me over the radio that he was going out to see what was happening. I watched him slowly get out of his vehicle and walk over to an Iraqi soldier. He stood talking for a moment, then turned and indicated that I should meet him at the back of his vehicle. I got out and started to walk towards A.O. I heard him say *VBIED*, and a car further down the road blew up. The engine block hurtled thirty feet into the air.

As that happened, I said, 'What, that one.' This happened very quickly, and all that was said was right in place at the right time – quite funny, really. I asked an Iraqi soldier if it was clear to proceed, to which he made a sign that we could move on.

This was obviously the secondary device meant to cause more death and destruction to me and my team. Nearly every attack on the coalition and security men had involved some sort of secondary device. We found that most attacks were initiated by an explosion, and then automatic fire would engulf the convoy or team. Some attacks were initiated by automatic fire, and when people got out of perfectly good armoured vehicles to sort damaged vehicles out, they would be hit by some sort of IED. The insurgents must have thought the security men didn't know about secondary devices. They should have realized that the security men who served with the British Army were well accustomed to secondary's because we had all done tours of Northern Ireland and other hot spots in the world. British Army soldiers were, and still are, the best fighters in the world when it comes to terrorists, insurgents, or militia.

Anyway, we got to Al Kasik safely enough. On reaching the main entrance checkpoint, I saw it was crawling with Iraqi military, not a good sight. I spoke to the checkpoint commander and asked him if any Americans were around, as I had stores for them. Amazingly, he didn't speak a word of English. I got one of my Iraqi drivers to ask him to get the Americans to the checkpoint.

If anyone has ever tried to get Iraqi guards to do something as simple as make a phone call to summon an American to the checkpoint and had it done without a complete story, I will chew my head off. The checkpoint commander wanted to show how powerful he was in front of his men, and so he started to ask stupid questions.

What did we have? Where had we come from? Were we all armed? How much of this did we have? How much of that did we have? In the end, I got really fucking irritated and just told my guy to tell him to get the Americans.

What a wrong move that was! This dickhead decided that he wanted to search all the trucks and the security trucks also. I told my guy to tell this halfwit that he had better get an American soldier to the gate fucking pronto, or I was turning around and going back, and he could explain to his boss why it happened. I made it as plain as possible that he was not going to search any truck or security vehicle.

Evidently he was concerned that we might be bringing a bomb into the camp. What a fucking joker we had here. That little statement threw me over the edge. I had just driven for the last six hours through hell to deliver this kit to the Americans, and he was worried about us bringing a fucking bomb into an American camp. I told my interpreter to give this twat my message, word for word, as I said it. I told him that in the Western world, no Christian would do what he seemed to suspect I might do. Nor would any Christian ever blow himself up, because he values his life. I told him that blowing oneself up was a practice that started in the East, not in the West, and that he should look a little closer to home when the next expat was killed up in this area. I then told him to tell the commander to get the fucking gate open before I rammed it off its hinges.

I think that last statement convinced him somewhat, for he ordered his men to open the gates and let us in. As we drove in, we saw an American vehicle driving towards us. When it reached my gun truck, I stopped, got out, and saw a smiling American soldier. He grabbed my hand and nearly shook it out of joint; he was that glad to see us. From then on, nothing was a problem, and we received anything we wanted from this guy, a real diamond geezer. He arranged for us to be fed and watered, then showed us to some billets so we could get our heads down. Unfortunately there was only enough room for the expats, and he said that the lads could sleep outside in the car park. I looked him in the eyes, thanked him, and said that if my guys had to sleep outside, then so would everybody else, and could he lead the way to the car park? I had to laugh because this really threw him, but to his credit, he understood and led the way. Later I asked him if he could give us some ammo to get us back down to Taji because we had nearly run out on the way up. He couldn't believe the battle we'd fought to get his stores to him. He left and returned with more than enough ammo – in fact, quite a bit of ammo, an amount that would see us through anything.

We all got sorted on the car park, and after posting sentries, we got our bedding out and placed it out on the ground. One of the Gurkhas was a Christian, and without me ever saying anything to him he decided to get my bedroll and American cot out and made everything up for me. He made some tea for me and the lads and then got his Bible out and read it for a while on his own. I asked Rabi what all this was about, and he said, 'He will look after your needs, as you are the boss.' This Gurkha turned out to be what I can only describe as an army officer's batman. We called it a night and got our heads down. The trip back down would be a night move, with us leaving there at 2330 hours. I couldn't sleep. I just lay there thinking of everything that might go wrong while going through Mosul and how I would combat it, if possible, because night fighting is very different from day fighting. I knew the insurgents, if they were still awake, would have the upper hand, quite a worrisome idea when I thought about it.

I got everyone up at about 2230 hours and gave everyone orders for the return journey. I would take point from here to Mosul and beyond because it was pitch black, and I knew the way without having to shine any light inside the vehicle onto a map. A.O would take over the point the other end of Mosul and take us all the way to Taji. A.O had been through all this before, and I realized it might be wearing him down. A.O was a real tough Welshman and had seen his mate burn to death in his gun truck after it hit a mine. For a convoy going through Mosul in the dark, anything could happen, because insurgents didn't observe curfews. Anyway, at the end of the day, I think A.O knew the reason why I was doing it; he wasn't stupid, but he went along with it. We left the camp, and I thought that if anything were to happen, I would be the first to know.

A.O was in the gun truck behind me about forty metres away. We arrived at the outskirts of Mosul, and I honestly thought something was going to happen. To my utter dismay, nothing at all happened, and we wound our way through the carnage left on the streets and out the other end. A.O and I could not believe it. The route back to Taji was the same route we had used earlier, all the way down, it was quiet. We passed the spot where we had been stopped by the Americans when they battled with the insurgents, and we saw only burnt-out vehicles – no soldiers and civilians, no traffic, nothing except for the odd convoy heading north, where we'd started.

We arrived at Taji just after seven in the morning, completely drained. I gave the DD250 form to A.O to hand in and told the guys to give the weapons a good clean and get them handed in to the armoury, then get to bed. I went to my room, took my kit off, and had a well-earned shower. I then stripped my weapon down, gave it a good clean, put it back together, and put it at the side of my bed. After a quick cup of tea, I visited the guys' rooms to see if everything was going well and that all the weapons had been handed in. Everything necessary had been done, so I told them to get some sleep after thanking them for yesterday's events.

What nobody realized was that A. W. would redirect a convoy team from one task straight onto another when they were heading back towards camp. In other words a task was to go from Taji to Buckmaster with ammunition. When the job had been completed, the team still had to get the empty trucks back down to Taji safely. A. W. would call the team leader and tell him to go to another destination, pick up some stores, and then drop it at some other FOB. This routine exposed the team to the insurgents by making them do a double job.

This practice was strictly against company orders. The double job never got put through the company books; the money for that job went straight into A. W.'s bank account. One of the team leaders mistakenly picked up a DD250, a form which had to be signed by an American who was accepting the stores, and on the form were the bank details of A. W.'s bank account. The fat bastard was double-hatting every job, and fortunately for him, the boss was out of the country and knew nothing of it. When he came back, he was informed of what Fatty was doing and released him from his contract.

I was glad A.W got sacked because unbeknown to him or

anyone else he was going to be killed. I and one other person decided he was too dangerous and that given the first opportunity he would be shot dead. A.W had always told me in the past that if we required his assistance on a convoy he would drop everything to help out. One day I told him that one of the ex pats was feeling under the weather and had been bedded down. I asked him if he was up for assisting us on a convoy to Ramadi to which he replied that he was. What he didn't know was that I and another guy had planned his death the previous night. The plan was for him to travel in my vehicle with me, outside of Baghdad we would fake a contact and a broken down vehicle. The team would obviously fire at fake targets out in the desert and whilst this was going on I would order A.W out of the vehicle to give cover whilst the damaged vehicle was repaired. It would be at that time when he was to be shot.

While we were still in camp A.W got his kit on and waited next to my truck but unfortunately he saw me speaking to one of the other ex pats over the other side of the compound, this must have sent shivers up his spine because when I got to the vehicle he must have sensed something was wrong and he told me he had been summoned to the contracts officer for a meeting and had to go straight away. What a complete load of bullshit. Anyway when R.R sacked him he also saved his life.

One task we had was to take some vehicles to Habbinayah. We got passed Fallujah and Ramadi without a problem then turned onto the desert route, Long Island. About four kilometers into the desert I heard J.S say over the radio for the convoy to stop. The whole convoy went static and I told everyone to remain in the vehicles until I sorted out whatever the problem was. I was informed that one of the Iraqi truck drivers had stopped and was now out on the narrow road and looking in his food bins. I told J.S to get the guy back in his truck and get him moving. J.S told me he had already tried and that the driver had told him he was hungry and tired. I thought I had heard it wrong and asked him to repeat what he had just said because I couldn't believe that anyone would want to stop here for a feed and a sleep. This area was particularly dangerous because you were right out in the open and wouldn't see anyone who was looking at you for a potential attack further down. The driver was adamant that he was going to have a feed and a sleep before he moved anywhere. The problem was that some of these drivers thought we were out on a Sunday stroll and just because they had armed security they could do what they wanted, fucking wrong. I told my driver to reverse as far as the first truck. Once I was at the front truck I got out and started to walk towards the rear of the convoy where the driver was situated. As I neared his truck I told J.S to take cover, he never asked why but just moved out of the line of fire. I shouted to the driver that he had better get back into his truck and get moving or I would shoot him and burn his truck. I was now about seventy metre's away from him and all he did was look at me and smile. I drew my pistol out of my holster and fired a shot in his direction. I have never seen anyone move so quickly before, his kettle and food got thrown into his vehicle, his side bins secured and all the time he was saying, ok Mr. Jack, ok Mr. Jack, no problem. When I got down to him I put my arm around his shoulders and asked him why he had put the entire convoy at risk. He never answered but just kept repeating ok Mr. Jack. I told him that we would stop shortly for food and a sleep and that he should keep up or wee would leave him on his own. He started his engine and waited for the convoy to get on the move. I met up with J.S out of sight of the driver and we both laughed our heads off. I never had any more problems from this guy on that trip. That driver turned out to be one of the better guys and stayed with us right until we all left, even through all the contacts we were about to have.

One day we got a job to Numaniya, a place south of Baghdad. This place was off Route Kiev and out in the middle of nowhere, an Iraqi camp with a small detachment of American soldiers. The trip down Route Tampa went without a hitch. We got into Camp Scania and rested for half an hour for refueling and a brew of tea. We set off again and left Scania by the south gate and proceeded out onto the open highway. A few miles down the road, we had to take a flyover because our route went left. We travelled through a small shanty village and then turned left along Route Kiev.

This route always gave me shudders because they were rebuilding it, and at the side of the road were heaps of sand and gravel. This area was well known for EFP attacks. It didn't matter how thick your armoured vehicle was; an EFP would go straight through it and out the other end. It passed through everything in its way. Anyone caught in its path would be instantly mashed to a pulp, dead or very badly injured. Travelling along the road, we came to the area where they were rebuilding. They had taken up the entire road, and we travelled along for about three miles on sand. Since our trucks were heavy, they sank into the sand, so this stretch got very dangerous for the security men. They had to dismount from their vehicles and walk through the sand, trying to get a hard bit of ground so the trucks could move forward. Unfortunately, however, the trucks could only move at a snail's pace, which added more pressure for the men.

We eventually made it to the camp. I made contact with an American major and handed over all the trucks laden with his kit. He told me we would have to sleep outside, as no contractor was allowed inside the camp – Iraqi policy, not his. I believed him because I knew what the Iraqi military men were like.

We all settled down for a night under the stars. I put a sentry out and made a duty roster for the guys. Morning came, and we got the empty trucks back from the Americans. As we travelled down the road towards the checkpoint, I noticed there was not much traffic on the road, and the traffic that was travelling was going very slowly. I had been to this camp quite a few times, and the road was always busy. Cars travelled fast on that straight road. I told my 2i/c to stop the convoy and to get up to my vehicle. When he arrived, I told him my feelings and said we were going to stay inside the perimeter for at least another hour, as I wanted to see if the traffic went any faster or stayed the same.

About forty-five minutes later, the traffic started to get faster, and there was more of it on the road. I decided that the time was right for us to go, so without further ado, we got started and moved off. We pulled out onto the road and turned right, heading in the direction of Scania. After about an hour on the road, we came up to a part that had large humps of gravel. As far as I was concerned, this area was the dangerous part.

About five hundred metres in front, I noticed a traffic jam, and on this part of the road, jams were very rare. As we neared the traffic, I noticed a nine-seat minibus that appeared mangled. On reaching the minibus, I saw that it had been hit by an EFP. The minibus was full, and all the passengers were dead. As I slowly passed the minibus, I saw that the people inside were mutilated beyond recognition. Blood was all over the place and arms and legs were scattered on the road. A head of a female dangled from a smashed window. The females head was still connected to her body by a few strands of muscle; the face had been smashed and had a big hole right through her head from ear to ear. Other bodies were just as bad, if not worse. Another body I saw was of another female, the top half of the body was cut right through at about breast level. A hole which entered through her back exited through the front, bringing everything with it, including the breast bone. Her chin had been shattered completely, leaving a gaping hole that should have been her mouth. Her eyes were partially open and had that glazed look that I had seen many times before. Both sides of the minibus had huge holes all the way along its length. The driver had been knocked out of his seat and across to the other side of the vehicle; he had massive holes all over his body. One good thing for all the passengers was that they wouldn't have felt anything, death must have been instantaneous and as far as I was concerned it was an own goal, in other words the insurgents had killed their own people even though the bomb was meant for us or someone else.

I gave a sigh of relief that we didn't get that lot because I honestly think the bomb was meant for us, if we had of been attacked the unfortunate thing is there would not have been any backup for us. However, looking at the spread of shrapnel, it would have only taken out one vehicle. The question on everyone's lips was 'Whose vehicle?' There was absolutely nothing we could do, and I certainly wasn't putting guys' lives at risk; these people were dead, and that was that. This was something that the Iraqi people had to come to terms with on their own. Either they accepted the risks on a day-to-day basis, or they helped the coalition to do something about the terrorist situation. Violent death was a daily occurrence throughout Iraq. People were horribly mutilated there. People were murdered for being in the wrong tribe or simply being in the wrong place at the wrong time.

We carried on towards Scania without a second glance back. On reaching Scania, I booked in with the movements section and then reported the events to the Americans. They were not too bothered about it. However, they took my report and filed it away. Civilian-on-civilian violence is a problem for the Iraqi Police. The Americans only got involved when security men were injured or dead.

All the guys got fed and watered, and off we went, heading for Baghdad. On the outskirts of Baghdad, the trucks split from the convoy and headed off to their homes, leaving only the security vehicles. We picked up speed and headed back towards Taji. To our advantage, we didn't comply with the rules of the road. When travelling with trucks or on our own, I would use both sides of the road, either with or against the flow of traffic. Either way, I would always make sure that no car, bus, truck, horse and cart, or walking civilian came anywhere near my convoy.

One day R.R decided to bring in Iraqi guys, he expected us to train them up and get them on the convoy teams. I was very much against the idea for various reasons, which included security breaches and the possibility of laziness, troublemaking, and theft.

Breached security was the worst. All the trucks that I took on convoys had Iraqi drivers. When they turned up for work, I made sure they were not told where they were going. All their mobile phones were taken from them and locked away in a metal box until after the job, when they would have the phones returned. You could guarantee that within an hour, the drivers knew where we were going. Even after searching them and their trucks one or two of them would have a phone hidden somewhere. They were crafty bastards. In the heat of the day, they would want to rest, and they would come out with any story they could think of to get me to stop the convoy. After a while, they all knew well that no story got any sympathy from me. I had a job to do, and I was going to do it, whatever the cost.

The drivers were either all Shia or Sunni, never mixed. The two types did not work well together. I could never understand why they couldn't work together. One convoy we did was for the Americans, transporting supplies to an Iraqi Army camp. The stores consisted of military clothing. All the boxes were sealed when they were loaded; I know this because I was there when they were loaded.

When we got to our destination, I noticed that the boxes had fist-sized holes in the sides. I got all the drivers out of their trucks and asked each and every one of them if they had taken any kit from the boxes, and all denied having anything to do with it. I told the drivers to stand to one side and then got all my team prepared to search each vehicle. I then asked all the drivers again and told them that if they gave me back the stores they had stolen, I would forget the whole saga. If they didn't, my team would search the vehicles, and whatever stolen kit they found would be put in front of the truck where it was found. I would then get the Iraqi Police involved.

All said they had taken nothing. I got the team to search the trucks one by one. Within a couple of minutes, one of the team threw out some training shoes and clothing; those items were then placed in front of that truck. We did the same with the next truck and the next and the next until all the trucks had been searched. The drivers were going mad, saying that we had planted the items inside the trucks; I reminded them that not one of my team had ever been near any of the trucks and that all the stolen kit had been found inside the cabs. Each claimed that he was not an Ali Baba, a thief, and that the kit was planted. I told them that issue would be sorted out by the Iraqi Police when they arrived.

Nearly all of them went white when they heard that; others thought I was calling their bluff. About fifteen minutes later, the Iraqi Police turned up, and I went off to speak to the officer. I told him exactly what had happened and pointed out all the kit in front of the trucks. He was obviously disgusted with the drivers and couldn't believe what he was hearing. However, he did act. He got a few of his officers to take down the names and addresses of all the drivers, and each and every one of them had to report to his police station when the job was finished. He then instructed his officers to take the truck drivers' *gensia*, or Iraqi ID documents. They would get their documents back at the police station.

Once the job was finished, the drivers went their separate ways. I only saw half the drivers on future jobs, and I was quite happy that they knew that if they stole from my convoy, they would be handed over to the police.

We had about eight Iraqi guys who wanted to do convoy work. They all said they were ex-military and had done convoys before, which I doubted very much. Hardly any company employed Iraqis as convoy security. We trained this bunch of guys as best we could, a serious challenge because they didn't speak or understand English. After two weeks of training, I decided to give them a trial out on the ground, which was a bad mistake.

The trip was an easy run to FOB Ramadi with stores for the US Army. I made sure the team had an ex pat medic and that the rear truck was commanded by an expat. There were also experienced guys in the convoy just in case we got into trouble.

We left the Taji base and turned right down Tampa, heading towards Baghdad. On the outskirts of Baghdad, we took a right along Sword, then on to Mobile, in the direction of Ramadi.

First we had to get past Fallujah, not a nice thought because the insurgents in Fallujah were absolutely mental. In Fallujah there were suicide bombers on foot and in vehicles, and they were mad people. Just before we hit the outskirts of Fallujah, all hell broke loose. The centre truck took a direct hit straight in the fuel tank; it didn't blow up, but fuel poured out, and I knew we wouldn't make it to FOB Ramadi because the truck would run out of fuel well before we got anywhere near the place.

I ordered the convoy to stop so we could improvise repairs. I had quite a bit of chewing gum in my vehicle, so I decided to give each person a stick of it to chew. Once the gum was nice and soft, I would collect it all in and make a seal around the hole in the fuel tank – a simple task, I thought. I started handing out gum, not noticing that the new Iraqi security men were watching me rather than doing surveillance. About four trucks down the convoy, bullets started to ping off the trucks and security vehicles. The experienced guys started to return fire in the direction of the insurgents, but the Iraqi guys got right down in the gun tub, afraid they would get hit.

I was in full view of the insurgents but had to get this small task done to be able to get the hell out of there. Dashing around the vehicles for cover, I collected all the chewed gum and kneaded it, meanwhile avoiding incoming fire. Once I had the gum nice and soft, I called all the security guys on the radio and told them to get as much fire down as possible because I was going to plug the hole. All the security gun trucks upped their firing from twenty round bursts to God knows how many rounds per burst. The firing sounded continuous. I dashed out in full view again, trying to calm down so I could seal the hole up. However, the bloody gum wouldn't take hold of the fuel tank and kept dropping off. The firing was still at its height, and the noise was deafening; all I could hear was the clatter of rounds going in the direction of the insurgents. Or so I hoped.

After many attempts to seal the fuel tank hole, I told the driver to get his towing pole out. We quickly attached the long metal pole to the front of his vehicle and the rear of the vehicle in front of him. Once secure, I dashed to my vehicle and ordered the convoy to move. A call came over the radio for the convoy to stay still. When I asked why, I was told the Iraqi security had left their vehicles and run off into the desert in the direction of a village.

'Fuck them,' I said. 'If they want to run, then that's their problem.' I then ordered the convoy forward. We managed to get out of the kill zone intact and headed off along the road. We managed to get past Fallujah without any more problems. Between Fallujah and Ramadi, there is an American outpost about forty metres off the motorway where I meant to stop and try again to get the hole sealed.

The stop came well before the outpost because one of the gun trucks had taken a bullet in the front tyre, and as we travelled along, the air seeped out because we had run flat tyres. The run flats are awesome. They can take a hit from a bullet without the tyre exploding because a substance inside the tyre seals the hole, and the tyre goes down gradually, this was a great advantage to any security company because you could drive a further 25km before the tyre was completely flat, if anything it would certainly get you out of the immediate gun battle. We had to stop to change the tyre. The crew got out and worked frantically to change the flat tyre. The area on both sides of the motorway was barren and just desert. I thought it would be okay but told all the security guys to keep a sharp lookout. I asked the tail end Charlie commander what had occurred and why the Iraqi guys had run away. He told me that they hadn't fired a shot at the insurgents, just gotten their heads well down. As the firefight got going and the rounds were whizzing back and forth, one of the Iraqi guys had jumped down off the gun truck and shouted something to the next gun truck driver, and the word to run had been passed down through all the Iraqi drivers. After hearing this, I wasn't really bothered whether they survived or got themselves killed; that would be their call, good or bad.

As we changed the tyre, a black BMW slowly approached the convoy from the rear. I told the rear gunner to signal for the car to stop. I saw the rear gunner waving his arms in an attempt to stop the car, and I saw the car stop. I then saw four men get out of the car and start firing at the rear gunner, a scene right out of a comic book. All I heard the gunner say over the radio was the word *bastards*. I then heard his machine gun going off; seconds later he stopped firing, and all four of the insurgents lay on the ground in pools of their own blood, one looked like he was dead, the others wounded. Just then and from nowhere, three humvees came up to my position and enquired if everything was all right. I told the commander what had happened and that there were four insurgents next to the black BMW. The commander got out of his vehicle and looked down the road towards the car, then looked back at me and said the Iraqi Police would have to sort them out. With that, he told me to get on my way as soon as the tyre change had taken place. It took about six minutes for the old tyre to taken off and the new tyre to be put on. We then headed off, leaving the Americans to sort the dead and wounded out with the Iraqi Police.

We completed the job and returned back to Taji and our small camp. We parked up, and I went straight to see the boss. He enquired about how the Iraqis had performed on the contact. I said I didn't know because they didn't stick around too long – as the tempo of the contact increased, they buggered off into the desert. The shock on his face was a picture. I filled out my report sheet and handed it in to the boss, and from there, a copy had to go to the US military for filing and any possible intelligence they could get from it.

That night the Iraqi Police came and enquired about the whereabouts of two of the Iraqi guys; they told us that they hadn't returned home, and we responded with the usual 'Oh, I am sorry to hear that' and the usual look of shock, but we all suspected they had been caught and killed.

The next day the boss decided to cancel any further Iraqi security. I just wish some people would listen to what experienced blokes are saying instead of always trying to save a dollar here and there. If the boss had taken heed of what I had said about the performance of Iraqis in security work, those two guys would still be alive today. One of the main problems with having an Iraqi security team was the US Army. No American soldier in his right mind would let an Iraqi security team onto his base without orders from a higher command, even if it was controlled by a British expat. Neither the British nor the Americans trusted Iraqis in security work.

Soon after that the boss decided he didn't want to carry on with convoy work. He fully intended to sell up the company and return to England. I liked the boss and felt really sorry for him. When Bob was serving in the army, he had done a tour of Bosnia, and by all accounts he had a bad time. He got all the expats together and told us all that he was selling, thanked everyone for their hard work, and brought the company to a close there and then.

Well, I suppose all good things eventually come to an end. I had really enjoyed myself on the convoys. I met some real good guys from all over the world. I fought some good battles with the insurgents and won. In the camp we always had a laugh, even after a gun battle earlier on in the day. Rabi had to go back to Nepal to sort out his paperwork for his British citizenship. Other lads decided they had made enough money and left for home. I can honestly say that these guys who went with me on the convoys were the best. I will miss them all.

R.R's announcement came near Christmas, and I was glad for the eventual break; at least I would have Christmas at home. All the expats collected their things, and we gave the locals what we couldn't pack. After a few days of packing, unpacking, and cleaning up the camp, we got our flight details finalized. From Taji, we would fly out in a Blackhawk to the APOD inside the BIAP. The APOD was where all the military flew into and out of Iraq. From there we would fly to Kuwait, where we would catch the long flight back to Heathrow in London, England. At LHR we all separated and went on our ways.

Results of an EFP

J.S. A very brave and fearsome fighter

A very brave man. He gave up Iraq later on in the year and settled down in civvie street with his young son and girlfriend. A diamond geezer.

Chapter 5 (2007)

SALRISK

I had an e-mail from one person I never expected to contact me, A. W. He was part of the management of a new company called SALRISK – Sea, Air & Land. The owner of the company was S. F., an ex-marine, the fattest bloke I had ever met. He and A. W. was a complete match. S. F. worked with A. W. in a company called Global in Afghanistan, and from what I heard they were both pushed out of the country for being, shall we say, a bit light-fingered. As far as I am concerned, there is no smoke without fire.

They had both talked a company called Raints of Dubai into lending them four million dollars to set up and run a convoy company. Raints was already active in Iraq, supplying the Americans with accommodation and D Facs (mess halls) and wanted to branch out into the dangerous world of convoys. I suspect they really didn't have a clue what they were letting themselves in for, especially with A. W., who could talk a good story but couldn't actually deliver. S. F., on the other hand, was a mystery to me. I had never met the guy and knew nothing of his past, although after a while and many enquiries I soon found out, the hard way, that he was worse than A. W. – something I never even thought possible.

I arrived in Kuwait in February 2007. There I was met by A. W. I had very serious problems with this man. He had shown in the past that he was dangerously inept and lacking regard for the men's safety. He failed to provide accurate intelligence briefings in situations where accuracy could make the difference between life and death. The only reason I decided to work for him again was because he did not own the company but was a partner, the other reason was because I knew he couldn't get involved in the day to day operations because he worked out of Kuwait. He drove me to a villa that SALRISK had rented. It was a nice villa in a quiet area and had four large bedrooms, a large lounge, and a small office/bedroom downstairs. I was shown to a bedroom, where I dumped my kit on the floor. A. W. told me to get my head down for a while, so I had a shower and jumped into bed, where I immediately fell asleep. My flight over was a night flight, and it had knackered me.

I awoke about midday and had another shower to jump-start my batteries before going downstairs. I met A. W. in the kitchen, where he was filling his fat face with anything he could get into his mouth. He was eating sausages straight from a tin he must have just opened, and one after the other disappeared down that gaping hole other people call a mouth. Looking at him from the doorway, I couldn't understand why he had been in touch with me to work for him; he must have known I hated him. In all honesty, I hated him with a passion. I loved waking up in the morning and thinking how great it was that I still hated him. He turned around when I coughed and looked surprised to see me; he then said that S. F. was due back from town any minute.

We sat and waited for S. F. to arrive. A. W. told me a little of S. F.'s background. He told me that S. F. was a former captain from the British Army. I already knew that A.W had reached the rank of corporal. He was divorced with two sons, and his ex-wife lived in Canada on his five-hundred-acre farm that he owned whilst he lived in France in a very large villa with his parents. God only knows how he produced two sons. I wondered how an ex British Army corporal had partnered up with an ex British Army Captain.

S. F. arrived at the villa, and A. W. introduced us. All three of us sat outside in the sun and chatted before A. W. decided to make a cup of tea. When A. W. was out of earshot, I began questioning S. F. about how he knew A. W., where he had met him, and how did he find him as a person. All the answers were positive, which made me think that I had really been wrong about him. S. F. was another large guy, about twenty stone in weight, and he had short, spiky, fair hair that looked like a grenade had gone off on top of his head. He sat with his great big stomach resting on his thighs. He was another one who was divorced with two kids; his ex lived in one of his houses whilst he lived with his girlfriend in another property he owned. He chatted about how he did this and that in Afghanistan and how he went out on jobs by himself – what a complete load of bullshit he came out with. These two fat, useless bastards were going to try and run a company based in Iraq from Kuwait, and I just couldn't wait to see the outcome.

I had already been briefed about S.F and knew he was an ex corporal from the Royal Marines and that he had been out of the forces for quite a number of years.

S. F. gave me the rundown on what was going to happen. They had borrowed four million dollars from a fronting company and were going to start up a convoy company working out of a place called Taji. I told him I knew Taji very well and had worked out of there for the last year. This news seemed to startle him somewhat, and he asked me who I had worked for. I told him I had been a team leader for a company called RGS. He then said that he was in negotiations with R. R. to take over the lease and buy the equipment from him, but R. R. was stalling. One of the guys I had worked with before, Mickey was already in the country and in Taji, trying to move things along. I was to join Mickey in a couple of days and sort the teams out and get ready for convoy work, as they already had a contract with the MNFI, Multi National Force Iraq.

To say that I was shocked at this news would have been the understatement of the decade. I nearly fell off my seat. Here was this guy with A. W, and they had a contract. Neither of them had ever been on the ground or had anything to do with the contracts office inside the Green Zone. Neither had a clue on how to run a convoy, and here they were with a bloody contract, for God's sake! There must have been some cutting and pasting going on.

Well, I didn't have to wait too long for the answer. When A. W., came out with the tea, he let it all slip out. They had used the RGS arming authority to get the contract by cutting and pasting, adding things into the authority and taking things out to suit their needs. This was, and still is, highly illegal, and if the American contract officer ever found out, heads would roll. Some people might find themselves in an

American jail. A. W. boasted about how easy he had found it to obtain that contract and even showed me a copy of the finished document. I couldn't see anything wrong with it initially but when I looked closely at it I could see what they had been up to. One part of the document was slightly lighter than the other part, and as I went through it, I could see where he had added things and taken things out; he was quite the magician.

I pretended that I thought this was great and he was fantastic. Now, could they get me a flight to the APOD in Baghdad? If A. W was involved it wouldn't be a problem. Knowing A. W. of old, I had serious concerns about how the pair of them was going to run this operation. I suspected that there would be a load of intelligence doctoring, and I also suspected that when they saw the dollars flowing in, they would get more and greedier, which could lead to casualties or deaths. I also knew the pressure would be on for them to repay the four million dollars, with interest.

On day three at the villa in Kuwait, A. W. informed me that I had been booked onto a military flight that night from Kuwait up to Baghdad. From there I would have to make my way across the airport to Camp Slayer, where the team would pick me up, all easier said than done. The documents they gave me were forged, cut and pasted; the LOA which served as a movements order was also cut and pasted. I was told that since I would come in on a night flight, the movement's cell guys would be tired and wouldn't take much notice of the form beyond a quick glance at it.

I turned up at the Kuwait APOD and waited for the movement's people to turn up. After about an hour of waiting the movement's people turned up, they set themselves up, and started to process people for the flight to Baghdad. When I got to the front of the queue, a female lance corporal, a little blonde, scanned my LOA form and immediately told me that it was wrong. She said that whoever gave me this form had cut and pasted material from an original form and that she couldn't accept my form. This didn't bother me, but it did make me wonder what else Fatboy would do to scupper plans.

I returned to the Kuwaiti villa and informed them that their ruse hadn't worked. S. F. was shocked, but A. W. was quite cool about it. Next day I got another LOA form and scanned it over and over.

I placed the forged one next to it, and for the life of me, I couldn't see any difference at all. That night I got a lift again to the APOD in Kuwait and again waited for the movements guys to show up. When they did, I made sure I was the last in the queue.

When my turn came, I gave my new form to the same girl I had encountered the previous night. She smiled and said, 'Let's see if this one is any good,' before scanning it very closely. She gave me the nod that everything was in order and processed me onto the flight. As usual, the flight north was uneventful, and we touched down in the American military APOD in Baghdad. Here we were met by a U.S. sergeant, who gave instructions. I needed to get on a bus from here to Camp Slayer, where I would be met by a team. I didn't expect the team to be there as it was dark, and I knew there were no moves during dark hours.

I eventually arrived at Camp Slayer and didn't see anyone resembling security personnel. I just got a place out of the wind, huddled up, and slipped in and out of sleep. The night was bitterly cold, and I shivered all night long. Morning came with the sun to thaw out everyone who had been sleeping outside. The heat made me feel like a lizard, stretching out to get as much sun and warmth as possible so I could move.

As I didn't have a phone, I couldn't make any calls to the ops room to see what time the team would be arriving. I saw a woman in civilian clothing using a phone, and with my kind manners and charm, I managed to talk her into letting me use it to make a call. I was told by the ops room that a team would be down to pick me up at about 1000 hours that morning.

The team arrived early. I met up with the usual crowd that I had worked with in the past, had a ten-minute chat and laugh, and got ready for the trip to Taji. An AK-47 was thrust into my hands, along with five full magazines. I checked the weapon over as usual, checked to see that the magazines were all right, and jumped into one of the new F-350 armoured gun trucks. The drive was only about half an hour from the BIAP, and it went very smoothly. Arriving at Taji, we went through the normal hassle with the Iraqi gate guard but eventually got through at the cost of twenty dollars. It's a scary business when you have to pay to get into your own camp. I often wondered what the guards would do if an insurgent offered them money to get inside.

The camp was exactly the same shithole I recalled. Raw sewage still seeped out of the sewage pits onto the road and left a stench. The porta-cabins were still up, but cold and wet because their roofs were not sealed. I dumped my kit and went over to the ops room to introduce myself to the new ops manager, P. G. Here was a great guy who knew his business and was very much up to the job, an ex captain from the Parachute Regiment. P. G. told me to get my head down and that he would call a meeting later on in the day to let everyone know exactly what was going on in the coming weeks.

I had a shower and unpacked my kit, then got my head down. I was wakened up about 1600 hours and told to be in the ops room at 1630 hours for a meeting. P. G. outlined a plan, he stressed he would look more towards safety rather than profit and would abide by the intelligence we would get on a daily basis. After talking for a while he asked us if any of us had any points we wanted to put forward; nobody said a word. All the following day, we would be training on contact drills and vehicle maintenance in the form of tyre changing. The team was well-drilled in many procedures, which made orientation a lot easier for all concerned. We trained hard putting in long hours for the next few days until everyone was happy with what they had to do in the event of something serious happening. We built their fitness up from nothing to being able to run 6 kms, I thought that was a great achievement because half the guys had never ran for years and were fast becoming couch potatoes.

The first job we had to do was a gravel run from Taji to FOB Ramadi, an American base just off the motorway outside Ramadi. The Americans at Ramadi were expanding the FOB and needed truck loads of gravel to enable them to achieve this. This location was not the best of places to go because we had to negotiate Fallujah to get there, and Fallujah was no walk in the park. Mick and I got our heads together and went through all the intelligence reports for the past two months for the entire route. We worked it out that if we left Taji at 0400 hours in the morning, we would hit the problem areas at about six, and we hoped that at that hour the bad guys would still be asleep.

Orders were given to the team the night before the move.

Everyone got themselves sorted with extra ammunition, and all the vehicles got the once-over. At 0300 hours I got up and woke all the guys. At 0330 hours we all paraded and put the final touches to the vehicles. At 0400 hours we rolled out of our little camp and headed towards the main gate, which was about a kilometre up the road. As we went through the main gates, the American sentry put his thumb in the air and wished us good luck and a safe trip.

We headed out onto the main road, where we turned left and headed south to the outskirts of Baghdad. Once we reached the outskirts of Baghdad, we turned right onto Route Sword and up past Abu Ghraib, area of the infamous prison. This was a nasty area where there was a great deal of activity by both day and night. We got to the main checkpoint just before we hit the massive warehouses on the right. There the Iraqi military sentry waved me through. When I looked closely at him, he appeared to be drunk. I even mentioned to my driver that the guard looked drunk.

As the convoy snaked its way through the checkpoint, I heard the distinctive sound of an AK-47 going off. Luckily Mick was in close proximity to the location where the shot was fired, and he immediately shouted on the radio not to fire, as the shot was a negligent discharge from the sentry. My heart missed a beat when I heard the shot because I had expected a massive return of fire. Imagine my relief when I heard Mick shout his instructions down the radio! Mick later confirmed that the guard was drunk and was trying to act as brave as he could; the bloody idiot nearly got himself shot.

We carried on along Route Sword before turning right onto Route Mobile and heading out towards Fallujah. This part of the route is quite open, but in the dark, it shouldn't be much of a problem because we would be able to see the muzzle flashes of any attack. Passing Fallujah, we went onto overdrive; everyone was on extra alert because this area was where suicide bombers operated. With only one chance, they would do anything to explode themselves right next to your vehicle, getting maximum impact when they pulled the plug. The number of burnt-out cars and security vehicles on the hard shoulder of this road was just unreal. My mind was buzzing at what could happen. I was trying to think of any eventuality and how I could combat it; I was getting a headache. All I was thinking on the drive was what if this happened, what I would do and how would I do it, what if that happened, what would I do and how would I do it. We got through without incident, but both Mick and I knew this road well and knew what could happen.

Reaching FOB Ramadi, we had to park on the side of the road and wait for the Americans inside the base to get clearance for us to enter. I didn't like this delay one bit; it was too bloody dangerous for my liking. This was the first time the Americans had made us wait outside a camp, especially on a busy road where anything could happen. The traffic started to move out of Ramadi and passed us. I told the guys to stay inside the armoured vehicles and that the only cover I wanted was a gun at the front and one at the rear.

After about an hour, a car stopped at the side of my vehicle. Inside were a driver and an important-looking man in the back. I took no chances and remained inside my armoured vehicle, waiting for the bomb to go off. The old gentleman in the rear of the car got out and walked over to my vehicle; I quickly gave him the once-over, finding no unexpected bulges around his waist and no wires. He knocked on my window to get my attention, and I wound the window down a little and asked in a polite manner how I could help him. He told me in good English that I shouldn't park here because suicide bombers operated in this area and wouldn't think twice about having a go at us. I thanked him for his information and told him we were just leaving, and with that, he got into his car, and the driver drove off.

What the hell could I do since the Americans wouldn't let us in and we had nowhere else to go? We could only sit there and wait.

Another hour went by, and then the radio crackled into life. It was the American sentry, now telling me to bring my convoy through to the inner checkpoint. This was not soon enough for me, so I got everybody moving, with Mick bringing up the rear. Inside, we had to dismount from all the vehicles, leave all weapons inside, and walk unarmed across a dust bowl to the sentry. The vehicles had to go through an x-ray machine along with the Iraqi drivers; they would link up with us at the inner checkpoint. Eventually the vehicles passed through the x-ray machine, and all the Iraqi drivers were searched. They drove their trucks up to our position, only to be told they would have to wait for an escort to take them to the unloading yard.

Another hour passed, and the escort arrived. He told me that I wasn't allowed any further into the camp and that the team would have to wait until all the trucks had been unloaded. Bloody hell – time was pushing, and I really didn't want to stay in this camp longer than necessary because that would give any potential attacker longer to sort something out for us. Two hours later the trucks started appearing at the far end of the camp, and I told the team to prepare to move. All the guys put their body armour and helmets back on and mounted up in their vehicles. As soon as I had counted twelve trucks, I gave the order to move out and take the same route. On the route back, we were in complete daylight and open to any attack. I ordered the drivers to drive faster to get us past Ramadi and Fallujah. We certainly didn't want to crawl by these two places. The speed of the trucks only reached 90 mph. I suppose that was fast enough to avoid any trouble, but I knew that if any car was intent on doing harm to the convoy that speed wouldn't be good enough, the problem was that some of the trucks could not reach 90 mph which meant we could only go as fast as the slowest truck. Some of the trucks were quite old and looking at them you could see that they were never maintained. Mick was doing my point, and a medic was looking after my back door, just in case.

The return trip went without a hitch, and the trucks left us on Route Sword. The drivers went their separate ways, heading for their homes. We carried on at breakneck speed towards Taji.

Arriving at Taji, we got through the Iraqi guards without any problems, and then sped off towards our small camp. In camp, Mick took charge of the guys while I wrote a report and filed it away with the watch keeper. It was time for a cup of tea, a shower, and some sleep because we were going to do the same thing the next morning.

The next morning we all got up and went through the same. We set off again down towards Baghdad, turned right onto Sword, and then onto Mobile, heading east towards Fallujah and Ramadi. Arriving at FOB Ramadi, we went through the same routine again with the trucks, had them all unloaded, and headed back to Taji. The following morning we ramped up again to take a convoy back to Ramadi. About 15 kilometres before Ramadi we had to pass under a bridge with a small American camp on top of it however, when we arrived at the bridge we found it all over the highway. The previous day two trucks laden with explosives parked under the bridge and exploded taking the bridge and small camp with it, nothing was found of the trucks. A tank guarded one end of the highway while another guarded the far end of the highway. Me and Mick decided to walk to the tank and get some information on when the route would be reopened, what we forgot was that the Americans are very suspicious of everyone and while we walked towards the tank the commander turned his turret round to face us, my god my arse cheeks were clenched so tight, if they had of fired we would have ended up on the moon. The commander popped his head out of his hatch and ordered us to stop, turn around and fuck off, never one to disobey an order we did exactly what he said, very quickly. Arriving back at Taji I informed P.G what had occurred and said it looked like it would take a couple to three days for the route to be reopened. P.G reported this down to the fat bastards in Kuwait and was politely informed that they didn't give a fuck what had happened and that the convoy would have to go through Fallujah, which was out of bounds. Who the hell did these two fat twats think they were.?

I knew we would become an attractive and predictable target if we kept this routine going, so I spoke to P.G, the project manager. P.G agreed with me but said S.F and A.W wanted two convoys per day to Ramadi. This was an impossible task because the company only had one team, and that was us. We would leave at 0400 hours each morning and not get back to camp until 1500 hours. Apparently the bosses wanted us to run Monday to Sunday with two deliveries per day, which was not only impossible but downright dangerous. I knew A. W. didn't care if any of the guys got killed, but I honestly thought S. F. had bigger balls than that. Mick, P. G., and I had a meeting, and we told P. G. our concerns. We had been in this game longer than S. F. and A. W.; we had been along these roads and knew exactly what they were like; by our recollections, neither S. F. nor A. W. had ever been on the ground. They certainly didn't look at intelligence reports, which detailed exactly what happened on the ground each and every day. The main problem, other than the insurgents, was time. If we got back each day at 1500hrs it would take us another hour to switch over to another load of trucks, by the time we reached FOB Ramadi the camp would have locked down for the night, this meant that nobody gets in or out.

Obviously we would have had to sleep out in the desert. This proved to me that neither of those fat bastards had really thought this through and were chasing the dollar.

On one trip to FOB Ramadi, we saw the dust from a massive explosion in the far distance. It would take us another hour or so to get there, though, and I hoped that whatever happened would be over because I didn't really want to drive into a shit storm. Everyone was at top alert. When we eventually arrived, there was a crater in the middle of the road as big as a crater on the moon. If one of our gun trucks had fallen into that crater, it we would have never seen the truck or the men again.

We saw vehicle skid marks going into the crater but could not find any remains of any sort of vehicle. We could only hope it had missed the explosion.

Considering the thickness of the tarmac in front of the vehicle, the explosion had been huge, and any vehicle on top of the bomb would have been blown to pieces.

The remainder of the trip to Ramadi went without any hitch. The usual crap happened when we arrived with the Americans, but once it was over, everything ran smoothly.

We left the FOB and headed back towards Taji via Fallujah. I was carrying out point vehicle when, in the far distance, I saw quite a few policemen on the motorway. There seemed to be a bit of a battle going on, but I couldn't make it out. I called Mick on the radio and told him what lay ahead. He said that going or stopping was my call. Assessing the situation as I got closer, I saw that the police were firing from the motorway out into the desert, so I told Mick we would push through.

When we eventually got to the firing line of policemen, I saw that the police on my side of the motorway were also firing. It was too late to stop the convoy, so I just decided to push on. As I got to the first policeman on the firing line, he looked at me with eyes wide open. He automatically stopped firing until I passed, then carried on firing when I had gone past him. He then stopped firing again when the main body of the convoy reached him. This happened all the way down the firing line; the policemen stopped firing until the whole convoy had passed them, and then resumed firing after the convoy had gone on.

As we passed their last vehicle, I noticed quite a lot of prisoners, who were bound, blindfolded, and made to kneel down in the central reservation. I thought to myself that these guys wouldn't see the light of day for a very long time. However, if they wanted to play with the big guys, they should be able to accept what was about to happen to them without complaining. No doubt some do-gooder in the UK would start complaining that these guys were innocent and try to get them freed, maybe even house them in the UK, why not, we house most terrorists anyway so a few more wouldn't go amiss. Every other spineless insurgent seems to be housed there. I would spend fifty cents on a 9 mm round and top the lot, bring the do-gooders out to Iraq, and top those wankers as well. It is people like these that have put the UK in the situation it is in now.

Further on down the motorway, we found another surprise for us. On the road where thousands of empty cases so someone had had a huge gun battle there during the day, good job someone else took the flack instead of us.

We reached Taji and got through the checkpoint without any major problems beyond the payment of another twenty dollars.

Another trip was planned for the following day, and I began to have bad thoughts. We had done quite a few trips to Ramadi and had been very lucky, but I knew our luck would change at some stage. I voiced my concerns to Mick, and after chatting for a while, we both voiced our concerns to P. G.

Unfortunately P. G. was in a *Catch-22* situation. He had to bring the business in to make the company some profit, but he also had the welfare and well-being of the guys to consider. P. G. knew we had set a pattern, but we couldn't stray from doing the job. So we came to a compromise. We would stagger the days from a trip every day to a trip four days in a row, then leave it for a couple of days, then do a three-day turnaround; we arranged the weeks into blocks and tried to keep our travel schedule unpredictable so that the insurgents could not predict our movements. The following day we remained in camp and prepared for the trip the next day. At first our illustrious cowardly leaders, who were all tucked up safely in Kuwait, accepted P. G.'s plan. However, when they realized that our plan would not produce the same profits as daily trips, they began demanding that we do daily trips... Any reasoning with these two fat, spineless tossers was fruitless. They just wouldn't listen. I understand, as well as anyone, that we are armed security consultants and that we should be able to take any crisis in our stride. Let's face it, though – if you can get a task done and bring everyone home safe that should be your aim. You should not aim to set patterns and get a contact every time you go out the gates. We are paid to assess the situation as best we can and then come up with a plan, not charge into a contact.

In the end, we had no option but to abide by the orders of the head shed in Kuwait and do the daily run. Mick and I contacted both S. F. and A. W. about our concerns for safety but got no replies. I made a point of mailing A. W, who was up to his usual intelligence-doctoring tricks again, and told him in no uncertain terms that if anything happened to any of our guys due to his greed, I would visit Kuwait and slot the fucker.

Early next morning we left Taji on task to Ramadi, and I couldn't help but think something was going to happen. Well, I was right. On our way to Fallujah, we encountered another security company having a bad time with some insurgents, who had gotten the better position. The insurgents held the high ground and were firing down towards the convoy which had stopped. Some of the convoy's trucks appeared badly damaged, which would have explained why they had halted to fight. We were lucky enough to approach from the rear, so the insurgents did not see my convoy due to them firing onto the static convoy with their backs to me. In hindsight what they should have done was have one of their men keep a watch on their rear which would have alerted them to my presence. I stopped the convoy quickly and gave a quick set of orders over the radio on how we were going to deal with this situation. I left a couple of gun trucks with my convoy to protect them, and the rest of the gun trucks followed me

We got up as far as we could to the rear of the insurgents before all the machine guns on the top cover opened up. My guys nearly took out every one of the four or five insurgents in a matter of seconds. The insurgents who survived that first burst from the three guns made a run for it and disappeared out of sight leaving the dead where they lay. This crisis turned out like a duck shoot because, as these insurgents ran away, my guys were standing on top of the gun trucks and still trying to pick them off. I ordered them to cease firing; there was no point in using any more ammunition than necessary. It was all over in a matter of minutes. I called my convoy up to my position; then we moved up very cautiously to the convoy ahead. On reaching the convoy, I ordered my trucks to move up alongside the damaged convoy to give it some protection until I found out how many injured or dead they had. I jumped out of my gun truck and met up with the team leader of the convoy, and was he glad to see me! Sheer relief etched on his face. He took my hand and gave me a hug, saying, 'Thanks for the assistance, mate!'

It appeared they had firstly encountered a roadside IED that blew out one of the tyres off one of his trucks. When they got out to fix it, all hell broke loose from the rear. They had been fighting for seven or eight minutes before we turned up. He had one guy injured, but not seriously. All he needed was to be looked at by the medic, and he was fine. The team leader told me he was on his way to Ramadi but had taken the wrong turn way back. After he found his bearings, he found himself on this motorway but didn't realize that Fallujah was that close. I told him to tag on at the end of my convoy, and we would head off as one. Nobody bothered about the dead of the insurgents or went anywhere near their firing position, the gun battle was reported by me when I next phoned my operations room.

Arriving at FOB Ramadi, I showed the TL what the correct procedure was to get into the camp and informed him that if he didn't use this procedure, the Americans wouldn't let him in. My convoy went in first to be unloaded, and once we finished, the other convoy headed in so it could be unloaded. We gave the TL instructions on how to get back to Baghdad and told him that we couldn't wait around for him, as we had to get back to load up again for the following day.

We started our return journey back to Taji. All was quiet right up until we were just about to meet up with Route Sword. A little scruffy village on the left had never been mentioned on the intreps (intelligence reports) but today that was about to change. In the convoy we had fourteen heavy trucks driven by Iraqi drivers and six security gun trucks, each with four armed men inside, two in the cab, and two as top cover inside the gun tub. All security gun trucks were armoured, but the civilian trucks were not, which made it very dangerous for the drivers. The pay was $1,400 per trip for the civilian drivers, quite a lot of money for about ten hours' work. My gun truck was out front as point vehicle. Then there was Mick behind me. Behind him were a few trucks, then a medical security gun truck. This went on right down the line until the last vehicle, a gun truck. This rear protection was under control of a guy called Jamie.

J.S was about twenty-four years old, an ex-Royal Marine and a good steady fighter. He was also one of the bravest young guys I had ever had the pleasure of meeting or been on the ground with. Nothing was a problem for him, and he obeyed orders right away. He lived in York and had a girlfriend and a little boy. Like everyone else out there, he was trying to make a living at something he knew and liked.

As you come down the road, the village is on the left, about a hundred metres away over open ground. The road at this point is very bad, and trucks always had to slow down to a crawl to negotiate the bad areas. This area, we always suspected, would bring trouble one day, but we never expected it that day. Further along the road, a road bridge crossed over it. On this bridge there was always American armour sat on top with its barrel pointing at the village. On the right of the road, the desert stretched out for miles, low and flat. Therefore, if any attack was to be mounted in this area, it would come from the village. As we passed this village many times previously, it had always seemed calm and very quiet.

As we neared the rough area of the road, we slowed down as usual to enable the heavy trucks to negotiate it. Half of the trucks had passed over this area when, all of a sudden, the firing started. The fire was very intense at all the trucks, and I could hear the cracking of rounds passing overhead. One bullet hit the armoured side window I sat next to, and other pinged off the side of the vehicle. All we could do was return fire and hope to get out of the area as quickly as possible. J.S came on the radio and told everyone that the truck in front of him had veered off to the right and was heading out into the desert, where it sank in the soft sand. Mick replied, asking if he could see the driver, to which J.S answered that the driver was slumped over his steering wheel. We battled through and headed for the bridge, which would have put us out of sight of the insurgents. It was then that I noticed there was no armour on top of the bridge. We corralled the trucks under the bridge, and I ran over to Mick. We decided we had to go back in to retrieve the driver, dead or alive.

While Mick battled with the crying Iraqi drivers, I gave a quick set of orders and ordered two gun trucks to remain with the trucks and keep them safe. No truck could leave until we returned because we still had a long, dangerous way to go. With everyone in position, we were now going back into the firing to attempt to retrieve the Iraqi driver.

Mick led the way. I was behind him and closely followed by J.S and C.D, our team trauma medic. The plan was to drive and put our vehicles in between the insurgents and the stricken truck in the desert. If any firing started, we would return heavier fire than we had when it first started.

As we came into view, the firing began. I think they knew we wouldn't leave anyone behind and waited for us to come out again. My window screen got hit by at least four bullets, Mick took a load of bullets to the side of his vehicle, and so did J.S and C.D. At one point I saw a large hole appear on my bonnet as a round ripped through it. At the designated area, we put the vehicles face on to the enemy. If we had parked broadside on, the damage to the vehicles would have been worse. We waited for our top gunners to get a tempo going with the guns before Mick and I got out and ran the 150 metres into the desert to the truck. J.S and C.D would remain with the gun trucks, J.S to direct fire and listen to us on the radio and C.D to remain in case of an injury to one of the guys.

Mick counted to three over the radio, and when he reached the dreaded number, he and I quickly got out of our gun trucks and raced to the rear of them and took cover. Another three and we would start the race to the truck in the desert. The gunners had a good rate of fire going into the village, so Mick and I decided it was now or never. We raced flat out over the sand with full body armour and assault vests on. The heat under all this kit was killing me; I thought I would melt before I got to the truck. We reached the truck and dashed around the other side of it and out of sight. Mick quickly jumped up into the cab while I kept an eye out into the desert. After checking the driver, Mick said he was dead, with an entry hole above his left ear and the exit hole just above his right eye.

Just as Mick was dragging the body over to the passenger side, all hell broke loose from the edge of the village straight at us. The number of rounds that hit the truck was fucking scary. I had never heard anything like it. There must have been 400–500 plus rounds hitting the truck all at the same time. I thought whoever was firing had fallen asleep on the trigger! Over the radio I told the top gunner of Mick's vehicle to switch targets and fire left into the bull rushes and to look out for my tracer, which would give him an idea of where to concentrate his fire. I saw the smoke coming from the insurgent's gun barrel, so I started firing in that direction. This obviously brought our gunner straight onto the target, because he must have given a 200-round belt directly into it. As quickly as that gun had started firing, it stopped.

I gave a radio call to J.S and told him we needed a stretcher here as soon as possible. Meanwhile, Mick had dragged the body out of the cab and onto the sand. Within minutes J.S and C.D turned up with the stretcher.

J.S had a big smile on his face and said, 'How you guys doing, need some help?' Mick just told him to fuck off and to get the body onto the stretcher. The look on Mick's face had me in stitches, so funny. The plan was that J.S and C.D were to carry the body and Mick and I were to give covering fire as we all dashed back to the safety of our vehicles. I got on the radio and gave the order to maximize the firepower because we were about to come back.

I had just gotten off the radio when all hell broke loose at the bridge, where the trucks were still waiting. We couldn't move from our position until they had that area under control. It seemed like ages. It was more a couple of minutes until one of the guys from the bridge area called me and said everything was under control. The four of us dashed out from the truck and ran as fast as we could towards our gun truck. While running, Mick and I fired in the direction of the village at likely enemy positions. At one point the body fell off the stretcher. J.S picked it up with both hands and flung it back on before we all started the mad dash again. I could not believe the number of rounds that hit the sand in front and to the sides of the four of us and the cracking of rounds overhead, yet not a single round hit its target.

We reached the gun trucks, absolutely soaked in sweat and gasping for breath. My legs ached, and my lungs heaved for more oxygen. C.D threw the body into the back of a gun truck along with the blood-soaked stretcher. We all got back into our vehicles. Then I noticed that Mick was still outside in the open! His driver was watching the insurgents firing and failed to realize that Mick was at the window. At times Mick had to get behind his vehicle because the insurgents had marked him and fired at him. I got on the radio and told the driver to get his fucking door open and let Mick inside, the third time I had to give that order. Finally the driver snapped out of his dream, and Mick was able to get to relative safety. We sped off towards the bridge and the waiting trucks.

When we got to the bridge, we stopped and reorganized ourselves. The Iraqi drivers were wailing and crying and thumping their chests; trying to calm them down was impossible. After three or four minutes of this crap, I grabbed one of them by the throat and shouted at him to get a grip and calm down because we were going to leave the area. The guy said something in Arabic to his fellow drivers, and then told me they were staying and that I had to go and get the dead driver's truck. I told him in no uncertain terms that I didn't mind putting my life on the line for a fellow human, but a fucking truck was out of the fucking question and that he should get into his truck and get ready to move. If he wanted the truck that badly, he could go and get it. We seemed to be hanging round for ages, waiting for these guys to get their act together, when Mick said, 'Fuck them, we are going.' That seemed to hit the button, and all the drivers stopped crying and wailing and got into their trucks. The body had been wound up in a blanket and placed at the rear of the gun tub on the outside.

We all moved off in an orderly fashion and headed towards Taji. We got through the main gates very quickly and without having to pay the normal twenty-dollar tax. Arriving at our camp, we were met by Paul, who ordered one of the guys there to take the body to the morgue.

P. G. took Mick and me into the operations room for a quick debriefing while Jamie sorted the team out.

Later on, a report was made, along with statements. All this paperwork went to the Americans for intelligence purposes; it would go under secret or confidential cover, and nobody else would be able to read it. A copy also went to the ROC, which was the security company's intelligence cell.

With all this done, I stripped off and stood in the lukewarm shower and thought about what had just happened. I believed it to be a well-rehearsed attack because they had hit us from three sides when we went back in. God only knew if we had hit anyone, and quite honestly I couldn't have cared less. My only worry was getting every one of the security guys out safely.

That night, after a good meal, I slept like a log. The next day was just another day in paradise, or so they keep telling me.

This year was not a good year for me because I learned that a very good friend of mine had been shot and killed in Tikrit. Swannie, Rob Swann, was looking after some American VIP's and was staying overnight in a camp just outside Tikrit when he was shot in the neck. Rob was one of the most professional guys I knew on the circuit.

I thought Rob had fallen out with me because I had been emailing him for a few months and had not had any replies from him. I emailed another friend of mine and mentioned this to him, in his reply he told me of the incident and of the death of Rob. To say I was shocked was an understatement. Rob was one of those guys who you thought would never die in Iraq purely because he was so professional about everything to do with the job. If he could die, anyone could die. After the incident quite a few guys left Iraq to find work in other countries, safer countries.

A few days later, P. G. was summoned to the American J.O.C. Nobody knew why, but off he went. P. G. returned about three hours later with a large grin on his face. Mick and I went into the operations room with him, and he told us the Americans wanted him to confirm what happened on the contact. P. G. had briefed them as to what we said about it, and when he finished, he said the Americans wanted Mick and me to write a white paper on exactly how we went back in for the Iraqi driver, as nobody had ever attempted going back into the kill zone before.

The next week became a nightmare of meetings with American

officers and intelligence officers. We wrote down exactly how the encounter happened not once, not twice or three times, but many times. Each time our story was the same, without variation or deviation from the truth. The questions of this and that, the questions of that and this became tiring. All they wanted to do was to see if we had made our story up. In the end I told them to look at the trackers on our vehicles and through the LMCC.

Each security vehicle had a tracker on it for tracking by the LMCC inside the Green Zone in case something happened to that particular call sign. When you got into trouble, all you had to do was press a red button inside the vehicle, and it instantly sent an alarm signal back to the LMCC. Here they monitored your every move before, during, and after the contact. If they needed to send out the QRF, they knew exactly where to send them.

One American officer said they had looked at the tracker and were able to plot our every move. Because nobody had ever tried such a move before, they found it hard to accept that someone had tried and succeeded and actually retrieved a body. When they realized we were telling the truth, which would have been hard to do with all the evidence they had, we became instant heroes. The Americans couldn't do enough for us. The word soon went around the Taji base that some ex-Brit soldiers working on convoys went back into the kill zone for a dead Iraqi driver. Mick and I even heard two officers discussing the incident at a table when we were at our evening meal. Another few guys were overheard talking about it at the PX. One of the American guards asked us who it was when we went through his checkpoint, and we said we didn't know. It seemed like everyone wanted to meet these guys, but nobody knew who they were. I was more than happy to keep it that way. The paper was written, and from what I was told, it would be sent back stateside and put into the training manuals for future courses. I doubt our names will ever be anywhere near the paper, for why would a couple of British expats be more professional than an American soldier?

That's life, I suppose, and if my contribution saves lives, I don't care who takes credit for it. I never did get to Kuwait to slot A. W., although I should have. If he had taken sound advice, one guy would still be walking today.

The arguments started between Taji and those cowards in Kuwait until we scored a victory.

Victory meant that we would run the convoys in the best way we could and as safely as we could as long as we brought in the money that paid the wages and the truck drivers. Since our last contact, we couldn't get any driver to drive for us because they said we were too dangerous, a comment not meant for the teams; it was earmarked for A.W and S.F in Kuwait. The main problem was that we still had only one team in the company. One team could bring in the wages, but you needed a second team to bring in the profit. Trying to get the Kuwait double act to realize this was impossible. All they wanted to do was run the existing team into the ground, either through complete exhaustion or by having a contact every day and losing guys. P. G., Mick, and I sat down and came up with a plan that would bring the company more profit with fewer trips to Ramadi. The way we did it was to take on extra work from a company in the Green Zone, which had approached us earlier in the week. The work was to FOB Normandy, which was north of Baqubah and in the opposite direction of Ramadi. We decided to do a couple of runs to FOB Normandy and then a couple of runs to Ramadi, and then take a couple of nights off. Then we'd try the same system again the following week. This worked well for the first month, and we didn't get into any trouble save for the odd brick thrown at us and abuse from the locals in a village called Mukdadiyah, which was right next to FOB Normandy. Mukdadiyah was a nasty village, and the Americans had more than enough to do trying to calm the locals down. It wasn't until much later that we found out how evil this village really was.

When the Kuwait double act found out we were doing this work to FOB Normandy, they put a stop to it immediately. Not that they thought we were dipping into the money, but because they wanted the higher price from Ramadi. Again the arguments started, and alas, in the end, the Kuwait double act won. Back to Ramadi we went.

Unbeknownst to anyone in Taji, the Kuwait double act had been in talks with the company from the Green Zone and set up a contract with them. They demanded that we do a trip to Ramadi, starting at 0330 hours in the morning and arriving back to Taji at about 1400 hours. We would then make a mad dash to the Green

Zone, where we would pick up a load for FOB Normandy. We would leave the Green Zone at 1600 hours for FOB Normandy, and then return to Taji to begin again for Ramadi.

If we left for Ramadi at 0330 hours, we would normally get back to Taji at around 1500 hours. With our kit sorted, on our way to the Green Zone, we would normally get there about 1600 hours. We would then wait up to three hours for this company to get itself sorted with a load. We would leave the Green Zone around 1800 hours for FOB Normandy. The drive to the FOB took between three and three and a half hours which would mean we arrived at 2130 hours. Then it took an hour to unload cargo there. We would then leave at about 0030 hours, arrive in the Green Zone at about 0430 hours, then go up to Taji to take another load to Ramadi. This was all to be done without sleep or a decent meal, and it was supposed to be done seven days per week. We decided, like fools, to try it for a week and see if we could make up time somewhere along the way. After the first week, we were all hanging out, absolutely knackered. Even P. G. was walking around in a daze because he and the watch keeper had to stay awake while we were on the ground. So, after the first week, we had a camp full of zombies.

P. G. put an end to this situation and informed the Kuwait double act that it could not and would not go on without them hiring another team. The Kuwait double act had gotten used to the big bucks they were earning and demanded that we carry on. After the first week, I think everyone slept for a full twenty-four hours. P. G. fought our corner with the Kuwait pair and won.

One trip to Mukdadiyah was to prove to us that this village was a nasty place to be. On leaving FOB Normandy, we headed out, with empty trucks, down the road that went through the village. All the people seemed to be out at the market, which we had to pass. That market would have been closed down anywhere else in the world, but here it was quite acceptable to have dead sheep hanging from hooks on the open street and flies and God only knew what else buzzing around the raw meat.

As we headed out of the village, one of the trucks blew a gasket, and the thick smoke from the engine made it impossible to see where we were going. I called a halt to the convoy. When the smoke eventually cleared, there were vehicles strewn out all over the place and pointing in all different directions, one of the funniest sights I had seen in a long time. Fred Karno's army at its best! I got out of the vehicle and gave orders to move the trucks closer together and to put the gun trucks in a circle to protect them. Nearing the broken-down truck, I found a local police officer already talking to the driver.

The policeman looked at me with sheer horror. I was quite surprised when he spoke in English and told me to leave the truck and go. I told him that I needed the truck and would try to fix it or drag it back with me. He demanded that I leave the truck and go, saying that a group of insurgents was already on the way to take us on. I asked him how many, but he said he didn't know, though it was a large force. I looked at the policeman, and something told me to believe what he was saying, so I asked if he would help if they turned up before we managed to get the truck ready for towing. His shocked look told me he wouldn't. I told the driver that he had ten seconds to gather anything he valued from the truck and to get into the back of my gun truck.

It wasn't that I was afraid to take these nutters on in a fight; what concerned me were the villagers and the police who had to guard this area. I suspected that in a fight in or on the outskirts of the village, we would be taking on more than we bargained for. The villagers and police would have to fight on the side of the insurgents or risk being killed at a later date. The place was small, surrounded by undulating farm land, and we would have to cross quite a bit of open land to get to the main highway.

After a little while, the truck driver got what he wanted and was seated in the rear of my vehicle. I ordered all the trucks to line up quickly and move off. I remained at the truck, waiting for the convoy to pass me. When the last vehicle had passed, I took out a grenade, threw it into the cab, and slammed the door shut, then sprinted off and got into my vehicle just as the grenade exploded. The cab instantly caught fire, so I told my driver to put his foot down.

We eventually reached the convoy and sped off towards the front. The rest of the trip back was done at speed; I didn't want the clowns from the village following us out into the open. Taji's main gate was a welcome sight. We sorted out all the kit. I made a report, had a shower, and went to bed for a few hours. The following day, in the intelligence report, there was a mention of a terrorist attack on the local police station.

Another time when we left FOB Normandy, we headed out on the same route, and to my horror, I saw about twelve heads lined up on the side of the road. These heads had not been there when we arrived there in the early morning, but they were certainly there now. As we slowly drove past, I looked for the bodies but didn't see any. The grass behind the heads hadn't been disturbed, so the only way they could have gotten there was by someone's car or van. The heads looked like Arab heads, tanned and wrinkled. Some had their eyes open, some had them closed. It was clear to me that all had been cut off with a knife.

Anyone caught by the insurgents normally lost his head. The whole scenario was filmed and normally put out on the television for the whole world to see. The culprit, dressed in orange coveralls, would be kneeling with his hands tied behind his back. A black cloth with white Arabic writing on it would be pinned to the wall behind him. In between the culprit and the wall, there would be a number of men with balaclavas on. The lead man would begin the chanting of *God is great, Allah Akbar*. This would lead the others into a bit of a frenzy, and the chanting would become louder and louder. The lead man would then take a knife and cut the culprit's head off either quickly or slowly, depending on his mood. Then he would put the head onto the small of the back of the culprit. End of film. Not a nice way to go, by any standards.

Returning to Taji, I made a report of my finding with approximate grid references. That sight has stayed with me to this day. I really do not understand anyone who could be so callous and do this sort of thing to another human. Whoever does this type of killing must be deranged.

Well, everyone realized that Christmas was just around the corner, and so a small committee of expats was started up to give the guys a good party. Most of the guys had not been home for a couple of years.

Taji was strictly a dry camp, with no alcohol at all. If the Americans suspected any company of having alcohol, they would ask that company to leave the base. This didn't stop the American soldiers or the private companies from smuggling some sort of alcoholic beverage onto the base.

Work carried on as normal, and as far as I was concerned, we were bringing in quite a lot of money for the company. We won another contract for the Americans to take equipment from the warehouses in the Taji base to the Iranian border, a place called Khanaquin. The only route we could go was up to Baqubah, then up north to FOB Normandy. We would then pass the FOB and take the desert road for three hours to the border. The delivery point was inside the customs post, where the Americans were building a small FOB. Because the site had no protection, they called it FOB Edge. The site was about thirty metres square and completely enclosed by twelve-foot T walls. There was one way in and one way out. The FOB was to be used by American Special Forces.

Since the route was a desert route, we had to plan how to get there and back safely. We had to go over intelligence reports from the previous four months and get information from anyone who had driven the route. What we found was not very comforting.

The desert route was called Route Jenna and extended right from FOB Normandy right up to the border crossing at Khanaquin. We had to negotiate five bridges across deep *wadis*. Once on the desert route, there was no assistance available at all. If you got into trouble, you were on your own to fight it out, as normal. The five bridges had all taken quite a lot of IEDs and also had pressure plate booby traps for the unsuspecting. This task started in January, and we only had ten days to get all the kit up to the FOB and in position. Ten days sounds like a long time, but this task would be run purely by intelligence personnel. If the intelligence guys said no, nobody would move.

We decided to do a route reconnaissance during the hours of darkness to see what we were going to encounter, since nobody had any pictures of the actual route that we could use. Not even the Americans had pictures of it. The American intelligence asked us to take as many pictures as possible and write a report on the route. We knew that the Americans would put whatever we gave them on the secret list, and we would never be able to see it again.

Planning started for the route recce, but first we had another trip to Ramadi, and nobody was looking forward to it. The Ramadi trip was confirmed, and we prepared the trucks and gun trucks for the inevitable, hoping that there would be no trouble.

We left the following morning at 0400 hours, and almost immediately our problems started. As you exit Taji, you turn left and head off in the direction of Baghdad. Then you pass a very small village, which was always completely blacked out. At the other end of the village, you had to cross over a bailey bridge that had been in place for a long time. The insurgents blew the concrete bridge a long time ago and due to it being the only way to cross over the river the Americans put this bridge in place, it was all to do with trying to keep the local villagers on side with the American forces...

A s we neared the bridge, we were stopped by an American soldier. He told us the bridge was closed because of vital repairs it needed. I asked him how long these repairs would take, and he told me they would take about another two hours or until the sun came up, whichever came first. When I looked around, I noticed American vehicles all over the place, providing security for the work party. I told my guys over the radio to remain in their vehicles and just relax, since we were inside the security cordon.

We eventually moved out over the bridge at about 0930 hours, in full daylight, with the sun beating down. This was certainly not what I had planned, but all good plans can go wrong. This one certainly was going wrong, and it was out of my control. I then knew it would be a different matter on the route, as the insurgents would be waiting. I knew they would be there somewhere.

Driving along Route Sword, I heard the unmistakable sound of an AK-47 going off and immediately got on the radio to see what was happening. The vehicle commander about three trucks to my rear answered and told me to look right. On looking right, I saw a school playground that stretched down from the school towards the road. There was a large group of school children, no older than about ten, and behind them were four gunmen who were doing all the shooting. My voice must have said it all, because I got on the radio and just told everyone to check fire. In other words, *don't bother shooting back.* All the top cover guys were already down and out of sight before I said anything. As we drove along, I watched these idiots shooting. To this day, I really don't know what they thought they were going to get out of it because between us and the playground were five-foot-high concrete T walls.

That is one contact that said it all! Here we have a freedom fighter, which is basically a terrorist, who has said that he will give his life for a free Iraq. How brave do you have to be to get a load of young school kids, put them in front of you, and shoot over their heads into an armoured vehicle that will bounce the rounds right off? That sort of cowardice didn't really surprise me one bit. I had heard many stories of how these cowards fight from behind innocent people, all in the cause of nothing.

I remember a march that went on in London, UK. It was conducted by British Muslims and was supposed to be a peaceful demonstration against the war in Iraq. It turned out to be an absolute disgrace in which banners were held high, bearing statements such as *death to all British and American soldiers* and *9/11 is on its way to Europe*. This attitude was from people who had adopted the UK as their home. We didn't ask them to come over; they decided that for themselves. If the British government had arrested the wrongdoers and threatened to deport them, it would have been a different matter. These people are no better than the ones we were fighting with in the streets of Iraq. However, the ones fighting in Iraq had more balls than the idiots in London. The cowardly bastards even covered their faces, a real hard bunch of fuckwits.

Needless to say no shots were returned by my men, who cannot be bothered fighting cowards.

During that trip, that was the only incident that happened. All was very quiet thereafter, and we all returned to Taji.

One other trip we did soon after that was a gravel run to Ramadi. This trip left the Taji camp at 0330 hours in the morning. Just as we were turning right onto Sword, I noticed a puppy cowering next to one of the many blast walls that surround various areas. Although I couldn't stop at the time, I did think of picking the little fella up on the way back. As I watched the little one in my rear view mirror, I saw a truck move out of the line and deliberately run over the dog, squashing it into the tarmac. To say I was furious was the understatement of the year. I noted the colour of the truck and fully intended to speak with the driver later in FOB Ramadi.

On reaching the FOB, I carried out the necessary routine, and then went on a quest to get the driver who killed the dog. On speaking to this guy, it was clear to me that he fully intended to kill the dog, especially when he said that dogs were vermin. This guy was going to realize the hard way, later in the day that I was not going to tolerate needless killing, even of a dog.

When we had unloaded all the gravel, I lined up all the trucks, ready to depart from the FOB. The driver who had killed the dog was put right at the back of the convoy. I spoke to the rear gun truck commander and told him we would pick up speed as we approached some open ground that we both knew; he was to get past the truck and leave him alone. I really didn't care what happened to him or his truck. I spoke to the driver again before we left and made it as plain as I could that the dog was more important than he was. It vexed him somewhat because he understood that I meant that he was lower than the dog, which he was. I told him that if he couldn't keep up, we would leave him to run the two hour journey back to Baghdad on his own.

As we approached the open ground, I increased the speed of the convoy, and the gap between the dog killer's truck and the rest of the convoy widened to about three hundred metres. I then saw the last gun truck pull out and pass the truck, leaving him to his own devices. That was the last I saw of the driver that day because we kept the breakneck speed up all the way to Baghdad. Next morning the truck and driver turned up for work. One of my guys told me he was coming in the main camp gate, so I made my way up there as quickly as I could. Luckily I got to the main gate just before his truck started the process of signing in. I ran over and told him he was sacked and wouldn't be allowed on camp ever again for what he had done the previous night. My God, he went absolutely mental. I thought the fat pig would keel over with a stroke. Well, I was hoping he would, but he didn't. He called me all the names under the sun, screaming and shouting verbal abuse at me. When he finished, I told him I valued the dog more than I valued him, and oh, my God, that set him off again. He was still screaming and shouting when I walked away, got into my vehicle, and drove away.

Christmas was just around the corner, and even though alcohol was strictly forbidden on the Taji base, we managed to smuggle some in for the guys to have a party and let their hair down for a few hours. The party the guys organized was quite spectacular, to say the least. It started off outside the ops room. Then, when all the food had been eaten and the presents given out, the guys retired to their rooms to carry on.

It was that time when we had to carry out the night route recce on Route Jenna. I was told route Jenna was named after one of President G.W Bush's twin daughters, strange to say the least. We were not looking forward to it, but it had to be done. We left our camp at 2330 hours and arrived at FOB Normandy, just outside the nasty village of Mukdadiyah. What a really nasty place that was! We carried on past Normandy and joined the desert road, one of the better roads in the whole of Iraq, as far as I was concerned.

As we drove along the road, I looked left and right and saw a vast open space; up ahead I could make out some village lights. We passed the village, and I knew, from looking at the map that day, that this village was the last one we would see until we got to Khanaquin. I marked the exact spot of the village centre on my GPS, which I would transfer across to my map the following day.

Up ahead was our first bridge. I decided to play it safe and stopped well short of it. I had guys on the ground and guys in the gun tubs watching out for danger. It wasn't that they would see any terrorist out there, but they would see the flash of his weapon if he fired it. Mick and I slowly walked up to the bridge and inspected it. We found that the bridge was intact and good enough to take the trucks with a load, even though the insurgents had tried to blow it up many times. Again I marked the centre of the bridge on my GPS. The second and third bridges were also good enough to pass over. The fourth bridge was another matter. This bridge was about halfway along the route and had been whacked quite a few times. There were large holes where the road meets the actual bridge, as if someone had tried to push the bridge into the *wadi* below. The fifth bridge was also okay. We carried on through Khanaquin and recce'd the route to the FOB. I had all I needed, so we turned round and headed back to Taji and arrived at 0715 hours the following morning.

I told the guys to get some rest because we were going to do the trip that night with five trucks. I went to my *basha* and had a shower and a few hours' sleep, and then went into the ops room, where I plotted all the information onto my map for future use. Later that day I briefed the team on timing and the order of march. We were going to leave at 2200 hours because, with laden trucks, it would take a while to get to Normandy along Route Jenna to Khanaquin.

We all met at 2100 hours at the trucks and loaded all our ammunition, water, and rations. I inspected the loads of the five trucks we were taking and found all the drivers in good spirits. At 2200 hours we left Taji and made our way at best speed towards FOB Normandy and Mukdadiyah. Along the route from Taji to the outskirts of Baqubah, we bumped into the rear of three American striker vehicles and had to stop. I walked forward to find out what was going on and spoke to an American officer. I was told that the Iraqi Army was pushing the insurgents north out of Baqubah and they were the cut-off in case the insurgents tried to make their way towards Baghdad.

Bloody hell, I thought. *This is going pear-shaped.* It would be another four to five hours before the Americans would let us pass, which was not bloody good as far as I was concerned.

We eventually passed FOB Normandy at about 0630 hours, which was daylight hours. I considered spending the day in Normandy and leaving later on that night, but after a quick powwow with my guys, we decided to push on. As I was going back to my gun truck, I noticed four Iraqi Army vehicles behind my small convoy. I walked up to the first vehicle, an armoured Land Rover, and spoke to the officer. He told me they were heading up to Khanaquin and would follow us. I didn't want to sound worried about the route and I never questioned him on the route because when he said he would follow us, I knew he had done the route before and that he was worried.

I got the convoy moving again and got as far as the small village. There I told my driver to stop the vehicle. He stopped immediately, and then asked why. I got on the radio and told everyone to stay in the gun trucks. I then told my driver to get out and open the bonnet and that he was to go along with everything I said if I was asked by the Iraqis. I and the driver had our heads inside the engine when the Iraqi officer turned up. He asked what the problem was, and I told him that our gun trucks have an automatic cut-out switch, and that if the engine got too hot, the cut-out switch would stall the engine. Unfortunately it could take a while for the engine to fire up again. He asked if I needed his mechanic to have a look at it. (Trust him to have a bloody mechanic.) I declined his offer, stating that I would give it time to cool down on its own, and that if it didn't, I would call the QRF out of Normandy to drag us in. I told him he might as well carry on with his journey because I didn't know how long I would be. At that he walked back to his vehicle, got inside, and after a minute or so, drove past me with his other vehicles following.

Basically I used him as a point vehicle. If anyone out there meant to pick someone off today, it wasn't going to be me or my convoy. I let the Iraqis move out of sight, and then told all the vehicle commanders to follow behind me. The first bridge wasn't all that far away, about one kilometre. In the distance I saw the plume of dust and smoke rise into the sky, then I heard the boom. Our Iraqi friends had found the ambush that had been waiting for us.

As we approached the bridge, I found the officer's vehicle static just on the bridge. The front wheel was further away, across the other side of the bridge. I got out of my vehicle and walked over to the officer, who stood outside of his vehicle, staring at the damage. I asked him if he had any casualties, but he seemed to ignore me. I tapped him on the arm to get his attention, and he nearly jumped out of his skin. The bang inside his vehicle had deafened him, and he couldn't hear what I was saying. Seeing the funny side of the situation, I laughed. After a couple of minutes, the officer could hear again and replied that he didn't have any casualties. He called into his HQ, wherever that was, and stated that a tow truck was on its way to him. I asked him were his other vehicles were, and he said he had told them to go on ahead. I told him our vehicle was all right and had started soon after he left and that I had tried to catch him up so I could take the lead again. He accepted what I told him. I said we would catch up with the other vehicles and go into Edge as one convoy, which seemed to please him. I left him a case of water and a ten-man ration pack and departed.

Just as I got to the top of the hill before the second bridge, I saw another plume of dust and smoke rise up. As I got over the brow of the hill I saw that the wrecker truck had been blown off the bridge and was down in the *wadi*. My God, what a mess. When I got down to the bridge and spoke to one of the soldiers, it turned out that the driver of the truck was dead. Looking around the area, I found wires that made up a pressure-pad IED.

I had the team medic look at the other guys who were in the truck when it went over the edge, but everyone was okay save for a few cuts and bruises, really nothing to write home about. I said the usual: how sorry I was to hear about the dead guy, and so forth. Quite honestly, I didn't care, but the Iraqi Army liked to hear stuff like that. These Iraqi soldiers were going to use me and my convoy as a point team, but I had turned the tables on them. They cleared the way for me. I know such a thing shouldn't happen, but that's life. When I think about it, I still cannot believe the officer fell for my limp story, but he did, and it cost him dearly. My guys, at least, were safe. I now had to travel the rest of the way without incident, and with my Iraqi clearing team gone; I knew I would have to think outside of the box. I still had a few bridges to cross, and without the knowledge or intelligence of the area, I didn't know if the local people or the insurgents were placing the mines.

I got all the guys to mount up in their vehicles, and we set off, I decided to take point in my vehicle. Taking point was not a good idea, but I knew what I was looking for, and I could give the normal point vehicle a rest.

A little way further along, I came across the other bridge. There I stopped short. I got out and had a good look around with my binoculars. I was looking for a glimmer of metal or any sign of anyone out there in the desert. Not finding any signs, I knew I would have to walk to the bridge and have a look for myself. The other two IEDs we had observed had been pressure switch types, so perhaps the rest might be the same. Time would tell.

As I neared the bridge, I kept a good look out at the part where the road meets the bridge for any signs of the earth being disturbed.

I visualized the other two bridges and realized one mistake that the insurgents had made. When they directed the wire away from the bridge, they did it in a straight line, and this line was visible. I walked off the road and inspected the ground either side of the bridge but found no straight lines of disturbed earth.

Not one for taking chances (that's a laugh), I returned to the vehicles and told my vehicle commanders we would draw straws to see who went on a recce of the *wadi* to see where we could pass, reminding them that the trucks also had to pass safely. One guy said he would do it, and off he went. The rest of the team covered his every move when he left and when he returned. I spoke to him, and he said there was good firm ground approximately a hundred metres down a track, that the river bed was firm, and that trucks would be able to pass, even with a load. We drove down to the crossing point, and I checked it out myself. I didn't want to start sending trucks over and see one sink. I didn't want to burn another truck, although I would have if necessary.

The bank on the other side looked quite steep, so I got one of the truck drivers to have a look. If he said yes, then I would do it; if he said no, then I would scrap the idea and begin the search again.

The truck driver was a young lad, and he listened to what I said; you could see the cogs turning round in his head as he rubbed his chin and scratched his head. Fucking hell, I was only after a yes or no, and here was this guy taking ages! Eventually I told him that I would appreciate an answer this year, not next, and it was early January. After another few minutes, the driver made his call. We would do it, and thank God, for I had begun to think I had asked the wrong person. Looking at the steepness of the climb on the other side, I honestly doubted the trucks would make it, but he had made his call, and I was going to go with that.

The first truck that tried dug itself in on the other bank. Shit, we were in trouble now. The driver I had asked went mad and ran over to the truck, cursing and swearing. I looked at one of my team guys and told him that this was where the fun would start. The driver jumped up onto the step of the truck and cursed its driver before pulling him out and taking the wheel himself.

I couldn't believe what I saw! This guy revved the engine of the truck until I thought it was going to blow a gasket, and the truck lurched forward. In a cloud of dust and sand, the truck disappeared. When we next saw it, the driver had parked it on the road and was walking back for the next truck. To say I was shocked was an understatement, I was amazed. I couldn't believe what I saw. The driver had my respect. In the end, this young lad drove all the trucks over, one by one.

We carried on with our journey and conquered the other bridges in the same fashion. We hit the checkpoint at the other end of the desert route and then carried on to our destination, FOB Edge. We met with the client, and he pointed out where he wanted the kit placed. I didn't really listen to him and just told the crane driver to drop it wherever he could. He and the client could place it later when I had gone. That is, if we were going to leave. I got all the vehicle commanders together and had a sort of Chinese parliament, an open forum where they had a say in whether we returned to Taji or stayed overnight. I let them have their say, and then reminded them that the damage had been done to the Iraqis and that I couldn't really imagine any insurgent planting mines during the day. I said that if we left at present, we had a very good chance of getting through unscathed, and that if we waited until morning, we would stand a chance of getting hit. *Your call, guys*, I told them. Then I left them and went to have a chat to the American client, who seemed quite happy now that he had his equipment and was looking forward to getting down to some work. We chatted for about ten minutes, and then I returned to the guys to see what they had decided. The guys had decided to take the chance and go, as they didn't want to pick up any packages the following day. We packed up the vehicles, got the truck drivers sorted, and left the area. As we passed the checkpoint that signaled the start of the desert route, I saw a truck making its way across about a kilometre ahead of us. If we could keep that truck in our sights, and if it didn't leave the route, we would be fine. I just hoped our luck would hold out.

Well, we eventually reached Mukdadiyah before the truck left us halfway through the village. From there it was a straight, fast run to Taji, and as it was getting dark, I didn't see any problems ahead. That area was heavily patrolled by the Iraqi Army at night.

We arrived back in the Taji camp about 2200 hours, and when we tried to get through the American checkpoint, we were turned away. When I asked why they wouldn't let us in, they cited orders from the

Beadock, the Americans operations room, which nobody disobeyed. The checkpoint was told not to let us in, and even though they knew us well, they did not. The only place we could go was onto the car park yet again. We were certainly in for a rough night, and after posting sentries and making out a stag list, we all attempted to get our heads down. Morning couldn't come quickly enough, as far as I was concerned, because the car park was a dangerous place at the best of times. I never did find out why they wouldn't let us in. This denial widened the gap between me and the soldiers, guys whom I used to sit next to at meals and who were part of the guard force. I began to ignore them and sit on my own. All these guys saw the change, and all said they had been only carrying out orders, but I could not accept what they said. Here I was with my team, on an American contract, and we had been treated like hostiles. I wouldn't hold out much hope for the coalition relations if such treatment was what we had to expect.

The days went by. The team and I were stuck in this hellhole of a camp. I trained with the guys every day. We played sport in the afternoon, and after our evening meal, we watched a film. Most of the films the guys had were in their native tongue, Sinhala, which is one of the languages spoken in Sri Lanka, so I couldn't understand what the film was about, only that it was some sort of love story, that's all I needed a fucking love story in a camp full of men. My God, here we were in the most dangerous place in the world, and here I had grown-up guys watching a fucking love story! Whatever next?

The next task we had was to take a few truckloads of ammunition up to Al Kasik. I hated doing the ammo trips because if one of the trucks got hit, it would be good night for everyone. The usual ammo consisted of RPG rockets and normal rifle ammo, 7.62 mm and 9 mm. We planned the route. Again it led north up Route Tampa as far as Mosul and then swing left out onto the desert road towards Al Kasik. We learned that Mosul was OOB, out of bounds, so we had to sort out another plan. The only route we could go was Route ASR Reno. This route had been closed for years because every time a convoy or PSD travelled along it, they would get hit. The private security companies lost quite a few guys on this route before it was designated OOB by the Americans. This route was a desert route and started about ten kilometres south of Mosul and brought you out about three kilometres south of Al Kasik.

One major concern was the actual route. The communications along the route were zero, which meant that if you got into any fire fight, you were on your own. The route had one Iraqi outpost, which was situated right in the middle. They had placed the guard building right on the road, and then built a small ring road round the building. How sad is that? This layout was meant to show how much power they had.

Small villages spanned either side of the road all the way along it. I did some research on the route and realized that the local villagers, rather than the insurgents, were the ones attacking the convoys. They were in rebellion against the Americans because of lack of work. They had thought that because the Americans were in the area, they (the villagers) would have first consideration for any opportunity to work. Unfortunately, that had not happened. It didn't work out that way because the nearest FOB was in the opposite direction and about thirty kilometres away, and it would have been a nightmare to get villagers from the area of Reno down to the FOB and back. Also the FOB had to employ the men from local villages in that area.

The scenario was very, very complicated. In the end, everything that travelled along that route was shot up, so it was closed and made OOB. Obviously some companies ignored the American advice and travelled along it so they wouldn't have to go through Mosul. That proved to be a wrong decision because these companies lost men left, right, and centre. Obviously the penny dropped, but too late for some.

Looking at the map, I estimated about an hour of driving, and the only obstacles we would have to negotiate were three checkpoints: one at the beginning, one dead centre, and one at the end... We would have to deal with anything else that we encountered ourselves.

We left Taji at 2300 hours and headed off north up Route Tampa. The roads were empty of civilian traffic, and the only other traffic we encountered was military.

We arrived at the left-hand turn and approached the checkpoint. A couple of minutes went by, and I wasn't sure if the checkpoint was closed or manned twenty-four hours a day. Just when I was about to get out of my vehicle, the sentry turned up, looking as if he'd just wakened. That didn't give me reason to hope that insurgents hadn't already been along the route. This was the most annoying thing about the Iraqi military and police: They would sleep at night though they were on duty, trying to protect a route of facility. When you challenged them about it, all they would say was *no problem*. Fucking *no problem*, what sort of answer was that in a country were insurgents might cut your bloody head off?

The guard didn't check us or anything we were transporting, just opened the barrier and let us through. This was the first time I had ever been on this route, and it was quite worrying not to know what lay ahead. It was now 0400 hours in the morning, and I was leading a small convoy laden with ammo along a desert route without proper ground forces, QRF, or even top cover, which I should have had in case of trouble. The top cover is a helicopter that shadows you as you travel along a route, especially when carrying ammo. If you got hit and had to leave a truck behind, the chopper would take it out when you were at a safe distance. The Americans hated the fact that their ammo could end up in the hands of the insurgents.

Moving during the night was a decision I made purely because I thought all the villagers would be in bed and sound asleep, or should have been. Driving along the route and looking out into the darkness to the west, I saw small fires every kilometre about two hundred metres from the road. I couldn't work out what the fires meant, and I sure as hell wasn't going to stop and have a look.

We reached the guard house, which was dead centre, and took the small ring road around it. The ring road wasn't a road, but a dust track the local drivers had made in going to and from their villages. No guard was seen, and the building was in darkness.

I saw the shapes of the farms and mud huts in the villages as we carried on towards the furthest checkpoint. Reaching this checkpoint at about 0530 hours, we again had to wake the guard from a heavy sleep. Bloody hell, whatever next? Luckily we were only about five kilometres from our drop-off at Al Kasik.

Reaching the main checkpoint at Al Kasik, we seemed to have alarmed the guards on the gate. They complained that I didn't inform them earlier of the date and time of my arrival. I spoke to the checkpoint officer, whom I had never seen before, and instantly thought to myself that I would be in for a hard time. How right I was! This guy was a fat, squat guy who oozed authority and lack of man management. What a bastard this guy was!

He first demanded to know what was on my trucks. Then, when I wouldn't tell him, he went crazy and demanded to search the containers. When I said no, he again lost the plot and wanted to search the security vehicles and the security team also. I knew I would get nowhere with this guy, so I tried to play to him. I told him that I didn't know what was in the containers and that they were all locked with huge padlocks. If he could get the padlocks off, he could search them, but he was to take full responsibility for his actions. I showed him my paperwork, which basically told him nothing except that the load was to be handed over to the Americans, who would sign for it. He took the paperwork from me and stood next to me. I asked him if he could read English, and he assured me he could and told me he had studied in London.

I watched as he read the form but didn't have the heart to tell him it was upside down. That's as much English as he knew: basically none. He told me the form was correct but still wouldn't let me through without a complete search of the security vehicles. The answer to that request was a straight no. I asked him why he wanted to search the vehicles, and he stood and just stood and gave me a blank stare as if trying to find an answer. Minutes passed, and still he didn't give me an answer.

I wasn't being difficult with this guy, just security-minded. If I had let him see what I had in my vehicles, he could have passed it on to anyone, even people whom we were fighting. I still had no trust whatsoever in either the Iraqis' military or their police.

After a while I decided that enough was enough, and even though I had asked him more than once for the Americans to come to the gate, he ignored my request. He seemed to feel that he was losing authority in front of his men who were stood about fifteen feet behind him, and he didn't like it one bit. To lose face in front of your juniors is a sin in the Arab world, where a man had to be tough and strong in front of everyone. To lose face in front of his subordinates who were stood behind him would have brought great shame to him and the authority he held.

I decided that I was wasting my time with this guy because he had stopped speaking to me and begun to wander around the checkpoint aimlessly. He told me he had no intention of calling the American duty officer until he searched my security vehicles and team.

I told the guys to mount up and move out and that we were going back to Taji with our stores due to the pigheadedness of this guy. If the Americans wanted this stuff, they would have to arrange for us to bring it at a later date, a date when this guy was on leave or posted to a far-off desert post. I managed to get in touch with my operations room, and even though the signal kept dropping out, I managed to relay what happening and what I was doing. The ops manager told me to go static for five minutes while he tried to assist me. A few minutes later I got a call and was told to return to the base, where there would be an American waiting.

I met an American sergeant at the checkpoint, and even before he opened his mouth, I told him my vehicles and men would not be searched under any circumstances. This shocked the sergeant a little, but he assured me that nothing like that would be allowed to happen. He then invited us through the checkpoint; much to the disgust of the Iraqi commander, and off we drove into the camp. The sergeant then directed the trucks to one part of the camp while he took us to another part of the camp. We ate breakfast at the American defac before meeting up with the empty trucks again. I checked with the drivers to see if they had been fed and all was well, and they told me the Americans had looked after them, and everything was good.

I told the sergeant that we would get back on the road as soon as possible and that I wanted to check the route out in daylight. He called the main checkpoint and told them to let us straight out.

When we arrived at the checkpoint, we were stopped by the commander. He asked us where we were going, so I told him that we were heading to Mosul to pick up stores bound for Erbil. He gave us the once-over and signaled for us to leave. We were not going to Mosul or Erbil. I never told any Iraqi with authority where we were going or anything that might compromise the task ahead of us. They didn't need to know, as far as I was concerned. The less an Iraqi knew of our future plans, the better I felt.

As we passed through the first checkpoint that led onto ASR Reno, the security guard stopped us. I thought he would give us a hard time, but he didn't. He told us, in broken English, to be careful. Jesus Christ, I really didn't want to hear that, because we were all tired and I didn't want a gun battle in the middle of nowhere without any backup. That comment did get us into high alert; the tiredness left us all in an instant. We passed all the little villages with the usual football game between the kids, the farmers out with sheep in the countryside, and the women walking back from the village store with small kids and shopping.

We reached the checkpoint that was directly in the centre of the route and swung around the dust track they called a ring road. When we got completely clear of this point, I noticed small outposts along the route; these were the ones that I saw in the dark with the fires going. They were as they had been before, but closer together, with eight hundred metres between them. The structure was simple, a shack of sorts with an earth bank at the sides up to roof level and an earth bank at the front, up as far as the lookout porthole.

We neared the end of the desert route, and then everything went pear-shaped. One of the trucks blew its engine. One of the main problems with these Iraqi trucks was roadworthiness; they were death traps, to say the least.

Drivers who wanted the work would turn up in all different types of trucks. Some would be new, some would be old, and some should have been scrapped. I didn't mind the drivers trying to make some cash for their families; I was in favour of that, but I had to draw the line at some of the vehicles that turned up. Some of those vehicles were not only dangerous for the driver, but even more dangerous for my team and me. Well, we tried to get this truck going, but every time we tried, it blew black smoke out of the exhaust. There was only one thing for it, and that was to burn it. Like the ammo, I couldn't allow insurgents to take the truck and use it for a VBIED or something similar. The driver was told to get his valuables out and to get his arse into my truck. When that had happened, I lit a piece of paper and ignited the driver and passenger seat. This truck wouldn't have been able to hold a grenade because it would have blown the flimsy driver's cabin apart. Once the fire caught, we departed the area. With no communications,

I couldn't inform anyone of what I had done. That would have been the normal practice so people could inform the Americans with a grid of the vehicle. When I returned to the Taji camp, I reported the incident to the ops manager, whose intern reported it to the Americans.

The next few days, we remained in camp with the usual training and sports to keep us busy so boredom didn't set in. One day I was asked to take a Pajero 4 x 4 to Erbil for the Americans. It was a simple case of driving it to the destination along with my team. After dropping it off, we were to return to Taji. A very simple job, I thought. However, it turned out not to be that simple.

I planned a route after looking at all the intelligence for the last two months. The easiest way was to go directly towards Mosul, use the ASR Reno route, and skirt around the top end of Mosul through the mountains. We decided to take this long route so we would not hit Kirkuk, where teams were getting hammered when going through at that time. We left Taji with four gun trucks with the Pajero 4 x 4 in the centre. Before I left, the boss gave me strict instructions not to get the vehicle damaged in any way. It was a gift from the Americans to some embassy in Erbil. I told him that I couldn't guarantee that request. Although I was going by the safest route, I couldn't foresee what was going to happen. I told him that the vehicle would be delivered, even if I just had the four tyres left.

Because we were freewheeling, with no trucks to hamper us, we could go faster. In the event of a contact, we would just be able to drive through the kill zone, at least if they didn't blow one of the vehicles up. We made it up to the north end of Mosul without a problem. Then, in the mountains, we had to cross over a dam, which would enable us to get onto the road where we needed to be. This road would take us to the police station where I needed to be for the handover.

When we arrived at the road that led to the dam, I found it completely blocked by earth mounds. I checked my map and GPS and verified that I was in the correct place. About three hundred metres away, I saw some armed men walking towards us. I got my binoculars out and saw they were Iraqi military. With one of the vehicle commanders, I started to walk towards the group. When we met up with them, we gave the normal handshake and greetings. I asked them if anyone spoke English. One guy said he did, so I asked him why I couldn't pass to get to the dam, and all he said was 'No good.'

Puzzled at that answer, I asked him again, and he gave the same answer. I then pointed towards the direction of the dam and told him I need to pass over the dam. He shrugged his shoulders and, looking sorry, told me the dam had been blown and that we couldn't pass. The penny dropped, and after saying thanks and good-bye, we made our way back to the team.

I got all the vehicle commanders to my vehicle and gave them the bad news and said we would have to go via Kirkuk and take our chances. As we drove back through the mountains, we came across a police vehicle checkpoint that had not been there when we came though earlier in the day. Something just didn't look right; all the officers were in civilian clothing, and when I asked them for some sort of identification, they showed me their Iraqi *Gensia*, which is their normal identity document and was not what I was looking for. Alarm bells rang for me. One of them asked me where we were headed, and I skirted round the answer. He told me they knew a quicker way out of the mountains and that if we followed them, they would guide us to the main road.

I told them we were heading to Al Kasik, which was the nearest place. I knew they would recognize the name of the place. I told them we were all right and had to meet another team further down the way. With that we said our good-byes and left, and because there was only one main route, I decided to turn off and head further into the mountains and hide out. It was getting dark, and I didn't need to be hit further along the route, especially up here.

I found a good spot that we could defend if attacked and set a camp up. It was obviously very basic. The vehicles were parked for a rapid escape if I thought we would be overrun, sentry positions were put out, and then everyone went fully tactical. That meant no engines running and, most importantly, no lights. The darkness came upon us, and in our little camp it was very quiet. Up in the mountains, noise travels; although you can hear far-off noises, you can't really tell which direction the noise comes from. Another thing that throws you is that the noise seems to be far closer than it really is.

We could hear the unmistakable sound of cars, and we could see the headlights from them, so direction was not a problem. Distance, however, was. With two of the guys, I left the camp and walked out towards the cars. We got to some high ground and stopped, and what we saw was pure, unmistakable trouble. Through the binoculars I saw three cars, all black. Each car had four armed men outside and talking. This place was not a place where lovers came or young guys gathered to show off their cars. It was in the mountains, so these guys looked well out of place. After they spoke for a while, all the cars drove off in different directions, obviously searching for us. At this point, I honestly didn't know if they were friendly or not, but from what I had experienced so far in Iraq, I was not taking any chances. We didn't want anything to do with them, and we certainly had no business with them, so why would they be looking around for us?

I managed to inform our operations room of what had happened at the dam and what was occurring here. I asked them if any reports had come in, through the Americans, of a search in my area, to which they answered 'no.' I was told the ops manager would speak to the Americans and find out for certain. Half an hour later, the ops manager spoke to me on the phone and told me to sit tight and not move. The Americans had no reports from the Iraqi police about any searches in the area. What the ops manager told me was that insurgents from Mosul were reportedly looking for silver gun truck type vehicles around the Mosul area.

Bloody hell, we seemed to have hit the jackpot. I relayed my conversation to the other vehicle commanders and told them I would remain where I was as a forward observation post until I was happy that the area was clear after these halfwits had left. These cars searched nearly all night for us and, at one point, got within a hundred metres of our position before turning around and heading back in the direction from which they came.

What a relief that was! The search for us finished about at 0330 hours, and we watched the headlights as they left the area and headed back in the direction of Mosul. The two guys and I made our way back to the main team, but not before calling the others on the radio to give them advance warning that we were heading back. We didn't want any mistakes at this stage. I told the guy on the other end of the radio what direction we would be coming from, reminding him of how many we were and the approximate time when we would be there with them,

Even though I informed them, I was still a little hesitant because I knew they would be on a high with all that had happened.

Next morning we got up at first light, which meant that everyone didn't really have a decent sleep. I got on the phone to the ops manager and asked him for advice on what to do. He told me to return to Taji and that we would try the trip some other day. We then hightailed it out of our makeshift camp and headed back towards Taji at best speed.

Once back at Taji, I made a report of what happened the previous night and how I was told the situation of the dam. This update went straight to the Americans.

I then had a shower, had a cup of tea, and got my head down. I was awakened after only a few hours of sleep, which seemed like a few minutes. I had to go to the ops room. When I arrived there, I was introduced to two American military guys who wanted to know about the cars and men who had searched for us the previous night. I told them the entire story, which one wrote down while the other did all the questioning. Once both guys were happy and had what they wanted, they excused themselves and left, and I excused myself by going straight back to bed.

I got up at mid afternoon and jumped straight back into the shower to wake myself up and snap me out of my sleeping stupor. I went into the operations room to see what was happening and to find out what I was to do about the Pajero. The ops manager told me to give it a few days and then try to get it to Erbil. I left the ops room and spoke to my vehicle commanders on when and how we were going to get this vehicle up to Erbil. They told me that if everything was quiet, we should make a dash through Kirkuk. I wasn't happy about that plan, but gave it some thought.

That night I checked the intelligence for Kirkuk and found that all the trouble was happening around one particular area the southeast, especially around the Tuz area on ASR Clemson. I decided to have a look at the southwest area and found it pretty quiet. I would have to get onto ASR Clemson, which I would join north of Tuz if I was heading that way. ASR Clemson takes you all the way from Tikrit to Kirkuk; you pass a safe haven, FOB Warrior, and then connect with Route One, which takes you directly into Erbil.

I decided to have a go at ASR Clemson. If I moved at speed, I could get through Tikrit before anyone knew I was there. If anything did happen in Tikrit, I could always move to FOB Scimitar and go to ground there.

In the early morning of the following day, we departed from the Taji base and raced up Tampa northward. We passed Samarra by way of the Hershey bypass, and then carried on towards Tikrit. We then located and turned onto ASR Clemson and raced through the town at breakneck speed until we reached the other end, which brought us out into open country. I couldn't believe I had travelled this far up without any sort of problem. However, by this time the traffic was running in and out of Tikrit quite heavily, which meant we had to slow down quite a lot and was something I hadn't bargained for. We got about fifteen kilometres north of Tikrit when we got hit by an ambush. Our speed was down to about sixty kilometres per hour, too slow for my liking.

A bongo truck passed us on the left, doing about ninety kilometres per hour. I looked and thought something was wrong because the oncoming traffic had to swerve to miss it. Just as I was reaching for my radio, the cover on the back of the bongo lifted up, and two guys appeared. They sat down behind a machine gun, and this all seemed to happen in slow motion, but when the rounds started to bounce off my window screen, everything went back to normal time. All I saw were bits of glass disappearing as the round struck the window. The driver flapped and nearly took us into the traffic in front of us before composing himself and attempting to get us out of this mess. Cars and lorries swerved, and brakes were slammed all around us as the gunmen kept shooting at us. I know innocent drivers were hit because I saw cars swerve off the road into the desert and just stop. My top gunners couldn't fire and risk hitting the other cars, so here we were, being fired upon from close range and unable to return fire! A right mess, to say the least.

I told my driver to get off the road and head out into the desert. I thought that if they wanted a fight, I would take them somewhere we could control events. I also needed to show the civilian drivers that I was taking a major problem away from them. We headed out into the wilderness and away from the roads, and when I was happy that the firing had stopped and that we were out of view from the other cars,

I brought the vehicles to a halt. I told everyone over the radio to keep alert while I went around every vehicle and checked for major damage myself. I met up with one of the other vehicle commanders, and we just looked at each other before laughing.

A load of people reading this will think I had lost the plot because I did not react quicker, but believe me, you had to be there to experience it and see it all unfold; you couldn't even dream this, never mind write it. The sheer neck of the bongo truck driver to overtake us and push all oncoming traffic away before the insurgents in the back of the vehicle opened fire was class! We were watching it all unfold and not doing anything about it because half of us could not believe what we were seeing.

I had a look around the vehicles and realized the damage was quite bad because some of the rounds had gone through the bonnets and into the engine blocks. The vehicles had burst pipes spraying fluids everywhere. I had a look at the Pajero and couldn't believe what I saw; it had not a single hole anywhere, and what a relief that was. I told all the drivers to keep their engines running and to follow my vehicle to FOB Scimitar. When we arrived in the FOB, I asked for assistance from the American soldiers, who pointed me in the direction of the mechanics yard. I had a mechanic look over the engines first before he gave me spare pipes; my drivers took off the ones with holes in and replaced them with the new ones. The American mechanics told me to get back to my camp and get one of our mechanics onto the task and then gave me a list of things for them to do. I thanked the guy for his assistance, left the camp, and told my operations room that I was returning to them.

Arriving at Taji, we limped into our camp. All the mechanics came out and took the vehicles away to the sheds for repairs while I went to the ops room to fill out yet another report.

The following day, with all vehicles fixed, we headed off again in a final attempt to deliver this bloody vehicle. This time I decided to go around the northern edge of Baghdad, and then turn left and head north up ASR Cheyenne. This meant we would have to go through Tuz. We made good speed north and passed through a village called Kalis; this village was not far from FOB Anaconda or FOB Grizzly. As we headed out north of Kalis into the open, I could see the outline of FOB

Grizzly. The traffic coming towards us was quite heavy and running quite well. We got up to about eighty kilometres per hour when, all of a sudden, I heard the repeated words *convoy stop*. I immediately stopped and looked in my rearview mirror and could not see anything behind me except a cloud of dust. I quickly told the driver to turn around and head back. On reaching the area of dust, I saw a sight that has stayed with me right up until this day.

An oncoming truck had swerved right across the road while carrying a full load of gravel. The driver had obviously tried to brake. Braking at such momentum made the truck tip over onto its side. As the truck was tipping over, one of our gun trucks drove right into its path. The results were fatal. The armoured gun truck was ripped to shreds. The front armoured window was nowhere to be seen and had been ripped away, the engine was inside the front cab, and both the front cab and engine were nearly on the rear seats. The driver, Joe, and the commander, Perry, were both dead with massive head trauma. The two guys in the gun tub, Sanjay and Umesh, were badly injured, and gravel was everywhere. I immediately got onto my operations room to tell them exactly what had happened and what I was doing about it. I told them I had two dead guys but didn't give any names over the net. I requested a helivac as soon as possible for the two injured guys. The ops manager told me he would get a helivac to me immediately.

We were not very far from the village of Kalis or FOB Grizzly. The police from Kalis came out but proved no help whatsoever. They just wanted to look at the dead bodies, which were lying out of the doors but still trapped in the vehicles by their legs. I saw one officer taking pictures on his mobile, and I told one of my guys to get the phone from him and smash it. I then directed another one of my guys to get two blankets and cover both Perry and Joe. The driver of the truck ran off into the reeds and was never seen again.

We managed to get the two top cover guys out of the back of the gun truck where the team medic could administer first aid. Both guys were in a bad way; one had internal breathing and bleeding problems, while the other was well broken up. The medic set to work on both guys. I set about trying to get Joe and Perry out of the gun truck. I told one of the guys to set out a roadblock and to place sentries out, as I knew this area was not a good place to be. Kalis was only a small place, but it had quite a few insurgents living there, insurgents who had killed the village mayor about a month ago because he wanted to assist the Americans.

After a while, my medic came over to me and gave me more bad news. Although he could save one guy, he doubted the other would make it, as he was broken up inside and had severe internal bleeding. I heard the helicopter about twenty minutes after I made the call to the ops room. The pilot was given our frequency and my call sign and got in touch with me. He wanted to know if the area was hot or cold. I told him it was cold; he then asked me if the area was secure, to which I replied that it was. The next time he spoke to me, he told me to drop purple smoke in a position he could land the helicopter. Looking around, all I saw was wires going in all directions, and I thought that he would have to land further away and walk in. The ground on either side of the road was just reed beds as far as the eye could see. I then looked straight up from the place I was standing and saw a large opening where I hoped the pilot could land. I had heard that these pilots were good.

I dropped the smoke at my feet and moved away to a safe area. The pilot confirmed that he could see purple smoke and told me to clear the immediate area, which I did. I watched in utter amazement as the pilot hovered above us. Then, very slowly, he dropped the helicopter straight down in between the many wires. What a perfect landing! He had about a foot to spare. The medic jumped out with his bag and ran over to the two injured guys. He then took the lead, and with my medic assisting; they got the two guys stable, onto stretchers, and into the helicopter.

He then came over to me, and I showed him the two dead guys. He told me he couldn't help me with them, as he wanted to get the two injured men to the base hospital immediately. He shook my hand and said *good luck* before he jumped back into the helicopter. The pilot lifted off, and away it went towards FOB Anaconda.

With my two injured guys out of the way and heading to safety, I now had the task of getting my two dead guys out of the wreckage before anything else happened. I asked one of the local police to get me a large truck and a chain, and he was only too pleased to help me. Off he went. Half an hour later, he returned with a huge truck and a very thick chain. Just then, a fire started in the engine compartment, so I shouted at all the guys to douse it. Once the fire was out, I made one guy stand by the engine with a fire extinguisher just in case it fired up again. I told him I was not going to take two charred bodies back to camp, and that if the fire started again, he had better put it out.

We attached the chain to the rear part of the truck and then told the driver to take up the slack before he revved up in an attempt to drag the truck off the gun truck. Slowly he took up the slack in the chain, and then revved the engine, which pulled the truck slightly off the gun truck bonnet. We all tried to release Joe and Perry from the carnage, but we still needed another foot or so. The driver again revved and pulled the truck off about another six inches. The problem was the gravel, because it was all over the place. The truck couldn't get any traction on the ground. We tried again to get Joe and Perry out but again failed.

Next we chained the truck to the rear of the gun truck, and again he took up the slack and then revved his engine until, very slowly, we saw the gun truck move slightly. Then it moved a little more until we had enough space to get Joe and Perry out. Before we got them out, I had another two blankets laid out on the ground to wrap them up. Two guys worked on Perry while I and another guy worked on Joe until we had them both out. I cut the body armour off Joe and then took his magazine pouches off him. I told one of the lads to grab him by the shoulders so we could lift him onto the blanket.

As I grabbed his feet to lift him, his feet started to come away from his legs. I cut his trousers open to find both his tibia and fibula broken in two. Every time I pulled his feet, his legs stretched like elastic because there was no bone to keep them straight and rigid. I grabbed Joe behind his knees and lifted him up and placed him gently onto the blanket on the ground. Looking at him, I saw that the top of his head was smashed open, exposing his brain. His face was not on the front, but had been pushed slightly round to the side of his head. Blood and brain seeped out of the opening and flowed onto the gravel and blanket. I was only glad that his eyes were closed because that sight would have stayed with me.

I remember one insurgent whom I had shot in the neck and chest, and when I went to look at him, his eyes were open and looking back at me. His face is firmly etched on my mind. The smell of a body when it has been in the sun for a while was quite nauseating, to say the least. It was a sweaty, musty smell. The body was cold to the touch but still wet with sweat, which wasn't due to the drive because they had air conditioning inside the cab. Joe was Fijian, and his black skin looked a lot paler now that he was dead, a sort of lighter shade, almost grey.

I reached into Joe's pockets and took out his wallet and notebook and his identity cards and Iraqi money, which I put into a plastic bag. He was wrapped up, and the blanket was secured around his broken body; he was then put into the back of one of the gun trucks.

The other two guys brought Perry onto the road. Perry was Sri Lankan. His colour was again very light and almost grey, and he was cold to the touch. His broken body had the aroma of stale urine, quite nauseating. His poor face was smashed, and the top of his head was shattered, exposing the brain. Again I was lucky; his eyes were closed. I took all his personal items and placed them in another plastic bag and secured it before putting it into my gun truck. Perry was wrapped up in the blanket and secured and then, like Joe, placed in the back of another gun truck.

I went over to the wrecked gun truck and looked inside to find blood and brain matter everywhere. I climbed into the front cab and ripped out the vehicle radio and the tracker unit. I collected these and any other usable components and placed them in a gun truck.

The police asked what I was going to do with the wreck and I told them they could have it; it was absolutely useless. I was assured that the vehicle would be placed in a police compound and would still be there when we decided what to do with it. With that, I got all the guys to mount up, and we headed off towards Taji. The trip back was very silent because of what had happened, but we still had to be alert just in case someone had been watching and decided they would give us another hammering. I knew the guys in the other gun trucks would be saddened and would have their heads down, but I had to keep them going for another hour or so. Arriving at the camp gate, I spoke to one of the American guards, who gave me directions to the mortuary. I decided to put the two men into one truck and take them myself. I told the other guys to head off to our camp.

With a couple of guys to help me, I took Joe and Perry to the mortuary. What a horrible place this was! It was situated in a building that looked drab from the outside, but once you got inside, it was all medical kit. We put the bodies onto a couple of stretchers and took them inside, where we were directed to put them where the Americans wanted them.

I gave one of the Americans a briefing on exactly what happened, thanked him for his time, and left. Again the drive back to our camp was quiet.

Reaching our little camp, I reported directly to the ops room and filled in my report while having a sandwich and cup of tea. The number of other team guys who came in and wanted to know what had happened was getting annoying, and I told them all to fuck off.

Later on in the day, when I had finished my reports and briefed the ops manager, I went over to my team and got them all together in one room. I said how saddened I was at the loss but reminded them that if they wanted to stay, they had better get used to this sort of thing happening. If they wanted to go, that was a decision only they could make. One of the lads asked if he could say a few words, and of course, I said yes. He stood and prayed in his own tongue for both Perry and Joe. Before I left them to go back to my room, I reminded them that my door was always open and if any of them wanted to chat, they were more than welcome.

Meeting up with my team medic outside my room, I asked him to find out where Umesh and Sanjay had been taken and to call the hospital for an update on their conditions.

I sat in my room and thought through what had happened. Was my luck running out? If I stayed, would it get worse? All kinds of thoughts went through my head. What was I to do, stay? Or had I had enough?

The leader of the Sri Lankans turned up at my room, and the knock brought me back down to earth. He told me that the team wanted to finish and go home. I respected their decision and told him I would speak to the ops manager and get things moving. He told me the team wouldn't participate in any more work and that he hoped the boss respected the decision they had made.

Well, I am sad and annoyed to say that this is not what happened. After I spoke to P.G, who was always onside he spoke to the boss in Kuwait. After a long conversation with him, he told me the boss was spitting bullets and would not agree to release the guys. Who the hell did he think he was, fucking God? He said the boss told him that we would go out the following day and deliver that bastard Pajero to Erbil even if it cost the whole team.

I told the ops manager that I would not lead a team of men who didn't have the heart for another fight and that if the boss thought that was inappropriate, I suggested he come and take the fucking job on himself.

I learnt that day that we lost one of the Gurkha team guys who were injured in the gun truck fiasco. Although I had been given daily updates on how the two of them were faring, I wasn't prepared for the outcome. Sanjay had been patched up and was doing well enough to send home to Nepal, whereas poor little Umesh had given up the fight and died. Umesh was a great guy, thin, about 5' 5u tall, and always had a smile. I used to rib him about being a military policeman. I didn't know if he was married or not. I really felt sorry for his family back in Nepal. I suppose one good thing came out of all this for the families, and that was the insurance money; each guy who died got $50k. I understand that in the countries the guys came from, that sort of money would keep their families comfortable for a long time. However, their deaths made for a very sad ending.

It took nearly two weeks for the company to arrange flights for the guys to get back to Sri Lanka and Fiji. I and the other expats decided to get the hell out of this company before we became statistics, so we resigned. The boss was absolutely livid with our decision, which was no surprise. With us gone, he didn't have anyone to run his suicidal convoys. Within a week he was in country and up to Taji. He met with the ops manager and then with me. I told him directly that some of his ideas were stupid and that although he had said he would listen to reason, he never did. He told me he needed the team out as much as possible for the money to repay the four million dollar debt he still had. I pointed out that in one week I had made $1.2 million for him and asked where that money had gone. He told me he had to pay off people whom he owed first, meaning the investors. I told him that I had checked my online banking and that I was alarmed to find that I hadn't been paid for two months, and I asked him why. All he said was that he couldn't afford to pay me until he paid off his investors. What did he think I would do, work for free? I am not the sort of guy to get angry and can keep my calm in any situation but this fat bastard was making my fucking blood boil to the point that if I had of had a knife I would have stuck it straight in his throat.

His answers didn't fill me with confidence, and I told him that without the team, I wasn't prepared to continue with the convoys. To my horror, he told me that if I left, he wouldn't pay me. He owed me a total of thirty thousand dollars. I told him that if I wanted to resign, I could, and reminded him that he couldn't do anything about it except find someone else to run his madhouse. Then he lost the plot completely and started ranting and raving of how I and the other expats were trying to wreck his company, and he was still wailing when I walked away to my room. I never spoke to him again until I left Taji, and that was after all the Sri Lankan guys had left. All I said to him was that I knew where he lived and that if he didn't pay what he owed, I would visit his home. He told me that if he saw me anywhere near his house, he would call the police. I told him that the police couldn't do anything to me; I would just be visiting the area, and there was no harm in that. I told him that for 30k I would risk everything and even put him in a wheelchair for the rest of his life which he sniggered at, he then went to walk away so I just told him if I didn't get him I could always get his girlfriend and laughed. He turned back and hit the roof but I didn't move position but just stared him out. I honestly think he thought I was some sort of crackpot because he started shaking and spluttering his words. In the end I just reminded him that for the sake of everyone he had better pay me. It took me nearly a year to get my pay by getting a solicitor involved. That year anything could have happened to anyone and the only person to blame was that fat useless twat.

Mickey and I left Taji with our eticket numbers and got on the Blackhawk helicopter to go to the Baghdad airport. From there we would take a military flight to Kuwait, where we would meet up with our Sri Lankan guys. We meant to go to Sri Lanka and visit Perry's wife and kids. At least she wouldn't feel that his effort was all for nothing. We went because Fatboy S .F. wouldn't go to see her, even though he had said he would.

Mickey and I went to get our etickets confirmed with British. Airways. Well, S. F. had the last laugh! Our tickets were no good at all! The numbers on them were not valid. They weren't even correct ticket numbers; they were more like bloody phone numbers. We had to laugh. The flight back home was going to cost us between £300 and £400 one-way.

We bought our Sri Lankan air tickets but had to spend a couple of nights in Kuwait. The layover was not a problem, as a bit of relaxed sightseeing wouldn't go amiss. We would also be able to shower in clean water and get the smell of Iraq out of our systems.

We boarded the flight at about 1500 hrs in the afternoon. About three hours later, we touched down in Colombo, the capital of Sri Lanka. Once outside the arrivals area, we were met by other team members who had seen the light a few months previously and left Iraq. It was great to see them again. After much handshaking, we were taken to a minibus. The plan was to go directly to see Perry's family, as they were expecting us. We arrived in a small village about 1900 hours and went straight to the house. We didn't get to see the actual village because it was pitch black, and with no lighting, anything past about 6' away was invisible. Inside and at the back of the house, the situation was completely different; the entire village had turned out to see these two white strangers who had come to pay their respects to a fallen comrade. It was the most humbling experience I have ever had. As soon as his wife saw us, she broke down in tears and came over to us. She said that she knew Perry wouldn't come back to her and that she had tried on many occasions to get him to remain with her and the children, but he wouldn't. I could understand where she was coming from, and I also understood Perry's motivations. She wanted stability, whereas Perry had still craved excitement. Perry was ex-Sri Lankan Commando and had fought for years against the Tamil Tigers further up north, so he would have found it very hard to settle down to a mundane job. We were introduced to his young son and his young, beautiful daughter. The son was about nine and the daughter about five, and both fit and healthy.

We stayed with Perry's family until about 2100 hours that night and then had to leave. We said our good-byes and departed for Colombo.

Arriving at Colombo, we were booked into a fantastic hotel, an old colonial hotel that had been modernized. This place was utterly beautiful, with spacious bedrooms and a bar downstairs, along with a nightclub. The only thing that spoilt it all was that there were no women, just men. To see a nightclub with men only was very strange to both of us. Some of the music was slow dance music, and when we saw two guys get up and dance, we knew that was no place for us and left.

We planned a little sightseeing around the capital the next morning. Even though the Tamil problem was further north, the number of roadblocks was amazing. Because we were with ex-military commandos who still had their identity cards, we were waved through without any problems. Most of the soldiers guarding the capital knew our guys, so nothing was a problem.

We eventually spent four days in the capital before we had to get back to the UK, but first we had to get to Kuwait to pick up our kit, which we had left at a friend's house.

The flight to London's Heathrow Airport was a boring six-hour flight. Arriving at the airport, Mickey and I had to part company because he was going to Belfast and I was heading for Manchester. Waiting in this queue was painful, to say the least. It was agonizingly slow. We cleared immigration and headed straight for another terminal to catch our domestic flights, and there Mickey and I parted.

I eventually arrived home, very tired but happy to see my wife. I hadn't seen her for about two and a half months, nearly three. After a shower and a meal, I sat her down and told her that I had finished with Iraq. I wanted nothing more to do with it, and as far as I was concerned, they could do with it as they wish. The end had to come sometime, and this was it. I was not prepared to risk my life or anyone else's life for people who did not appreciate what we were trying to do. To me, they were people who just would not stand up and be counted except for trying to get to the front of the queue to kill you, and that included both male and female. This was the end of an adventure that I just wanted to forget. I had no respect for any local person living in Iraq, and I had begun to hate them for what they did and also for what they said about the coalition. If the truth was known, most Iraqis didn't want Saddam out of power, and they certainly didn't want the Americans in the country. In the beginning, all the Iraqis had thought that the coalition would sort out all the major problems their country was experiencing, all their issues with trains, roads, food, and, most of all oil. When the Americans didn't deliver all these fixes by the following month, unrest started to creep in. Basically, the Iraqi people wanted everything sorted out in very short time and without having to lift a finger themselves, mainly because it was too hot to lift a finger. More to the point, I had found that they were just too lazy to do anything themselves.

We decided to spend a couple of days in England, then get out and have a two-week holiday in Spain.

During our first couple of days in Spain, I just relaxed and took things at a slow pace. At the beginning of the second week, we were in a furniture shop when my mobile rang, and I naturally thought it was one of our sons. Answering it, I heard a familiar voice that I hadn't heard for a few years. The caller was the boss of a company who had been trying to get hold of me for a while. What he wanted was pretty simple; he wanted me to go back over to Iraq and work for him. I had to go outside for the rest of the phone call, away from my wife. Speaking to my friend, I told him that I wasn't really interested and had just gotten back from a long stint. He kept on and on until I asked him what the daily rate was. I told him that if he wanted me that much, he had better raise the compensation quite a bit and then said my good-byes.

I told my wife about the conversation and that I had declined the offer, much to her relief. What I didn't tell her was that if he offered me sufficient money, I might well go back to Iraq.

ROAD TRAFFIC ACCIDENT

8 JANUARY 2008
TEAM LEADER: JACK HERON

INTRODUCTION
On Monday 8 January, the team task was to deliver a vehicle from Camp Taji, northwest of Baghdad, to Erbil, southeast of Mosul. Departure time from Camp Taji was approximately 0830 hours. The estimated time of the journey was calculated at 6 (six) to 7 (seven) hours' drive. The team consisted of five gun trucks with four men in each, total twenty men. A rest stop of one hour was to occur at Kirkuk.

ROUTE
Depart Camp Taji and head south down route Tampa, then onto Route Pluto; use the canal road from Route Pluto to get onto Route Cheyenne. Once on Route Cheyenne, we head north towards Kirkuk. Once through Kirkuk, we remain on Route Cheyenne, still heading north to Erbil.

ORDER OF MARCH
Vehicle No. 1 – Point vehicle, *Anura*
Vehicle No. 2 – Command vehicle, J. Heron
Vehicle No. 3 – Delivery vehicle, Dan Rai
Vehicle No. 4 – Centre protection, Perry
Vehicle No. 5 – Medical support, Terence
Vehicle No. 6 – Rear protection, Pitamber

INCIDENT
On Route Cheyenne, I found the oncoming traffic to be fair to medium. We had just passed through a small village called Kalis. At 0956 hours, approximately 8 kilometres north of Kalis at grid MC

214

55416–50862, I heard a call over the radio to stop the convoy, as an accident had occurred. I immediately halted the convoy and directed my driver to turn around and head back to the accident scene.

On arriving at the scene, I found that a truck laden with gravel had swerved in front of one of my gun trucks. The truck was on its side and had crushed the front of the gun truck. I immediately put out local protection and directed other team members to assist in getting the injured personnel out of the damaged vehicle. Whilst this was going on, I made a phone call at 1000 hours to my operations room, informing him of the accident, and I told him further details would be sent when I knew the full extent.

Injured personnel were Sanjay Kumar Chetri and Umesh Kumar Karkri.

The team medic, Terence Clarke, administered aid to the injured at the side of the road.

On looking inside the vehicle, I saw the driver, Joseph Tikoivuna, had been trapped by his legs due to the engine block moving into the front cab. Joseph had severe head injuries and was dead at the scene. The ops room was informed. On moving to the other side of the vehicle, I saw the commander, R. W. L Perera, had also been trapped and had suffered serious head injuries, and he, too, was dead. The ops room was also informed of this death and asked to task a Medivac to my location to get the injured to hospital.

At approximately 1010 hours, an Iraqi Army patrol arrived and took over as local protection. This released other team members to bring a cordon closer into the accident scene.

At approximately 1012 hours, the Iraqi Police arrived. I informed them of what had happened and requested a crane or vehicle capable of getting the truck off the gun truck so I could get my men out. At almost the same time, a fire started in the engine and spread quickly; team members rushed with fire extinguishers and managed to put the fire out. An Iraqi Police officer called the Kalis Fire and Rescue team out from the local village. They arrived at approximately 1019 hours.

My team medic had stabilised the two injured and assisted me in trying to get the two dead men out of the vehicle.

At approximately 1040 hours, the helicopter Medivac arrived and landed on my green smoke. I linked up with the American medic and gave a brief outline of what happened before handing him over to my team medic for an update on the injuries sustained by my two team members.

At approximately 1044 hours, the helicopter lifted off with the two injured men on board en route to hospital; the American medic told me he could not help me with the dead before leaving the scene.

With the assistance of the Iraqi Army continuing to support me by holding the outer cordon in place and the Iraqi Police and Fire and Rescue assisting me inside the inner cordon, we eventually moved the huge truck enough to get the two bodies out. Each body was carefully wrapped in a blanket and put on the rear of a gun truck.

On looking at the scene more carefully, I saw that the armoured front window screen was missing; the entire engine block was shattered, with some of it inside the front driver's cab. The passenger's armoured door had also been ripped off its hinges and, like the armoured front window, was nowhere to be seen. Gravel was strewn all over the accident area.

All equipment from the damaged gun truck was collected and shared out with other gun trucks for safekeeping.

A final headcount was completed by Anura whilst I obtained permission to leave the site from the Iraq Police Commander. On gaining permission, we left the scene and returned to Camp Taji. Departure from the scene was approximately 1156 hours; arrival at Camp Taji was approximately 1317 hours.

NOTES

The Iraqi driver who caused the accident was only seen once by myself when I helped him out of his truck; he had no injuries, and I sat him down at the front of his truck and motioned for him to remain there. Unfortunately, whilst I was directing my men in getting injured people away and attempting to get the dead out, the Iraqi driver disappeared. He was either arrested by the police or just walked away.

My special thanks must go to the Iraqi Army, the Kalis Fire and Rescue, and the Kalis Police. Without their unreserved commitment to assist us, the task would have taken many more painful hours.

The damaged gun truck will be taken to the Kalis Police compound. In my opinion, the vehicle is beyond repair, a total write-off.

This is a statement which I found in a prominent British newspaper, which I kept as a reminder of what could happen to any expat ever caught and sold on to insurgents. It also made me think twice about a faith that is supposed to be peaceful and loving to its fellow humans. The statement is quite gruesome, and I would warn anyone who is of a nervous disposition not to read it. Those who are brave enough to read it do so at their own peril.

The statement concerns a female journalist who obviously loved her country and wanted nothing more than peace, which peace she never had when she was kidnapped.

Part of me died when I saw this cruel killing

EVEN *by the stupefying standards of Iraq's unspeakable violence, the murder of Atwar Bahjat, one of the country's top television journalists, was an act of exceptional cruelty.*
Nobody but her killers knew just how much she had suffered until a film showing her death on February 22 at the hands of two muscle-bound men in military uniforms emerged last week.
Her family's worst fears of what might have happened have been far exceeded by the reality.

Bahjat was abducted after making three live broadcasts from the edge of her native city of Samarra on the day its golden-domed Shi'ite mosque was blown up, allegedly by Sunni terrorists.
Roadblocks prevented her from entering the city, and her anxiety was obvious to everyone who saw her final report. Night was falling and tensions were high.

Two men drove up in a pickup truck, asking for her. She appealed to a small crowd that had gathered around her crew, but nobody was willing to help her. It was reported at the time that she had been shot dead with her cameraman and sound man.

We now know that it was not that swift for Bahjat. First she was stripped to the waist, a humiliation for any woman, but particularly so for a pious Muslim who concealed her hair, arms, and legs from men other than her father and brother.

Then her arms were bound behind her back. A golden locket in the shape of Iraq that became her glittering trademark in front of the television cameras must have been removed at some point – it is nowhere to be seen in the grainy film, which was made by someone who pointed a mobile phone at her as she lay on a patch of earth in mortal terror.

By the time filming begins, the condemned woman has been blindfolded with a white bandage.
It is stained with blood that trickles from a wound on the left side of her head. She is moaning, although whether from the pain of what has already been done to her or from the fear of what is about to be inflicted is unclear.

Just as Bahjat bore witness to countless atrocities that she covered for her television station,Al-Arabiya, during Iraq's descent into sectarian conflict, so the recording of her execution embodies the depths of the country's depravity after three years of war.

A large man dressed in military fatigues, boots, and cap approaches from behind and covers her mouth with his left hand. In his right hand, he clutches a large knife with a black handle and an 8-inch blade. He proceeds to cut her throat from the middle, slicing from side to side.
Her cries – "Ah, ah, ah" – can be heard above the "Allah Akbar" (God is greatest) intoned by the holder of the mobile phone.
Even then, there is no quick release for Bahjat. Her executioner suddenly stands up, his job only half done. A second man in a dark T-shirt and camouflage trousers places his right khaki boot on her abdomen and pushes down hard eight times, forcing a rush of blood from her wounds as she moves her head from right to left.

Only now does the executioner return to finish the task. He hacks off her head and drops it to the ground and then picks it up again and perches it on her bare chest so that it faces the filmmaker in a grotesque parody of one of her pieces to camera.

The voice of one of the Arab world's most highly regarded and outspoken journalists has been silenced. She was thirty.

As a friend of Bahjat who had worked with her on a variety of tough assignments, I found it hard enough to bear the news of her murder.

When I saw it replayed, it was as if part of me had died with her. How much more grueling it must have been for a close family friend who watched the film this weekend and cried when he heard her voice.

The friend, who cannot be identified, knew nothing of her beheading but had been guarding other horrifying details of Bahjat's ordeal.

She had nine drill holes in her right arm and ten in her left, he said. The drill had also been applied to to her legs, her navel, and her right eye. One can only hope that these mutilations were made after her death.

There is a wider significance to the appalling footage and the accompanying details. The film appears to show, for the first time, an Iraqi death squad in action.

The death squads have proliferated in recent months, spreading terror on both sides of the sectarian divide. The clothes worn by Bahjat's killers are bound to be scrutinised for clues to their identity.
Bahjat, with her professionalism and impartiality as a half-Shi'ite, half-Sunni, would have been the first to warn against any hasty conclusions, however. The uniforms seem to be those of the Iraqi National Guard but that does not mean she was murdered by guardsmen. The fatigues could have been stolen for disguise.

A source linked to the Sunni insurgency who supplied the film to London claimed it had come from a mobile phone found on the body of a Shi'ite Badr Brigade member killed during fighting in Baghdad.

But there is no evidence the Iranian-backed Badr militia was responsible. Indeed, there are conflicting indications. The drill is said to be a popular tool of torture with the Badr Brigade. But beheading is a hallmark of Al-Qaeda in Iraq, led by the Sunni Abu Musab al-Zarqawi.

According to a report that was circulating after Bahjat's murder, she had enraged the Shi'ite militias during her coverage of the bombing of the Samarra shrine by filming the interior minister, Bayan Jabr, ordering police to release two Iranians they had arrested.

There is no confirmation of this, and the Badr Brigade, with which she maintained good relations, protected her family after her funeral came under attack in Baghdad from a bomber and then from a gunman. Three people died that day.

Bahjat's reporting of terrorist attacks and denunciations of violence to a wide audience across the Middle East made her plenty of enemies among both Shi'ite and Sunni gunmen. Death threats from Sunnis drove her away to Qatar for a spell, but she believed her place was in Iraq, and she returned to frontline reporting despite the risks.

We may never know who killed Bahjat or why. But the manner of her death testifies to the breakdown of law, order, and justice that she so bravely highlighted and illustrates the importance of a cause she espoused with passion.

Bahjat advocated the unity of Iraq and saw her golden locket as a symbol of her belief. She put it with her customary on-air eloquence on the last day of her life: "Whether you are a Sunni, a Shi'ite or a Kurd, there is no difference between Iraqis united in fear for this nation."

I really enjoyed myself in Iraq. The jobs I carried out were dangerous, to say the least, but I had luck on my side and came through my experience there all right.

I know we lost a lot of guys within our industry, and I hope it was not in vain. I honestly thought we were doing a good job in the reconstruction of the country. Unfortunately, some people there obviously didn't think so, hence the trouble. The troubles only began when supporters of Saddam Hussain from both inside the country and outside the country decided to fight the foreign forces occupying Iraq. If they had of stood back and watched what was going on they would have realized that the Americans and British, along with other countries, only had good intentions for Iraq. We encountered fighters from many Middle Eastern countries who obviously thought they were coming to the aid of Iraq when in actual fact they were disrupting the rebuild in a massive way. I cannot believe that they thought the Americans and British would pull out of Iraq when they turned up and started fighting. Whatever gave them that idea?

I never agreed with the war from the start but like many ex soldiers I would never miss the chance of a good fight. I never gave the civilian deaths a second thought because they were killed by their own people, what used to goad me, and still does is the deaths of so many young men, be they American or British.

If it were not for the Security Contractor aiding the coalition I think the death rate would have been double what it is today because even in the security industry out here we have lost many men ourselves. Hardly any death of a security contractor made headline news save for the guys who were kidnapped and murdered.

I still work in the security industry in foreign lands and hope to carry on for a few more years.

I have the utmost respect for all the American soldiers, both male and female, who served in Iraq, whatever their job entailed. I never once expected any assistance when I was out on the ground but was very thankful when it came.

One thing I will say is the American Security Company's operating in Iraq are nothing more than a bunch of failed Rambo's. These guys were hated by the British Security Company's because they were all "royd men", in other words they used steroids because some most of them were absolutely massive. It doesn't matter how muscular you are it won't stop a bullet from going right through you. These guys made life harder for the forces by causing mayhem out on the streets and then expecting the U.S Forces to come to their aid and get them out of trouble. Some of us even saw an American Security guy with two swords strapped to his back, what the fuck this meat head thought he was doing is beyond me, what a complete tosser. One American security man I spoke to had a huge "Bowie Knife" strapped to his shoulder strap. When I asked him what it was for he told me it was for use when the insurgents got too close, I said to him that if they got that close he wouldn't know anything about it because he would be dead, much to his shock. What I really couldn't get my head round was why people like this were doing out in Iraq ? who let them out of the nut house ?. they obviously thought they were on some Vietnam trip.

I know for a fact that if they were shot at they would just open up on anything that moved which was a far cry from what the British Security guys would do, we need to see smoke or gunmen before we opened fire in Baghdad city, out in the desert was completely different, mind you, American private security didn't go out that far because it was far too dangerous

Al Hateem Truck after attack

Typical Convoy heading to Mosul

Mick in Camp Taji

Jack, M.A and P.G. Christmas 2007/2008

Christmas party 2007/2008

Night brief by Mick

Mine and Mick's room. Notice the derlict buildings.

Fallujah crater

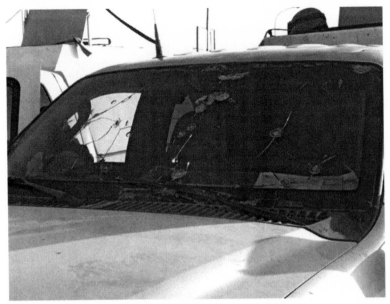

My window screen after gun battle

J.S vehicle after gun battle

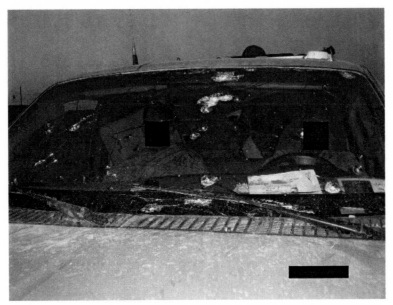

Anura's vehicle after gun battle

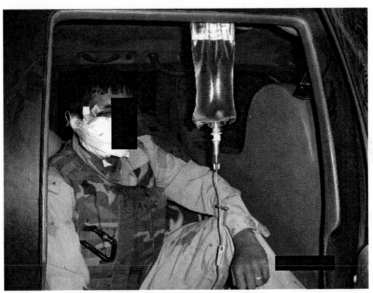

Manju with shrapnel wound to face

One of our burnt out vehicles after gun battle

Mukdadiya village

Route Jenna, desert route

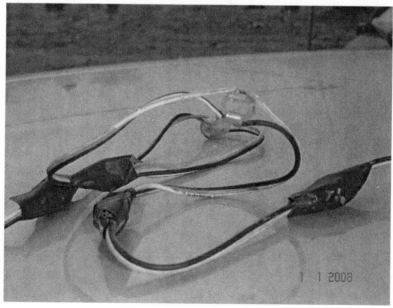

Pressure plate

Iraqi Officers vehicle after explosion

Iraqi truck blown off bridge, one dead

Looking for a way across the dry river bed

Waiting to move on that fateful day

Accident where Joe, Umesh and Perry died

Iraqi Police gun battle that we drove through.

Me and Rabi in Al Hateem

THREAT CONTINGENCIES AND EMERGENCY EVACUATION PLAN

Attachments

1. Name list of *principles*

2. Navigation plan for emergency evacuation by road

3. Security compound fire drills

4. Security and access control

5. Quick Reaction Force and composition

DOCUMENT PURPOSE

The purpose of this document is to clarify the threat contingencies and emergency evacuation plan for all principals in the event of a hostile and/or natural threat.

INTRODUCTION

It is of vital importance that detailed threat contingencies and an emergency evacuation be devised AND implemented to ensure organised reactive drills and contingencies for all possible threats to principals. This plan must include protection against all possible criminal, hostile, and natural physical threats to ensure that everyone enjoys full access to the best security measures, as contractually agreed upon.

It is thus necessary for all security to have an effective, well-organised plan, which should accommodate the following.

a. Discourage and/or prevent any attacks and threats to life and property.

b. Emergency assembly area for the gathering and/or preparation for evacuation of all principals.

c. Have an effective base defence plan in place until such time that emergency evacuation can commence.

d. Ensure that all members are safe during an indirect fire (IDF) attack.

e. Safe movement to an emergency RV.

f. Conduct evacuation of all casualties to the predetermined medical facility for treatment.

g. Deter any criminal acts threatening the efficiency of effort regarding the planned emergency procedures and resources.

POSSIBLE THREAT OVERTHROW

The biggest foreseen threat to personnel employed and/or contracted can be summarised as follows.

Hostile. The following hostile threats are considered major threat possibilities.

1. Abduction of foreign personnel.

2. Indirect fire attacks, which include all trajectory deployed weapons/ordinance, such as mortars and rockets.

3. Small arms fire, which includes sniper attacks.

4. Large-scale attacks on the base with an intent of overrunning it.

5. Complex attacks.

Criminal. The following criminal threats are assessed as being of importance.

1. Theft of personal and/or construction equipment and commodities belonging to the client/company.

2. Blackmail.

3. Threats to life and property of anyone employed and/or contracted by the client/company.

4. Theft of specialist security equipment such as weapons/ammunition.

5. Financially motivated abductions of senior personnel.

6. Sabotage.

Natural Fire is foreseen as the greatest natural threat to personnel.

It is important that these emergency plans be simple and functional, and it must be understood by all involved personnel that regular confirmation thereof must be done by means of rehearsal. These emergency plans also include all other possible emergency situations not covered by this document, for which the reactive drills will remain the same as the drills explained in this document, to include all situations that might be a direct result of any other hostile, criminal, negligent, or natural/uncontrolled actions/omissions.

Scope The following aspects will be discussed in the document.

a. Emergency procedure execution directive.

b. Command, control, and communication structures.

c. Emergency assembly area drills.

d. Emergency levels.

e. Evacuation drills.

f. Emergency procedures.

g. Collective emergency preparations.

h. Individual emergency preparations.

i. General.

EMERGENCY PROCEDURE EXECUTION DIRECTIVE

This directive is composed as a general guideline contingency plan to be executed during the event of any emergency situation. The basic drills are applicable to all described emergency possibilities, not only specific threats.

Detailed amendments will be made during the event of an emergency, depending upon the exact nature of such situation.

The basic drills of this plan must be regular rehearsals, meaning not less than once monthly and such rehearsals must be confirmed to the higher HQ. The plan must also be reviewed on a regular basis.

All planning and preparations must be made to be totally self-sufficient from any outside military formation.

COMMAND CONTROL AND COMMUNICATION STRUCTURE

The following command and control structures are effective within the compound.

1. Project manager. Responsible to oversee all contracted/ subcontracted activities.

2. Operations manager. Responsible for the daily operations. Reports to the PM, will step up when PM absent.

3. Security manager. Responsible for all related security aspects. Reports to the operations manager.

4. Supervisor. Responsible for his immediate teams. Reports to both security manager and operations manager.

5. Team Leader. Responsible for his immediate team.

Communications.

1. Internet. Required.

2. UHF/VHF Radios. Required.

3. Satellite phone. Required.

4. Local cellular phone. Required.

EMERGENCY ASSEMBLY AREA DRILLS

The emergency assembly area is the designated secure area gathering point for all management personnel during the event of any alarm or emergency.

Upon the activation of the emergency alarm, all principals, security, contractors and subcontractors withdraw to the assembly area.

Security must ensure that the assembly area is safe to enter before allowing the others to enter.

Once the principals, contractors, and subcontractors are safe in the assembly area, specific teams will be redeployed on specific tasks.

a. One team remains with the principles, contractors, and subcontractors.

b. Two teams as local defence.

c. One team as outer defence with a heavy machine gun, supported by the local static guard force.

d. One team preparing the vehicles for possible immediate extraction.

e.   Static guard deployed to main entrance/gate.

f.   Static guard deployed to secondary gate/exit.

g.   Roving guard to react to suppressed area.

The emergency area must be equipped with the following.

a.   Water.

b.   Radio with spare battery.

c.   Medical bag and stretcher.

d.   Emergency rations.

e.   Torches.

f.   Blankets.

g.   Extra ammunition.

EMERGENCY LEVELS

The following are the levels for emergency evacuation. The chosen level will depend on the situation and the support available. The option to evacuate will be chosen when the need exists after a good appreciation is made concerning information received, the threat, and required support.

LEVEL ONE Minor threat situation. All principles, contractors, and subcontractors to be evacuated to the emergency assembly area. Teams responsible to secure the assembly area and compound. Defensive positions must be manned until further instructions. All security personnel withdraw to the assembly area on command.

LEVEL TWO. Medium threat situation. All principals, contractors, and subcontractors are to be evacuated to the emergency assembly area. Escorted movement of all principals, contractors, and subcontractors only, until further notice.

LEVEL THREE High threat situation within the area or base area. Enemy base overrun foreseen. Immediate evacuation from area. All security personnel to withdraw to the compound HQ for preparations to evacuate rapidly to the nearest safe location.

If the threat is of such a nature that evacuation out of the compound is not necessary, level 1 emergency drills are to be applied. All will depend on accurate information and the current threat before considering another option.

If level 2 drills are applied, the evacuation will be executed according to the emergency plan. All movements will be coordinated with and relayed to HQ.

Level 3 emergency drills will be implemented if it is not possible to link up with any military forces.
It is of vital importance to keep close liaison with any military formations in the area of responsibility during all phases as to ensure that they are informed of all actions and deployments. All actions and intentions must also be liaised with HQ.

EVACUATION DRILLS

All vehicles available will be used if the situation allows evacuating.
High-profile tactics to be applied during all motorcade movements outside the security perimeters of the compound. All planning and preparations must be made according to the high profile concept.

The high profile motorcade may be made up as follows.

    a.   Point vehicle, security.

    b.   TL vehicle, security.

    c.   Principal vehicle with security.

    d.   Contractor vehicle with security.

    e.   Contractor vehicle with security.

    f.   Rear protection.

The size of the motorcade depends entirely on how many principals, contractors, and subcontractors we have at the time.

Only the minimum personal equipment will be allowed per person, also applicable to all principles, contractors, and subcontractors, during the evacuation phase.

The most senior man (security) on the ground at the time will take overall charge (convoy commander). He will report back to the HQ. He will ensure 100% accountability of all personnel.

All principals, contractors, and subcontractors will come under direct command of the senior security man organising the evacuation.

The following sequence of events will commence upon the decision to effect an emergency evacuation.

a. The project manager will inform all personnel of the decision to evacuate, to include a summary of the reasons for such a decision.

b. All evacuees will be assembled at the assembly area for a roll call, final inspection, and brief on convoy orders.

c. While gathering in the assembly area, all relating drills and procedure as applicable to the assembly area must be adhered to.

d. All vehicles must be completed as quickly as possible.

e. Vehicle commanders must report ready to move.

f. The evacuation will commence on command of the senior security man appointed convoy commander.

g. The convoy will move in bounds to predetermined RVs according to the navigation plane.

EMERGENCY PROCEDURES
When subject to any emergency situation, always remember the client depends on the professional attitude of the security. Remember the

following.

    a.   Do not panic.

    b.   Think logically.

    c.   Identify all danger points and threat areas.

    d.   Regular rehearsals ensure readiness, also with the client's participation.

    e.   Be observant; stay alert.

Possible situations. What can go wrong?

    a.   Fire.

    b.   Bomb/IED/VBIED/SUICIDE.

    c.   Accidents.

    d.   Natural disaster.

    e.   Attacks involving shootings, hostage-taking, armed robbery, and physical attacks.

Where can it take place?

    a.   In a building.

    b.   In a vehicle.

    c.   On foot.

Actions in case of fire

    a.   Sound alarm and try to extinguish the fire.

    b.   Evacuate the immediate area to a predetermined area.

    c.   Remain within the security perimeters, or within supporting range of the guard.

    d.   Notify the project manager.

e. Apply first aid to any injured.

Implications

a. Regularly inspect fire extinguishing equipment and ensure they are all serviceable and accessible.

b. Identify safe areas.

c. Know the telephone numbers, radio channels, and call signs of key support personnel.

d. Submit an incident report.

e. Assess the situation and try to determine whether the fire was caused intentionally as a possible diversion and react accordingly.

BOMB/VBIED/IED/SUICIDE

A. Take proper cover where possible.

B. Warn all stations of oncoming threat, if possible.

C. Apply first aid to the injured.

D. Evacuate the area to a predetermined safe area.

E. Notify the project manager.

F. Do not touch anything.

Implications

a. Be aware for other possible threats and keep the area safe.

b. Know telephone numbers, radio channels and call signs.

c. Ensure that you have a complete medical bag.

d. Inspect all emergency equipment.

e. Submit an incident report.

f. Assess the situation and determine whether the attack is a diversion for another attack.

Accident

a. Apply first aid.

b. Notify the project manager.

Implications

a. Know telephone numbers, radio call signs.

b. Ensure the medical equipment is at hand.

c. Submit an incident report.

Natural disasters

a. Apply first aid to anyone requiring it.

b. Evacuate the area to a predetermined area.

c. Notify the project manager.

Implications

a. Know the telephone numbers of key personnel, radio channels, and call signs.

b. Ensure medical bag is complete.

c. Submit incident report.

ATTACK

a. Apply self-defence measures and take proper cover from incoming effective enemy fire. When returning fire, ensure that all shots are aimed and controlled.

b. Positively identify the location of the threat and hold your ground where possible.

  c. Apply first aid to the injured.

  d. Request for reinforcements.

  e. Apply suppressing fire into the direction of the threat with the available support weapons.

  f. Withdraw safely and regroup to a predetermined secure area.

Golden rules during night attack.
  a. Deactivate all lighting of own position as not to be seen by the enemy.

  b. Only return fire at a clearly visible target, using controlled fire; remember to conserve your ammunition.

  c. Regularly change fire position.

  d. Only deliver controlled fire as not to give away your position by means of your muzzle flash.

  e. Remember that the use of tracers also gives away your position.

  f. Always stay down and observe.

Preventions of attack

  a. Guards must always be alert for possible attacks. Observation must be done to ensure that no grouping or attack/battle indications are overseen.

  b. If any indications are observed, the project manager must be informed; he will then inform the principals.

Handling suspicious persons/objects. All suspicious persons or objects, such as parcels or a person who observes the compound or base over a long period in a covert manner, must be dealt with as follows.

  a. It must be reported to the project manager, security manager, and security, or any other relevant person.

  b. In the case of a suspicious object, no personnel must be allowed to go anywhere near it or handle it.

c. The area where the suspicious object is located must be evacuated to a predetermined secure area as soon as possible.

d. Take proper cover.

e. No suspicious person must be confronted unless on command.

Collective evacuation preparations.
All vehicles must be equipped with the following serviceable equipment.

a. Tow rope.

b. Two spare wheels.

c. Onboard vehicle emergency equipment, jack/spanner.

d. One box emergency rations.

e. Water.

f. Complete medical bag.

g. Spare ammunition.

Weapons.
Personal weapons. During an emergency, each member of the security team must have in his possession the following, being the minimum requirement.

a. AK-47 assault rifle.

b. Minimum 5 full magazines.

c. PKC machine gun.

d. 150 spare machine gun rounds.

Support weapons

    a. PKC, PKM.

    b. 1,000 rounds.

Security store
The store must be prepared with the following equipment.

    a. Sufficient water.

    b. Emergency rations.

    c. Vehicle emergency equipment.

    d. First line ammunition and reserve.

    e. Engine oil, transmission fluid, weapon oil, and other lubricants.

    f. Extra jerry cans of fuel; this is to be replaced every two weeks.

All support weapons will be used as the support weapons in the vehicles during an emergency evacuation. The relevant support gunners must ensure that when the support weapons are loaded into the vehicles, the above scales of ammunition are adhered to.

No vehicle equipment will be carried on board each vehicle as described above during normal daily use. All the relevant emergency equipment will be locked up in safekeeping; this avoids any damage or theft. During the emergency, all such equipment will be loaded into the allocated vehicles. All such must, however, be prepared in such a manner as to be present and easily loadable when required. Monthly inspections must be done to ensure serviceability and completeness.

All vehicles must be refueled by 1600 hours daily and parked together within the confines of the compound perimeter. Vehicles must be parked in such a manner as to be easily driven out from their parked positions; no vehicle may be parked so as to block the movement of another vehicle.

INDIVIDUAL EVACUATION PREPARATIONS

Each evacuee must prepare the following individual equipment in the form of a single bail-out bag, and nothing more.

a. Passport.

b. Money in the denomination of the country, or dollars.

c. 2 litres of water.

d. Survival rations for 48 hours.

e. Spare ammunition.

f. Important medication.

g. First aid kit.

h. Field dressings.

i. Navigation aids.

j. Spare clothing.

k. Communication device.

l. Tactical light.

The following additional equipment will be allowed each principal, contractor, and subcontractor.

a. Laptop computers.

b. Important IT devices containing classified and/or sensitive material.

c. Any other item deemed of vital importance.

d. Important documents which cannot be destroyed.

The aim of the bail-out (bug-out) bag is to provide the carrier the basic equipment required to get along with ease for at least 48 hours. The size of the bail-out bag must not exceed the normal size of a day rucksack. The basic rule of thumb when preparing the bail-out bag is that you must be able to run with it without restrictions or discomfort. All personnel must also have the following.

a. Body armour.

b. Helmet.

c. Assault vest.

GENERAL

The main aim of these emergency contingencies and emergency evacuation plan is to ensure that all the basic requirements are adhered to by all involved ensuring the safe passage of all principals to a safe location during the event of an emergency and or threat.

These drills will be rehearsed regularly to ensure that all role players are informed and understand what is expected from them during the event of an emergency.

All security is asked to enforce this emergency contingency and evacuation plan to its fullest extent.

Attachment A to
Emergency Contingencies
Emergency Evacuation plan

NAME LIST OF PRINCIPALS TO BE EVACUATED

Attachment B
Emergency contingencies and
Emergency Evacuation plan

NAVIGATION PLAN FOR EMERGENCY EVACUATION PLAN BY ROAD

Attachment C
Emergency Contingencies and
Emergency Evacuation plan

OUTSIDE MILITARY/SECURITY CONTACT DETAILS

Attachment D
Emergency Contingencies and
Emergency Evacuation Plan

FIRE DRILL	MEDICAL	BOMB THREAT	
ON HEARING THE ALARM	MEDICAL ASSISTANCE	ACTIONS ON EXPLOSIVES	
Everybody within the compound	Determine how many and how serious the	Report it immediately.	
Gathers at the assembly area.	Casualties are, if any.		
		Immediate evac to the assembly area	
Each team leader reports to the	Execute first aid as required.		
Security manager.		Deploy guards around the compound	
	Remove casualties from danger.	to avoid any bystanders from	
Guards are deployed around the		entering the danger area.	
location to prevent theft or	Alert any Military if casualties are serious.		
unlawful entry.		DO NOT attempt to disarm the device.	
	Wait for additional medical assistance.		
ACTIONS OF DUTY PERS		ACTIONS OF DUTY PERS	
Team leader to inform		Team leader to inform	
security manager,		security manager,	

Operations manager		operations manager.	
Operations manager to inform PM.		Operations manager to inform PM,	
		medic.	
All guards remain at post.			
		Ensure guards remain at post behind	
Team leader to log incident.		cover.	
		Activate alarm.	
		Direct all to assembly area.	
		Ensure nobody enters cordon.	
		Take roll call of all people.	
		Hand the incident to the security	
		manager.	
		Be alert for possible attacks.	

FIRE DRILL	MEDICAL	BOMB THREAT	
Assembly Area	Medical	Actions at Assembly Area	
All personnel to gather at the		Roll call.	
assembly area for task allocation			
and specific instructions.		Remain calm and await further	
		instructions.	
Remain calm and stay within the			
safe area until further notice.		Evacuate all sleeping quarters and	
		report to the assembly area.	
Roll call of all personnel.			
		Remove all classified information	
		immediately.	
		Report :-	
		Size	
		Shape	
		Location	
		Material	
		Obstacles around device.	
		Colour	
		Exact position of device.	

Attachment E
Emergency Contingencies and
Emergency Evacuation Plan

SECURITY AND ACCESS CONTROL

SECURITY

Every day there are a number of situations or circumstances that will
challenge the security personnel therefore all members must be on their
guard and look for combat indicators, things that do not seem right. .

It is essential that every member of the team become acquainted with
each of these points so that all will be able to recognise all the situations
containing dangers to the security, to identify them, to be on guard
against these dangers, and then to react accordingly.

The aim of security orders is to inform all those concerned of the
rules and regulations concerning security within company-controlled
security perimeters.

Security can only be enforced effectively if everyone is security-conscious
and makes a united effort towards this goal.

SECURITY IS APPLICABLE TO

All personnel.
All visitors to the facilities/compound.
All emergency situations. During increased levels of security, additional
measures may be taken.

SECURITY OF INFORMATION

Security of information means guarding against unauthorised admission
to classified information, documents, or equipment controlled.

The following personnel must be informed immediately if there
is any suspicion that a person is not acting in accordance with the
abovementioned definition.
Project manager.

Operations manager.
Security manager.

SECURITY OF PERSONNEL

Members must not spread rumours or rash gossip, such as informing outside personnel of personnel status, number of vehicles held, serviceability of vehicles, weapon amounts, ammunition amounts, or the capabilities of the company.

Members must attempt to determine the source of rumours and then report it to the
following.
Project manager.
Security manager.
Operations manager.

COUNTERMEASURES

Security personnel must not brag or boast to anyone or try and bluff someone about how far or well they shoot with a certain type of weapon that is in use, or how many vehicles and or type of vehicles there are on location.

Do not supply information regarding types of weapons, vehicles, and characteristics thereof to anyone.

Do not cheerfully provide anyone with strengths, qualities, or organisations of personnel, weapons, and vehicles.

If any rumours are in circulation, which have an undesirable effect on members, immediate steps must be taken to put a stop to such rumours.

Many of the local nationals, whether employed as static guards or being local residents, are very curious and ask all sorts of questions which have reference to security such as strengths, weapons, vehicles, and personnel qualifications achieved within a certain period of time. No member must provide any information betraying the security of the compound, specifically in reference to the principals.

SECURITY OF EQUIPMENT AND MATERIALS
Security of materials includes the security of buildings, vehicles, equipment, stores, weapons, and ammunition.

It is imperative that before personnel leave their place of work, all buildings, vehicles, stores, and equipment are secure.

Ensure that all doors/windows are secure.

All heaters/lights/air conditioning and fans are to be switched off.

Classified documents and controlled stores are secure.

All cabinets, strong rooms, and safes are locked.

Always take immediate steps to get broken locks, latches, windows, and bolts for doors and windows repaired.

Ensure all computers are switched off and password-protected.
Ensure all equipment is under control, especially communication equipment.

CLOSED AREAS_
Only authorised personnel may enter these areas.
Weapon stores.
Construction sites.
Food stores.
Equipment stores.

PROTECTION OF VEHICLES
Vehicles not in use must be parked within the designated parking areas within the security compound. Vehicles must also be parked in such a manner as to be easily removed in the event of an emergency.

PROTECTION OF WEAPONS

Personnel are individually responsible for the safekeeping of weapons issued to them or assigned under their control.

A weapons register must be available at the weapon store to manage all weapons.

The project manager will exercise full accountability over all weapons and such ammunition under his control, and responsibility over proper care of such weapons and ammunition is delegated to the individuals in possession of such weapons.

Weapons may not be left unattended at any place except authorised storage facilities.

Do not remove or tamper with any weapon or ammunition not belonging to you.

SECURITY OF AMMUNITION

Ammunition must be locked away at all times.

Ammunition will only be issued to duty personnel. Additional ammunition requirements will. be determined and approved by the project manager.

Issuing and handing back to the stores rep must always occur.

Unaccounted ammunition must be returned to storage for safekeeping.

Regular equipment inspections must take place to ensure that no person is in the possession of unauthorised ammunition or unexploded devices.

Each individual must be issued with first-line ammunition, and it will be an individual's responsibility to safeguard that ammunition issued to him. First-line reserve ammunition must remain in storage until otherwise instructed.

Nobody is authorised to retain any ammunition/weapons/parts thereof confiscated from any belligerent grouping during the period of operations.

PROTECTION OF FUEL, OIL, AND LUBRICANTS

Oil and lubricants must be kept in a room on the floor, which is covered with river sand.

NO SMOKING notices must be visible to all.

Smoking is forbidden near fuel pumps, fuel storage points, or when vehicles are being refueled.

Drivers must ensure that the vehicles' fuel caps are locked when parked.

GENERAL

The human deviant plays a large role in security and always remains a dangerous security violation element. There always exists the danger that someone will say the wrong thing in the wrong place in a moment of weakness or thoughtlessness. For this reason it is absolutely imperative that every member of the security team be fully conversant with the principles of security, especially with the view to the dangers of negligent gossip. Clear information and strict discipline are of the greatest importance when enforcing security.

ACCESS CONTROL

It is of the utmost importance the effective access control measures exist at each security control point to restrict unauthorised entry/exit of unauthorised personnel, items, or suspicious objects.

Entrance control within the security compound can be done by means of the following methods.

Personnel control.

Vehicle control.

Roving security patrols.

Identification system.

Permit system.

Observation posts.

Escorts.

Cooperation with outside military formations and other security resources.

Static guards.

Regular searches and spot checks.

PERSONNEL CONTROL

Guards must be positively identify personnel before granting them entrance into the security perimeters.

Visitors must be issued visitor permits after stating their reason for the visit.

Searching must be done by the guards. Men may only search men, and only women may search women.

VEHICLE CONTROL

Civilian vehicles belonging to residents within the security perimeter must be identified, and permits must be issued to such owners.

ID documents of the driver and passengers must be controlled before allowing unknown civilian vehicles into the security perimeter.

Incoming vehicles must be registered in the vehicle access control register at the main search area before entering the security perimeters. The access control register must be compiled of the following information.

Date.

Time of entry.

Driver details.

Number of passengers.

Vehicle type.

Vehicle colour.

Vehicle registration number.

Reason for entry to security perimeter.

All vehicles must be searched thoroughly for explosive devices and unauthorised items, weapons, and ammunition. These searches are also applicable to all security vehicles entering the security perimeter.

All vehicles and personnel must be searched for unauthorised items and suspicious objects. If a vehicle is found with unauthorised items or suspicious objects, the following people must be notified immediately.
Security manager.
Operations manager.

Roving security patrols must be conducted to prevent unauthorised entrance to facilities by means of going over or through fences.

Guards will be reinforced by personnel of the Quick Reaction Force (QRF) when required during an emergency.

CONCLUSION
All security personnel must obey these entrance control measures to ensure that entrance control can be carried out effectively and efficiently.

Attachment F
Emergency Contingencies and
Emergency Evacuation Plan

QUICK REACTION FORCE AND COMPOSITION

INTRODUCTION

Upon consideration of the high threat level and the restricted availability of personnel, it is very important that a reaction force be available at short notice if the situation requires it. Such a force will then be referred to as the Quick Reaction Force, or QRF. The client must still be guarded if the QRF is activated.

The minimum reaction time must always be taken into consideration, and therefore an effective trained QRF must be available and combat-ready at any time to ensure quick follow-up of an incident within the security perimeters.

AIM

The aim of this plan is to explain the procedure for the implementation and utilization of a QRF within the security boundaries.

SCOPE

The following aspects must be discussed; however, they are not the DS solutions.
Command and control.
Composition and organisation.
Reaction for activation.
Utilisation of the QRF.
Training of the QRF.
Equipment and storage.

COMMAND AND CONTROL

The QRF grouping for the security boundaries may consist of the following.

    1. 2 x Nissan Patrols.

2. 1 x PSD team, acting as the QRF commander, and the vehicle commander of one of the vehicles.

3. 1 x static PSD, acting as a vehicle commander of the second vehicle, also being the alternative QRF commander.

4. 1 x support weapons gunner with a PKM/PKC and 1,000 rounds boxed and belted ammunition.

5. 4 x static guards from the main gate armed each with an AK-47 assault rifle with 150 rounds of ammunition.

The security project manager will appoint additional personnel as reserves if necessary. Sufficient security resources must, however, remain available to secure the principals at the compound facilities.

During the activation of the QRF, all personnel must be activated on full alert. All security personnel will be responsible for such preparedness as is required to protect the principals, as well as themselves. It must, however, be emphasised that the protection of the principals and their assets would enjoy the highest priority, and contingency planning must be done accordingly.

ACTIVATION OF THE QRF

The activation of the QRF will be on command of the project manager only, or in his absence, his appointed representative.

The QRF must be able to act within 10 minutes after activated. Regular rehearsals must be conducted to ensure fast reaction time.

The QRF will be activated in the following instances.
Reaction to incidents such as attacks, robberies and threats towards personnel and facilities.
Evacuation of personnel.
Natural disasters.

UTILISATION OF THE QRF

The QRF will be utilised primarily within the security boundaries for scenarios where control over or protection of personnel is required and during natural disasters.

The security manager or his appointed representative is the only person who may utilise and task the QRF.

TRAINING

Rehearsal is very important and must be done regularly to ensure and effective QRF, and the project manager will determine these times. Training in the following aspects must be done regularly.

Legal aspects.

Riot control.

Cordon and search.

Vehicle control.

Natural disaster management.

In order to maintain an effective QRF up to standard, rehearsals must be done during the day and at night.

QRF EQUIPMENT AND PLACING

The equipment listed below must be available for use by the QRF, and storage thereof must be in such a manner that issuing does not take longer than 10 minutes.

2 x binoculars.

2 x UHF hand held radios.

First line ammunition.

Smoke grenades.

2 x medical bags.

3 x blankets.

2 x fire blankets.

2 x high-power search lights.

1 x PKM/PKC machine gun.

1,000 rounds belted ammunition.

2 x boxes of water.

The abovementioned equipment must be controlled by the QRF commander.

The following equipment must be prepared by each member.

Chest webbing.

Drinking water.

5 x full magazines.

First line ammunition.

Personal assault rifle.

All personal weapons must be issued per individual, and it is that individual's own responsibility to exercise control over his personal weapon. Weapons will be handed out per register, which is the responsibility of the QRF commander to control.

CONCLUSION

The safety of your own forces is very important. However, the efficiency with which a task is executed must be professional, and that must be remembered at all times. Legal aspects must be kept in consideration continuously during situations.

I wrote these documents over a four-day period. They can be used for any camp or newly built camp. They are a sort of startup package for people who get promoted to the dizzy heights of operation manager. They can be adapted to suit the individual's needs by cutting and pasting. I think I covered everything. Hey, though, let's be fair. Nobody is perfect.

Many companies concentrate more and more on beefing up the security so an ant couldn't get in the place without a siren going off. The possibility that companies neglect is fire. Fire is also a killer, and many rockets or mortars start fires, so why is there not enough done to combat fires? I have seen before, and I suppose I will see again, that the fire side of the security is neglected.

Lightning Source UK Ltd.
Milton Keynes UK
24 January 2011

166253UK00002B/128/P

9 781452 082547